The Creative Vision

To
Judith and Isabella

The Creative Vision:

■

A Longitudinal Study
of Problem Finding in Art

JACOB W. GETZELS

MIHALY CSIKSZENTMIHALYI

A WILEY-INTERSCIENCE PUBLICATION

JOHN WILEY & SONS, New York • London • Sydney • Toronto

Parts of this book are based on previously published material in *Science Journal*, 1967, **3**, 9, 80–84; *Studies in Art Education*, 1968, **10**, 5–16; *Sociological Quarterly*, 1968, **9**, 516–530; *Public Opinion Quarterly*, 1969, **33**, 34–45; *Journal of Personality*, 1970, **38**, **1**, 91–105; *Journal of Personality and Social Psychology*, 1971, **19**, 1, 47–52; *British Journal of Psychology*, 1973, **64**, 1, 91–104; and in E. R. Hilgard (Ed.), *Theories of Learning and Instruction*, 63rd Yearbook of The National Society for The Study of Education, Part I, Chicago: The University of Chicago Press, 1964, 240–267.

Published by John Wiley & Sons, Inc.

Library of Congress Cataloging in Publication Data

Getzels, Jacob W.
  The Creative Vision

  "A Wiley-Interscience publication."
  Bibliography: p.
  Includes index.
  1. Artists—Psychology. 2. Creation (Literary, artistic, etc.) I. Csikszentmihalyi, Mihaly, joint author. II. Title.
  N71.G4   701'.15   76-16862
  ISBN 0-471-01486-9

Printed in the United States of America

10 9 8 7 6 5 4 3 2 1

■
Preface

The artist has been for centuries the archetype of creativity, at least in Western culture. The artist's ability to shape inert matter into lifelike forms that, once created, take on a life of their own, has become a symbol for the human power to change, order, and improve the environment.

From earliest times, the riddle of the world's origins has been explained symbolically, in terms of an act of artistic creation. The Teutonic tribes of Northern Europe held that Wotan carved the first human beings out of the trunk of fir trees with his sword. According to Hindu tradition, the universe is created and destroyed by the dance of Shiva. And many myths tell how man was first shaped out of a lump of clay: by Lao-Tien-Yeh, the Heavenly Father, in early Chinese legends; by Prometheus in the Greek creation stories; and by Jehova in the Bible. It is not surprising, therefore, that an aura of mysterious power has always surrounded the practitioners of art, and that the artist has been often seen as the creative person par excellence.

Although we were aware of and sympathetic with this august tradition, our decision to study creativity in a group of artists was based on practical considerations. Simply put, we studied a group of painters and sculptors because we expected to be able to observe the creative process more clearly with them than with any other group of potentially creative people. The media in which painters and sculptors work, and their behavior while working, are more accessible than the media and the behavior of scientists, poets, or musicians. We hoped that by observing and studying artists at work we would learn something concrete about the act of creation—something more than one can obtain through psychological tests, retrospective accounts, or intuitive leaps of the imagination.

Therefore, we began studying several hundred young artists who were still in school, and then followed the careers of a selected subgroup several years after graduation. Throughout this time we collected as much information as possible about them as persons, about the processes underlying their creative work, and about the social forces that eased or hindered the expression of their talent.

What resulted is, we believe, the first longitudinal study of artists and the first analytic description of the creative process in a true-to-life setting. This book attempts to present the often complex findings of more than 10 years of work in as systematic a form as possible. We begin with a psychometric description of young artists and their specialization and performance in art school (Part 1); proceed to an analytic description of the creative process, from the crucial stage of "problem finding" to the completion of a work of art (Part 2); and then present the longitudinal component of our research, in which we tested the predictive power of the "problem-finding" model, and showed that despite personal and social obstacles, young artists whose cognitive approach emphasizes problem finding over problem solving are more successful in their creative careers (Part 3).

At each step, the generous assistance of many persons and institutions made the difference between success and failure. First and foremost, the cooperation of the School of the Art Institute of Chicago has been invaluable. We were fortunate in having the fullest assistance of Dean Norman B. Boothby, of Thomas Lyman, Chairman of Admissions, and of the entire faculty and staff of the school. We wish in particular to thank the students, who may not always have agreed with the objectives and methods of empirical research, but who nevertheless took part in the time-consuming tests and experiments conscientiously and with goodwill.

We are indebted to several artists, gallery personnel, and art critics who evaluated the drawings produced in the experiments. Special thanks are due to Ruyell Ho, who helped us to develop the experimental procedures, and to Franz Schulze and Robert Nickle for their expert advice.

The U.S. Office of Education financed the first two parts of our study with Cooperative Research Grants E-008 and S-080. The support of the University of Chicago carried us through the last stages of research.

We wish to express appreciation to the staff who worked on this project: Jesse Hurley, Isabella Csikszentmihalyi, Naomi Steinfield, Sharon Avery, and Lonnie Bovar, who acted in various research capacities; and to Allen Herzog and Robert Panos, who contributed to the computer programming and statistical work.

JACOB W. GETZELS
MIHALY CSIKSZENTMIHALYI

University of Chicago,
Chicago, Illinois
June 1976

Contents

CHAPTER 1

■

Introduction

The life and work of artists have been studied many times in the hope of disclosing the secret origins of creativity. Most of these analyses have been retrospective, carried out after the artist had become worthy of biographical attention. Our study follows a different approach; here the development of a group of artists is seen prospectively, in order to determine the steps by which creative works come into being. Instead of attempting to reconstruct the genesis of completed works of art, we sought to observe the development of artists, and the production of their work as it was being created.

The subjects of our inquiry were devoting their lives to becoming, but had not yet become, recognized artists. They were *future* artists, or at least persons from among whom some might become creative artists. We felt that if we could ascertain their origins, their motivations, their mental and emotional traits, and especially how they conceive and produce their work, we would be able to shed light on what makes a person decide to become an artist, about which little is now known, and on the sources and processes of creativity, which the retrospective approach does little to clarify.

We thus decided to undertake a *longitudinal* study of artistic development—so far as we know, the first to be undertaken. From it we would learn not only who wants to become an artist but who does become one, and perhaps even why some aspiring artists succeed and others fail.

Who Would Become an Artist. We began our study by selecting a group of art students. Although one can become an artist without ever going to an art school, many aspiring artists make their first serious commitment by enrolling in one. Students enrolled in art schools are the kind of persons we wanted to know more about: They are manifestly committed to becoming artists, they are still in transition, and they have not yet attained a reputation in the art world. An incidental consideration was that they are easier to locate than individuals with similar aspirations who are not enrolled in a school.

The school we chose, the School of the Art Institute of Chicago, is one of the outstanding museum-connected art schools in the nation, and counts many renowned artists among its alumni. We began by observing, interviewing, and administering psychological instruments to the students. The initial questions we had in mind were quite simple: What are their family backgrounds? Do they differ from other students in mental and emotional characteristics? Are their values different from those of young people preparing for other professions? What are their motives for choosing a career in art?

We soon discovered that in addition to talent, which is a prerequisite for admission to the school, the students shared many personal traits, and differed remarkably in these traits from other students of the same age, sex, and educational level. Yet there were also substantial differences among art students, differences that were not random but that seemed to be related to the field of specialization a student selected. The choice of applying one's graphic talent to advertising art, industrial art, art education, or fine art became one of several unanticipated but fruitful subjects of investigation.

One can become a successful artist without being a good student, or even without going to art school at all. Nonetheless, when a person becomes an art student, his or her chances of future success depend in some measure on performance in art school. Adverse judgment of teachers, who are also practicing artists in their own right, is not only an obstacle to remaining in school, but may undermine the student's motivation to continue in a field that is hazardous at best. It is therefore important to ask whether there are differences in family background, intelligence, perceptual skills, values, and personality related to performance in art school. Although these issues appear to be related more to the success or failure of art students than to the success or failure of artists, they are also pertinent, as it turns out, to achievement after leaving school.

The Making of Art.   To know who chooses a career in art is a first step toward understanding artistic creativity. To specify relations between the characteristics of these people and their performance in art school is another. But knowledge of this order speaks only to the *correlates* of creativity. It does not in itself tell anything about the deeper issue of the process of creativity: What artists do when they paint, how a work of art is made.

Although there are many explanations of *why* a person may want to make a work of art, there are few observations about *how* it is produced. Psychoanalysts, for example, have written a great deal about the unconscious motivations underlying the creative process, and how the process serves the individual; sociologists have written about the social forces underlying the creative process, and how the process serves society. But systematic observation of the creative process itself, of what the artist actually does, has largely been neglected.

There are good reasons for this lack of evidence. A painting is easy to observe—one only needs to walk to the nearest gallery or museum, or look up a book of reproductions in the library. It may even be possible to *reconstruct,* from preliminary sketches or from the accounts of the artist and the artist's friends, the process by which the work was produced. But it is not so easy, and often not possible at all, to *observe* the process of creation while it is occurring, from the germ of an idea to its fruition as a finished painting or sculpture. And even when it is possible to observe the artist at work, there is a prior fundamental problem: No one knows exactly *what* to observe in order to record the essential features of the creative process.

There is one obvious firsthand source for knowing what artists do: artists themselves. But they are usually too involved in the doing to describe analytically what they do. Most often they give only tantalizing, inconclusive hints such as Kandinsky's observation about the artist's work as: "The expression of mystery in terms of mystery" (Overy, 1969, 77).

Virtually all accounts of artistic creativity agree that it springs from a subconscious inner impulse. But how does the impulse get translated into a concrete product? At what point is a connection established between the unconscious forces and the conscious artistic purpose?

The transition from formless impulse to controlled expression is well described by Henry Moore: "I sometimes begin a drawing with no pre-conceived problem to solve, with only the desire to use pencil on paper and make lines, tones and styles with no conscious aim, but as my mind takes in what is so produced a point arrives where some idea becomes conscious and crystallizes, and then a control and ordering begins to take place" (Moore, 1955, 77).

What Moore describes is the birth of a creative problem. Prior to its emergence, there is no structure and no task; only a desire to use pencil on paper, with no conscious aim. After the problem emerges, the skills of the artist take over. Control and ordering begins.

The crucial step, one to which little attention has been paid, is how a situation where there is no problem to be solved gets transformed into a situation where a problem ready for solution exists. What needs to be examined is not only how artists solve problems they are already working on, but how they envisage and then formulate such problems in the first place. For the formulation of a creative problem is the forerunner of a creative solution.

Although the skills involved differ, what Einstein said about the creative process in science holds true of the artistic process:

> The formulation of a problem is often more essential than its solution, which may be merely a matter of mathematical or experimental skill. To raise new questions, new problems, to regard old problems from a new angle, requires creative imagination and marks real advance in science. (Einstein and Infeld, 1938, 92)

Wertheimer makes the same point:

> The function of thinking is not just solving an actual problem but discovering, envisaging, going into deeper questions. Often in great discovery the most important thing is that a certain question is found. Envisaging, putting the productive question is often more important than the solution of a set question. (Wertheimer, 1945, 123)

In studying creativity, investigators have generally assumed that the crucial cognitive process is the one that starts to grapple with a task that is already defined. This assumption, however, implies that what is to be discovered is already present in the person's response repertory. But the definition of the task, as Mary Henle has pointed out, is really the central question to be investigated; it cannot be assumed at the outset. "These associationistic approaches," she writes, "eliminate the role of the problem or the question, which is usually the starting point for productive thinking . . . many scientists have pointed to the role of the problem in scientific work, and something analogous cannot be ignored in the arts." She concludes with a query almost identical to the one that prompted our work on this book: "Why have psychologists paid so little attention to the nature of the problem or of the question? Or to what precedes the problem; doubt, uneasiness, wonder?" (Henle, 1975, 798, 799).

If the process of artistic creativity, and of creativity in general, is to be understood more fully, the study of what the artist does cannot be restricted to the visible solution, the finished product. It must include the earlier, crucial step: formulation of the creative problem to which the solution is a response. At the same time, we must bear in mind that the emergence of a problem in art is seldom a single event but rather a continuous, cumulative process of discovery which begins before the artist picks up a brush, and often does not end even after the canvas is hung on the walls of a museum. Cézanne, for instance, repainted the same still life or mountain many times without exhausting the problems they posed for him. It is this process of *problem finding*—the way problems are envisaged, posed, formulated, created—that we decided to observe as a crucial element in creative work.

Thinking is known to behavioral scientists almost entirely under the guise of *problem solving*. This is understandable, since most of us most of the time are coping with problematic situations that must be faced. Hence, psychologists have been rightly interested in the cognitive events that take place after a person is presented with a problem. But the fact that most thinking gets done in the problem-solving mode does not mean that it is the only, or even the most important form that cognitive processes may take.

Too often thinking is equated with rationality, with the methodical if unadventurous unfolding of symbolic links from given premises to known conclusions. Yet we know that creative thinking, in art as well as science, does not seem to follow this route. Instead of accepting the premises of a structured problem, it fashions a new problematic configuration. Instead of striving to reach a known solution, the cognitive efforts of a creative person are often aimed at results that had been unconceivable before. To study the cognition of discovery, we were prepared to reopen the whole question of what thinking consists of, and of its salient characteristics. By the careful observation of artists at work, we hoped to gain insights into the dynamics of this problem-finding approach, and perhaps to enlarge accepted ideas about the nature of thinking.

The idea of studying how problems are found, obvious in retrospect, had not been pursued systematically before. Although there were numerous theories of problem solving on which to base an empirical study, there was no theory of problem finding. Methods for studying problem solving also abounded, but none for studying problem finding. One can present a problem to subjects, and observe how they solve it as has been done in innumerable studies of intelligence, concept formation, problem solving, and even creativity. But how is one to observe this hypothetical problem-finding process?

In the second phase of our work, we built a model of problem finding as a cognitive process. Then we devised an experimental setting in which art students doing a creative task could be observed in terms of the theoretical model, from the time they began formulating a problem to the completion of a drawing. We then attempted to answer the central question regarding the making of art and the process of creativity: What is the relation between the artist's problem-finding behavior and the originality of the work he or she produces?

Who Becomes an Artist? Five to six years after the art students were graduated, and seven years after our last contact with them in school, we undertook to discover what had happened to them. The initial questions were obvious: How many of the former art students are now full-time fine artists? Do any of the traits measured in school predict who becomes an artist? The most important question was whether the problem-finding behavior observed in the experimental setting, which theoretically should indicate higher originality, had anything to do with who is a successful artist seven years later. If it did, then the importance of problem finding as a cognitive concept for exploring creativity would gain strong support.

The former students were by now scattered across the country, but it was possible to visit many of them and talk about their experiences in attempting to become practicing artists. These conversations made it clear that beyond the various categories of data we had collected, some of which do in fact relate to success after leaving school, there are social issues that affect the fate of young artists. Thus we moved our inquiry into the area of social institutions and cultural conditions, as they impinge on the world of art. For to earn a livelihood in our society, artists must learn to negotiate forces that are often in conflict with their deepest values, personality traits, talents, and aspirations.

The cognitive abilities of the artist must be adapted to cope with the present sociocultural environment and its requirements. As social conditions change, so do the stresses that affect the manifestation of creativity. Therefore we could not limit ourselves to a study of the creative process as a cognitive phenomenon out of a context; we had to locate it instead within the historical reality of the "American Art Scene" with all its idiosyncrasies.

Much of the inquiry, in this as in the preceding phases, was objective and analytic, based on quantitative data. To provide a more subjective and holistic view, these results were rounded out with several case studies of individual artists. For each person we tried to describe the sources out of which creative problems emerge, against the background of his life, from earliest childhood to the present. A concluding chapter places our inquiry in the context of previous studies of creativity; it focuses on the nature of problem finding as a cognitive process, and on its role in creative achievement. A brief survey of the literature in creativity and the psychology of art is provided in Appendix 3.

PART 1

Who Would Become an Artist?

CHAPTER 2

■

The Study in Context:
Setting, Subjects, and Procedures

Visitors making their way through the halls of the Art Institute of Chicago to the eastern end of the museum finally find themselves in front of a small, unmarked door in a bare wall. The door is usually closed; should it open, all that visitors can see is a guard sitting on a stool just inside it. Open or closed, the door is uninviting. Visitors generally turn back without giving it a second thought.

But were they to cross the threshold and turn the corner they would be greatly surprised. The glow and space of the museum give way to a tunnellike passage, dim, low, and cramped by rows of beaten-up tin lockers along both walls. The stately silence and leisurely pace of the museum are replaced by the lively sounds and bustle of young people, hurrying up and down a long, narrow corridor. Farther along the passageway, doors open between the banks of lockers. In one room the flicker of a blowtorch outlines an unfinished metal sculpture. In another, the tall frame of a loom holds a many-colored rug at which a young woman is at work. Next door a dozen young men are hunched over drawings of an automobile. The center of the next room is taken up by a stand on which a model is posing, while all around intense young people try to capture the essential lines of her being with stubs of charcoal.

This meandering passageway with its studios and workshops, its cluttered offices and crowded cafeteria, is the approach to the School of the Art Institute of Chicago. An integral part of the museum, the school is one of the preeminent places for training in the visual arts. Young people with talent apply to it from every part of the nation and from abroad.

This was the setting for our study of the artistic process. We assumed that the School of the Art Institute would provide as representative a cross-section of talented people in the process of becoming artists as could be found anywhere.

The reason for choosing this school was its fame; many renowned artists had studied here. But why choose a school at all? For one thing, it presents a convenient location for observing a large number of artists-to-be—indeed, the only place for doing so. But there were more compelling reasons as well. Attendance in art school has become almost indispensable for those who aim to become artists. Not that they need the diploma. What the art school offers is an environment where they can learn techniques, strengthen their goals and values, and try their talent in a supportive institution.

In the past, other avenues were open to young persons with graphic talent. They could advance their techniques through apprenticeship to an established artist. In some historical periods, apprenticeship was formalized in variants of the guild system, where supervision of the young artist's progress was maintained by the craftsmen in the community. But from the eighteenth century, the training of artists, like training for other crafts and professions, has become centralized in educational institutions, and alternate choices have become less and less available.

This is not to say that it is now impossible for a person who has not attended art school to become an artist. Artists are surely less dependent on formal education than, say, doctors or lawyers. First of all, they can learn through trial and error, and be their own tutors. Then there has been a recent rebirth of community art workshops where one may learn and practice skills with other young artists. A few persons may still enter the art world through apprenticeship to a master. Finally, correspondence courses in art also seem to flourish.

Nonetheless, these alternatives to art school either provide less reliable training or are less widely available to prospective students. Hence, the great majority of youth seriously interested in art is likely to be found in art schools. And from this group, we expected to find in the School of the Art Institute some of the most talented and committed.

Given our interest in the creative process, and more specifically in the creation of works of art, art students provided an ideal sample. The practice of art by definition involves a creative process. Moreover, the process includes visible steps easier to observe than, say, the steps involved in creating poetry or mathematics. Inferences to the latent processes are more easily anchored in observation of the manifest processes, although of course the two are not assumed to be synonymous. And finally, young artists still in school are in a formative stage, presumably not yet committed to a style or ideology foreclosing the observation of development and change.

In some ways this was the crux: We wanted to start observing student artists while they had been practicing art only for a few years, and to follow their development until they became or—as was more likely—did not become independent artists. And so we began visiting the school, hoping to find answers to our three questions: Who are these people? How do they go about producing a creative object? What happens to them after they leave school?

Procedures. The first experiences in the school were exhilarating. Wonderful visual surprises in the studios, intriguing conversations with the students in the cafeteria, and the friendliness of the dean and the faculty made the research environment highly pleasant. Every day we came away with huge amounts of notes of what we saw and heard.

But our intent was not to produce a subjective and impressionistic account of art schools, art students, or artists, although we expected to make use of such observations. The lives of artists and the creation of art have been described by art historians, philosophers, and artists themselves for centuries. Our own intent was at once more modest and more risky. We wished to explore the possibilities of a systematic, and if possible even experimental, investigation of the development of artists and their work, using the concepts and methods of the behavioral sciences.

The specific concepts and methods, however, were not at hand ready to be applied to the phenomena we wished to understand. Few previous works and no explicit theoretical or methodological guidelines were available to give order to our observations, to say nothing of providing hypotheses for empirical test. We were forced to feel our way and develop procedures step by step as we went along over a period of years. New questions arose that had not occurred to us when we started; new methods evolved on the basis of results obtained from preceding methods. Each new pattern of findings helped to shape the next turn that the study was to take.

The inquiry focused on second- and third-year students. Freshmen were omitted since they had just entered the school and might not yet be clear in their commitment to art; seniors were excluded because most would be leaving the school after graduation, before the study was scheduled to end. When we started our work, there were 321 second- and third-year students in the school. This was the target population.

We wanted to describe this group as accurately as possible. We had learned much about them through observation and conversation. But we wanted to obtain descriptive measures that were as objective, as reliable, and as valid as the state of the art would allow, not because objective measures are necessarily more trustworthy than subjective accounts, but for two other reasons. There are as yet few studies of young artists based on the more recently available objective psychological tests and measurements. Even more important, these tests and measurements have "norms" by which the responses of the art students could be compared with some precision to the responses of other groups.

We selected a broad range of mental, perceptual, and personality tests. Six hours were needed to fill them out, so the set was divided into three batteries of two hours each to be given at weekly intervals. The testing was conducted in the lecture hall of the Art Institute. Recruitment of the students was handled by the dean of the school, who wrote a letter to each second- and third-year student inviting him or her to participate in the research project. Because of conflicts between class schedules and testing sessions, and in order to collect as many cases as possible, we repeated the first battery three times, the second five times, and the third five times over a two-month period.

Despite art students' justified jealousy of their time, their mistrust of objective psychological testing devices, the burden of two-hour sessions, and the voluntary conditions of participation, 88 percent of the 321 students in the target population took the first battery, 66 percent the second, and 65 percent the third. This is no mean achievement, and points to the seriousness with which the students participated in the study. Complete information from all three batteries was available for 179 students, that is, 56 percent of all second- and third-year students. The data are given in Table 2.1.

Table 2.1. *Composition of the Samples Tested*

Registered at the School (Population)		Took Test Battery No. 1 No. 2 No. 3			Took All Three Test Batteries (Core Sample)	Percentage of Population
Juniors						
Males	94	73	54	50	44	47
Females	81	69	60	59	48	59
Sophomores						
Males	75	57	45	46	42	56
Females	71	67	53	55	45	64
Total	321	266	212	210	179	56

These 179 students constituted the "core sample." So far as could be determined from the information in the student files (age, sex, course grades, teacher ratings), it was representative of the total population.

The core sample was composed of almost equal numbers of second- and third-year students, males and females, and represented the school's nine fields of specialization. Since it was cumbersome to deal with nine small subgroupings, for most purposes the fields were regrouped into the four "majors" recognized by the school: fine art, industrial art, advertising art, and art education. For certain analyses, the advertising and industrial art students were combined into a large applied art group, to which the fine art group could then be compared.

The fine art group included students in drawing, painting, sculpture, printmaking, and ceramics. The industrial art group included students in dress design, flat pattern and weaving, industrial design, and interior design. The other two groups—advertising art and art education —corresponded to the identical majors recognized by the school. By far the greatest number of students—35 males and 44 females—were in fine art, reflecting the noncommercial orientation of the school. The art education group included 12 males and 15 females; the industrial art group included 23 males and 27 females. The only significant sex difference was among students majoring in advertising art, where the ratio of males was twice that of females. The distribution of students in the core sample by major and sex is given in Table 2.2.

Although our focus was the fine art group, the availability of other curricular groups turned out to be a heuristic windfall. It permitted us to

Table 2.2.   Composition of the Core Sample in Terms of Sex and Field of Specialization

Specialization	Males	Females	Total
Fine arts	35	44	79
Art education	12	15	27
Advertising arts	16	7	23
Industrial arts	23	27	50
Total	86	93	179

ask and seek answers to a number of important questions regarding the choice of art as a career. A frequently made assumption is that these career choices are founded in technical competence: If one is not "good enough" to be a fine artist, one becomes an applied artist. This was not the case, at least not in this art school.

Admission here is highly selective. Regardless of their ultimate field of specialization, all applicants must meet the same requirements in technical skill before they can enter the school. During the first year all students, again regardless of field, must show proficiency in the same fundamental studio courses. Moreover, the art teachers repeatedly told us that differences in technical skill—or, as they said, "native talent"—did not distinguish students in one field of specialization from those in another. The choices were based on something else, they said, but just what else was not clear. If differences in technical skill or "talent" do not account for the choice of fine art or applied art as a career, how can the choices be accounted for?

The tests provided intriguing observations regarding biographical, mental, and emotional characteristics of young artists, and permitted some answers not only to the question as to who they were but also to why some choose fine art and others choose one of the applied arts. But tests cannot provide observations about the actual process of visual creation: what an artist does, how a drawing is produced. We decided, for reasons that are set forth later, to concentrate this aspect of the inquiry on the male fine art students. These students were observed as they worked on a drawing. The observations were complemented by photographs, controlled experimental procedures, and in-depth interviews. It is from this aspect of our work that the concept of problem finding, the mental process that appears so important in artistic activity (and in other kinds of creative activity as well) evolved.

Two years after the study was begun the preceding phases of the research were completed. But to obtain longitudinal observations—the information concerning what happened to fine art students after they left school, and the relation between what we had learned about them while they were still in school and their later success—some time had to pass. No new data were collected for the next six years; we waited until the students had a reasonable chance to establish themselves as independent artists. Then, five years after they had left art school, we again made contact with the subjects we had studied intensively during the first two years.

Details regarding the analysis of the test data, the methods devised for the problem-finding experiment and the evaluation of the student drawings, the procedures for locating and visiting the artists in their homes or studios five years after they left the school, and the assessment of their relative success or failure as independent artists, will be presented when the respective results are described. Here we turn to an introduction of the students themselves and then to some details about the tests they were given.

The Students.   Although the School of the Art Institute is a postsecondary, degree-granting institution, the majority of students did not enter art school directly from high school. Almost 10 percent had already completed college elsewhere, and 43 percent had other prior college experience. The students are thus somewhat older than many second- and third-year college students; the average age of male students is 22.78 (SD 4.70), and of females 23.78 (SD 6.92).

The social background of the students is varied. All social and economic strata are represented. Fourteen percent came from homes with an annual income of less than $5000 and 13 percent from homes with an annual income of more than $15,000. In general, the socioeconomic status of female students was somewhat higher than that of males. Thirty-seven percent of the males and 55 percent of the females reported that their fathers had some postsecondary school education.

Although no exact data about the number of students "working their way" through the art school were available, our impression was that the majority had some part-time employment and that there seemed to be little difference in this respect by social class. A number of students who had previously attended college made interesting comments about their parents' attitude toward art school and financial support. Although their parents had supported them willingly through college, the support was often withdrawn when they transferred to art school. As one of the students put it, "To my family and their friends I am a college dropout." Another said with bitter irony, "When I was goofing off in his college I was supported by my father in style, but now that I am working my heart out painting all day and driving a cab at night, he thinks I am goofing off."

Almost all the students come from intact families; only 10 percent report their parents divorced or separated. The breakdown of religious preference includes 39 percent Protestant, 26 percent Catholic, 13 percent Jewish, 5 percent scattered through other faiths, and 18 percent that declined stating any religious affiliation. Surprisingly for those who hold the stereotype of the free-thinking, bohemian artist, a large proportion—43 percent—reported attending religious worship at least once a month. But then a number of stereotypes concerning artists fall by the wayside under empirical scrutiny.

About half the students began thinking earnestly about art as a lifework between 14 and 19 years of age. But there are interesting differences in this respect also. Twenty-six percent of the females report they were considering art as a career before age 10; the corresponding figure for males is only 10 percent. Despite the preponderance of male professional artists, accepting an artistic identity seems to be easier for females than for males in our culture. A girl can think of herself and even announce publicly that she will be an artist, but a boy must wait before he can come to terms with an occupational role that is not seen as masculine or economically secure.

The age at which students remember beginning to work in art varies. Twenty-five percent of both male and female students state that they began doing art work on their own initiative before the fourth grade; about 13 percent said they did no art work during elementary or secondary school except that required in class. But whether involvement begins early or late, the intensity of the students' motivation while in art school is extraordinary. Although there is no way of making quantitative comparisons, our impression is that the motivation is far more intense—far more personal, far more intimate—than that of students in academic disciplines or other professions.

This is especially true of fine art students. They are perfectly aware that theirs is a hazardous undertaking. They know that in fine art there is no clear-cut route to a livelihood as there is in engineering, dentistry, English, or history—or, for that matter, in advertising art or art education, careers that also fit their unique technical talents.

Customary responses by other young people to the question "Why do you teach, or drive a truck, sell insurance, work for a company, and so on" include reference to money, security, social usefulness, a desire to get ahead, opportunities for leisure. Although "interest" may be mentioned, work is usually seen as a means to an end, the end being some form of reward extraneous to the work itself. Not one response from fine art students even remotely resembled the customary answers. They all responded in intrinsic terms—mentioning not rewards *from* the work but *in* the work, rewards derived not from the *product* but obtained in the *process* of production.

This is not to say that they did not hope to sell paintings, and if possible at good prices, nor that they did not aspire to win fame. But this was not primarily why they were "putting out," as one student put it. The process of painting itself, they insisted, must provide its own satisfaction or they surely could not bear investing themselves in products that might never be seen or appreciated, let alone rewarded materially. They felt that making art is its own reward.

The aesthetic ideology developed in the past 300 years has tended to reinforce the notion that art must be made for the sake of art. It is perhaps not surprising that art students give answers reflecting this ideology. Still, the unanimity with which extrinsic motivations were disregarded was striking. If the students really expect their rewards to come from the activity itself rather than from its results, then one can understand why they are able to persevere in their hazardous vocation—a vocation that is both without financial security or immediate social recognition.

But what exactly are these intrinsic rewards that artists obtain from the activity of making art? Some answers recur often enough to allow us to speak of "types" of motives related to "types" of rewards. In reporting these, we do not mean to imply that they are exhaustive or necessarily representative of any other group of young artists. They do represent, however, the range of answers our subjects gave to the question "Why do you paint [or sculpt]?"

One might expect that most of the answers would deal with the rewards the artist gets from creating "beauty," "harmony," "order," or some such aesthetic goal. This was not the case. Very few students mentioned anything of this kind at all, and only two with any explicitness. Instead, the most frequently mentioned reason for painting can be

categorized as entailing some form of "discovery" or "understanding."
Twelve of the 31 young male fine artists gave this as a reason for working
in art. Here are excerpts illustrating what they were talking about:

> I have a vague surrealistic feeling about all my work, a feeling of strange-
> ness. I paint common objects in unusual contexts. I recognize it's me, yet it
> surprises me, I didn't know it was in me . . . (S. 17)

> I paint because it's necessary, not because it's been taught to me . . . it's
> something you have to say. I can't say it any other way. I can't write. It's the
> only thing that ever comes close to me making anything. I want to say
> something, but don't know what. It's a basic questioning of what one wants
> . . . (S.06)

> I guess I don't know. I like it, I like to do it. Not knowing is part of why I do it
> . . . My intention is to discover what my intentions are, formulate my
> opinions . . . (S.01)

> Drawings are better than words, but even so I can't express what I want. I
> want to know what I am doing, trying to express myself emotionally. I want
> to draw what is in me, not what is there . . . Portraits are like psychological
> analyses of people. I like to look at people once removed, to understand and
> enjoy them, to probe, interpret their characters . . . (S.12)

> I try to define myself, on what terms do I fit in, and where . . . (S.26)

> Everyone has certain doubts about the reality of the world he lives in. I can't
> decide whether objects really exist . . . I want to state visually things that
> don't exist, and make them exist . . . (S.29)

These and similar answers suggest that one of the main rewards artists
obtain from their work is a stronger grasp on the world that surrounds
them. This is not an intellectual knowledge in the usual sense but an
existential, intuitive, visual understanding of themselves in relation to
other persons and objects. The discovery of how they relate to the rest of
the world through the process of artistic creation is an important source of
satisfaction for young artists.

What artists discover through painting is most often some facet of self.
Eleven students emphasized that the reason they painted was to understand themselves better, or to discover who they were. The purpose of
the revelation is, as one artist said, primarily private rather than public.
For instance:

> I also try to express myself, to express what I am conscious of —relate what I
> am struggling with. The paint gives me a physical freedom, it helps me in

mental, emotional freedom. My message is to myself, I am not talking to the public . . . (S.12)

In other kinds of jobs, you rarely see the outcome of what you have been doing. I guess actually the drawing is me. There was charcoal, paint—but without me nothing would have happened. It's an expression of individuality . . . (S.30)

The purpose of the artist is to show how he feels about nature, life, in a way that others can understand . . . the artist has to understand his own feelings about objects . . . the artist does not create anything new, he just discovers. (S.14)

I only paint objects that have a personal significance to me. They all have a meaning for me, I create with them a little world of my own. I like to look at these things, that's why I paint . . . (S.11)

I know the feelings I want to convey, but not the real reasons. All my work is related in the sense that they are areas of myself, facets of my personality. (S.05)

It is clear from these excerpts that discovery of self is one of the central goals of artists. In this sense, their work helps them in the pursuit of the oldest and most basic form of philosophy: the search for self-knowledge. But other areas of reality, although perhaps less central than self-discovery, are also important to them. These are knowledge of other people, an understanding of time and death, and an attempt to come to some understanding of the universe. Time and again, the young artists mention these as reasons for painting.

Here are some of the things they say regarding how their work relates to understanding other people:

I paint mostly figures: walking, standing, sitting, I am interested in human beings . . . (S.19)

I always sculpt human figures. I don't carve figures by choice, but because the power of sculpture is that people can relate to it, and one can relate best to figures. For instance, I made a little abstract dancing figure in copper, it made my friends dance too when they saw it . . . (S.08)

I just like to paint figures, it seems you can do more with them. I like to catch different aspects of different people: psychological, personality aspects . . . (S.13)

I am interested in portraits more than anything. In the universal concept of man: *The* man rather than *a* man. I don't know what this is, that's why I am searching . . . (S.25)

The searching after an understanding of *the* man often becomes extended to a search for universal laws underlying all of reality. Some of the artists voice their quest in words that would be appropriate to philosophers or to physical scientists:

> After reading Newton, that business about every action producing a reaction, I saw everything in those terms. I began putting one shape down, then other similar shapes reflecting other forces which counterblance the first . . . Like Newton established physical relationships in the universe, music and art reflect a similar kind of universal order. I enjoy the way that in science forces balance each other intricately to hold the universe together. Essentially the structure of the old masters' paintings is the same: ordering of space . . . of movement, of time. (S.23)

> I want to find out what reality is for me—like Plato did. Which is real, the concept or the object? The visual pleasure, the emotions are for me subordinated to the intellectual quest for reality. (S. 25)

> Fine art is close to science—it does research of the same nature but from a different point of view . . . (S.14)

One aspect of the laws of nature that many students were concerned with is death and time. Several mentioned that their work helps them to come to terms with these boundaries of human existence:

> That's what I am trying to express in my work: people's immortality and my own tombstone. Most of my prints have symbolic elements: clocks, skeletons, suns—time, death, and time again . . . people can look at them and understand . . . (S.19)

> I work mostly with portraits and busts. I enjoy reorganizing, distorting them. The idea is to assert mortality by breaking, distorting very unobtrusively the human form. (S.29)

The four major categories of reasons the artists gave for painting or sculpting—discovery in general, self-knowledge, understanding other people, and the quest for reality—are, of course, closely interrelated. Taken together, they seem to point to a deep existential commitment to coming to terms with life. If we are to trust the self-report of artists, this, and not the usual external rewards of a profession, is what motivates them to devote their lives to their vocation.

What these young artists find rewarding in their work also gives us a clue as to the sources of the problems they deal with. What they do is clearly problematic: Their answers usually begin with phrases such as "I want to," "I try to." Nor is what they want to do or try to do something relatively simple like "doing my job right" or "pleasing the boss" or "getting to be a vice-president in the company." The problems they are coping with are vague but extremely basic tensions inherent in the human condition.

Before artists—or anyone else—can begin to grapple with such vast problematic issues, they must somehow formulate them as concrete problems through the help of symbolic means, which in the case of artists involves the use of form, color, light, space, and other visual elements. To be able to formulate, and then resolve, a basic existential problem is the hallmark of creativity. The main goal of this book is to answer the question, how do people get to find and formulate such problems? The odds were that the kind of cognitive processes measured by standard tests of intelligence would not get us closer to an answer. Much of the research in creativity can be interpreted to mean that the problem-finding process involved in grappling with undefined problematic issues crucial to creativity is a different cognitive mode from the problem-solving process that is involved when one is presented with an already defined task.

Of course, the searching for basic problems is in part dictated by the ideology that surrounds art in our day. Perhaps the young artists' fundamental motives are different from what they consciously report. Yet the answers were so spontaneous and personal that one must assume they truly believe in what they are saying. Perhaps as they grow old, their motives and goals may change. But in the meantime it seems quite certain that what attracts young people to art is not money or fame, nor even the prospect of making objects of beauty. It is rather the attraction of discovering some meaning in life that seems to keep these people involved in an activity that has little external support.

One other important category of answers must be mentioned here. This does not involve some form of understanding or discovery, but the rewards that the artist obtains from the use of his talent, the ability to control his materials, the pleasure he derives from making something that did not exist before; and more, the use of this talent in a *free* rather than an assigned way. We shall return to this theme again and again in dealing with the distinction between working on problems that one discovers oneself as against working on problems that are presented by others.

Tests and Measures. Although personal interviews and firsthand observations will be the mainstay of our procedure, certain questions cannot be answered by interviews and observations alone. For example, what is the level of intelligence or perceptual skills among art students? How does it compare with that of other individuals of the same age, sex, and education? What are the values of art students and how do they compare with those of young people who do not plan to become artists? Is there a personality structure typical of art students, one that can be described more objectively than through interviews and observations? And if there is such artistic personality structure, how does it compare with the personality structure of other groups?

To answer questions of this order, recourse must be taken to standardized instruments such as commonly used intelligence tests, perceptual measures that have been given to a variety of groups, normative value questionnaires, and objective personality inventories. The problem, of course, is which instruments? Insofar as there is no generally accepted theoretical scheme applicable to artistic performance, we had no certain guidelines as to which instruments were likely to prove most fruitful. The early stages of the study were not designed to test hypotheses, but to explore possibilities. For every test eventually chosen, a dozen tests equally good (or poor) were rejected.

The instruments selected with much trial and trepidation were intended to provide objective data in three areas related to creativity and aesthetic performance: cognitive processes, perceptual skills, and personality attributes. In addition, biographical material was collected through questionnaires, and the school files yielded ratings in artistic potential as well as grades in studio and academic courses.

The following list of instruments indicates the characteristics each was supposed to measure according to the test manuals and reports in the literature. A fuller description of each instrument is provided in Appendix 2, along with information on the manual or bibliographic source of the instrument, the method of administration and scoring if other than that described in the source, and the interscorer reliability if there are subjective elements in the scoring. Although the instruments are grouped here according to the a priori notions of what they were measuring, in subsequent sections they may be regrouped according to the pattern of relationships that emerged from analyses of the responses.

1. *Cognitive instruments.* In addition to the usual tests of general intelligence, several tests designed to measure the process that Guilford has called "divergent" thinking were selected. The criteria for selecting any given instrument were the presumed relevance of what it measured to the

study of creativity in art students, its fruitfulness in previous work, the availability of comparative data from similar and other groups, the ease of administration in a group situation, and not least important, the suitability of the instrument to art students who made no secret of their skepticism of objective psychological tests.

The cognitive tests included: *Wonderlic Personnel Test I*, a speed test of intelligence; *16 Personality Factors Inventory, Form A, Factor B*, a power test of intelligence; *Unusual Uses*, a measure of "divergent spontaneous flexibility"; *Brick Uses* a measure of "divergent semantic fluency" and "flexibility"; *Thing Categories (Ideational Fluency)*, a measure of "divergent semantic fluency"; *Object-Question Test*, a measure of "divergent evaluative questioning power"; and *Word-Association Test*, a measure of "fluency and flexibility of associations."

2. *Perceptual instruments.* It was very difficult to find group instruments measuring purely perceptual aptitudes or aesthetic perceptions. Three of the tests expected to measure dimensions of perception are known also to measure dimensions of cognition. Indeed, the distinction between perception and cognition is a delicate theoretical issue, though it need not detain us here. The instruments in this category might most accurately be described as nonverbal tests of perception-cognition.

They included: *Hidden Shapes*, a measure of "convergent figural transformations"; *Match Problems III*, a measure of "cognitive figural transformations"; *Spatial Visualization*, a measure of "cognitive figural transformations"; *Perceptual Memory*, a measure of "memory of perceptual content, structure, and detail"; and *Welsh Figure Preference Test*, a measure of "visual aesthetic preference."

3. *Personality instruments.* In spite of its common usage, personality is an inordinately elusive concept, and the choice of instruments here was even more difficult than for the preceding categories. Many of the definitions of personality are contradictory, and instruments based on these various definitions of what is being measured frequently produce contradictory results. Gordon Allport once reported with dismay that he found 50 significantly different definitions of the term "personality."

In general, however, the more popular definitions may be classified into three main categories. First, there are what we may call *behavioral* definitions. Typical of these is Watson's position, who sees personality as the sum of a person's habit systems (Watson, 1930, 274). That is, personality is the totality of a person's usual behavior. *Self-report* inventories and questionnaires that require respondents to record their own behavior are often based on definitions of this type. Second, there are what one may call *social-stimulus* definitions of personality. Typical of these is the definition by Mark May: Personality is the social stimulus value of an individual. It is the responses made by others to the individual as a stimulus that defines his personality (May, 1932, 82). Here the focus is not the subjects' own statements about themselves but the impression they make on others. Deriving from this type of definition are the familiar *rating* scales where individuals who are presumed to know something about a particular person rank that person in terms of a set of variables. Third, there are what may be called *depth* definitions. Typical of these is the one by Gordon Allport: "Personality is the dynamic organization within the individual of those psychophysical systems that determine his unique adjustment to his environment" (Allport, 1937, 48). So-called depth or *projective* techniques are based on this definition, since they attempt to delve beneath the individual's manifest behavior to the underlying needs and covert motives of which the individual may be unaware.

Each of these conceptions of personality has its uses and misuses, and the instruments deriving from them have their advantages and disadvantages. All three types of instruments were used in this study, from self-report and projective instruments to observations of actual behavior and to ratings recorded in the school files. From the numerous possible personality instruments six were selected since they seemed to be most relevant to the study of artists, they could be given in a group setting, and they were worded so as not to antagonize a rather sensitive group of subjects.

They included the *Allport-Vernon-Lindzey Study of Values*, a measure of the relative strength of six values—the theoretical, economic, political, aesthetic, social, and religious—based on Spranger's personality typology; the *16 Personality Factors Inventory*, a self-report questionnaire covering 16 factors such as ego-strength, sensitivity, and self-sufficiency (a combination of 10 of these factors had also been used by the test-constructors to measure "creative personality"); *The Paired Direct and Projective Sentence Completion Test*, a measure of the self-report and projective reactions to the same objects of inquiry, previously used to study "levels of personality"; the *Semantic Differential,* a measure of "identity diffusion" based on Erikson's theory of ego identity; *The Group Thematic Apperception Test,* a projective measure of personality, scored especially for "novelty of production"; and *The Association of Colors,* a measure of "acceptance or rejection of stereotypes."

4. *Biographical Questionnaire.* Personal and family data were collected by means of a general questionnaire which included such items as the respondent's age, sibling position, and family income.

5. *Ratings: Originality and Artistic Potential.* Ratings in originality and artistic potential were already available in the files of the school, since the teachers of the school fill out a rating sheet for each student in their classes at the end of each semester, which together with the course grade becomes part of the student's permanent record. Ten variables, including reliability, working habits, common sense, originality, and artistic potential, are listed on the rating sheet. For each variable the student is rated from 1 (very low) to 4 (very high). In this study only the ratings on originality and artistic potential were used. Originality was defined by the teachers as: "Ability to originate ideas and draw on personal resources in preparing assignments." Artistic potential was defined by the teachers as: "Capacity for growth and development for innate talent in pursuit of positive professional success in chosen field." MacKinnon (1962) defines creativity as a response or idea that is novel or statistically infrequent; adaptive to reality; and that is carried out until it results in a tangible product. The "originality" rating meets MacKinnon's first requirement; the "artistic potential" rating meets the other two.

These teacher ratings yielded two measures: *Originality and Artistic Potential I,* an average of the ratings for the first year in school, and *Originality and Artistic Potential II,* an average for the second year. The ratings provided a more realistic assessment of the students than one could have hoped for. Ratings given for the student's permanent record are more likely to be considered seriously by the teachers than any evaluation they could make at our request. This functional advantage was, however, accompanied by an experimental disadvantage: It became difficult to estimate the internal reliability of the several ratings. The procedures for ascertaining the reliability and the reliability itself are given in Appendix 2.

6. *Grades.* Two separate grade-point averages were computed from the school's files: art grades and academic grades. Art grades are a grade-point average based on all the grades a student received in studio art course. In accordance with the grading system used by the school administration, a letter grade of "A" was given 12 points, "A−" 11 points, "B+" 10 points, and so on. "F" was given 0 points. Academic grades are a similar average based on all grades a student received in courses other than art (history, humanities, etc.).

As we have mentioned, the instruments were divided into three batteries, each administered in two-hour sessions. Within each battery, the cognitive and perceptual tests were alternated with personality inventories, timed tests with untimed tests, and so on, to achieve a maximum of diversity. Appendix 2 provides the details regarding the division of instruments into the three batteries.

In the chapter that follows, we present a profile of the future artist based on these instruments, including measures of intelligence, perception, values, and personality.

CHAPTER 3

■

A Profile of Future Artists

Young people who enroll in art school do so in the hope of living their adult lives as artists. They believe that they have the necessary talent; the fact that they were admitted to a prestigious art school confirms their estimate. But they also know that very few among them will ever get artistic recognition.

They may dream of becoming a Picasso, a Giacometti, a Calder, or a Warhol. Even industrial design majors think of themselves as being in the tradition of the creative masters; those in fine art follow directly in that tradition, even though few of them will find a livelihood as fine artists. There is perhaps no other course of professional training where the discrepancy between aspirations and achievement is so great.

Of those who hope to become painters and sculptors, most will eventually settle down in jobs related to art, but will not produce art themselves. They will find employment with architectural firms, with galleries, or most likely as schoolteachers. Others will drop out of the art world entirely. Nonetheless, even these will often preserve an artistic identity—latent perhaps but still essential to their self-concept. In this sense, for art students it is true that "although many are called, few are chosen." It is also true that "once an artist, always an artist." Whether one should or should not consider the unrecognized artist an "artist" is a metaphysical question beyond the scope of empirical inquiry.

What *can* be answered empirically is what kind of people attempt to become artists. It is possible to determine the way in which those who aspire to an artistic career differ—if they do differ—from others their own age.

The profile of the art student that will take form here will not reveal any essential traits of artistic accomplishment. Later we explore how certain traits are related to achievement within the school and in the world of art outside. At the moment, we are concerned with a far simpler task: to provide a psychometric description of young people who have decided to undertake training as artists. It is from among people of this kind that outstanding artists of the future may come. And the rest, the great majority who will never be publicly recognized, nonetheless will fulfill an important function, and therefore cannot be ignored. For without the many unknown artists, the few eminent ones would exist in a vacuum.

The greatness of an artist depends in large degree on the effect of that artist's work on lesser artists. Indeed, "greater" has no meaning except in relation to "lesser." Art as a cultural institution may survive without geniuses, but would not survive without dedicated craftsmen. Even though few will achieve their goal, and fewer still attain any measure of greatness, aspiring artists are worthy of study in their own right, as well as for being a prototype of what they might become.

Intelligence and Perception.   Perhaps the best way to begin drawing a profile of future artists is to sketch an outline of their ways of thinking and perceiving. It is true that standardized tests may not reveal the unique qualitative features of their mental processes, but even dry IQ scores can help settle some issues regarding the "intelligence" of artists.

Speculation about the intelligence of artists is hardly new. Plato, Aristotle, and their contemporaries did not have a high opinion of the visual arts or of those who practiced them. Throughout most of history it was generally believed that all artists did was to copy the visible attributes of reality. Far from requiring a high level of intelligence or imagination, the act of copying was thought to enslave the mind. By contrast, poets were truly creative; they transformed reality into the abstract medium of language. This judgment varied by circumstances of time and place: the status of the craftsmen, the value put on works of art, the style of the art, and types of people who were recruited into the artistic profession. Hence generalizations across time and place must take these conditions into account.

The pattern that emerges from our data is both simple and suggestive.

On both intelligence tests, the performance of art students was close to college norms (see Table A1.1 in Appendix). On the speed test, however, they did relatively less well than on the test where speed was not an issue. Male art students did significantly worse than other college students on the speed test, while female college students did significantly better than their comparison group on the power test of intelligence. Evidently quickness of response in standard intellectual tasks is not the forte of those who plan to become artists. Of course, speed in answering an IQ test is not the ultimate measure of a person's cognitive capacity, even if it might be its most obvious manifestation, the one on which popular judgment of intelligence is likely to be based.

In any case, these first results confirm the expectation that the standard reasoning process tapped by the usual cognitive tests cannot be the crucial ability that distinguishes people who are involved in creative tasks. Hence we need to look further to discover the source of their creative cognitive abilities.

The next area where one might look for characteristics that distinguish the artist is the perceptual domain. Here, one might suspect, large differences ought to be found between artists and "normal" students. This is in fact true for both measures of perception that were available. One tested the ability to see a three-dimensional object in two-dimensional space, and then to visualize the form of the object as it is rotated; it is a difficult task in space perception. The other was not a measure of perceptual skill per se but rather of aesthetic taste.

Art students outperformed the norms on both measures (see Table A1.2). The markedly superior space perception of female art students is particularly notable. Females are usually far less proficient on this task than males. Consequently the scores of female art students here were still far below those of male students, but they were very much higher relative to female norms than the scores of male art students were to male norms.

The results on the aesthetic judgment task are obvious. Art students score twice as high as the norms. This may seem almost too self-evident to report; of course art students should perform significantly better than nonartists on tasks requiring perceptual skills and aesthetic taste. But the matter is far more complex. It will be shown later that the relationship between such skills and artistic talent is not as straightforward as it appears to be. There are indications, in fact, that an excess of refinement in this area is detrimental to artistic achievement.

Taken together, this first pattern of results suggests that artists do possess very strong skills in the area of their expertise—visual perception. It is by manipulating visual forms that artists express their creativity; therefore it is quite appropriate that they should be unusually proficient in this respect. But neither spatial visualization nor aesthetic taste have much to do with creativity. The cognitive ability to ask new questions is independent of visual skills, which if indispensable to artists, are less relevant to musicians or mathematicians. Whatever this ability consists of, we know at this point that it is unlikely to be synonymous with so-called intelligence, a quality that artists, as we have seen, do not possess to an exhorbitant degree.

Values.   One's values give coherence to one's actions; they make our lives consistent and meaningful. This is not the place to become involved in the controversy about the origins of values—whether they are nothing but rationalizations of instinctual desires, or of economic interests, or of learned responses. However values become established, our actions are explicable by the values we hold. To know art students, one must know their values.

Here again we must call attention to the limitations of testing instruments. Individual value systems are enormously complex, and are in certain respects as unique as thumbprints. It is impossible to present a detailed analysis of all the values held by any one of our young artists, let alone of those held by all of them. Therefore we must be content to report their scores on the most widely used values instrument—the Allport-Vernon-Lindzey Study of Values—which includes six basic values postulated to represent the major human motivations.

The six values are: *theoretical,* that is, the pursuit of truth, the belief in the importance of abstract intellectual understanding; *economic,* or the propensity for achieving material rewards, attaining financial independence; *aesthetic,* the search for meaning through art, the belief that life without sensory harmony is wasted; *social,* the importance of interpersonal relationships, the fulfillment obtained through helping other human beings; *political,* the solution of problems through the use of interpersonal persuasion and power; *religious,* the emphasis on supernatural goals and spiritual rewards within a traditional religious context.

Table A1.3 in Appendix 1 makes it amply clear that the art students hold uniquely extreme values. The males differ significantly from norms on four, and females on five of the six basic values.

As was to be expected, the score on aesthetic value—the value most relevant to the artist's work—is by far the highest. In fact, it is higher than that of any group for which data are reported in the *Manual*. This comes as no surprise. But four additional observations regarding the value profile of young artists are noteworthy. First, compared with the values of students preparing for other professions, only those in theology have a higher peak on any value (the religious value). Second, the difference between the highest score (aesthetic value) and the next highest score (theoretical value) of art students is greater than the difference between the highest and next highest score of any of the 29 student and professional groups reported in the *Manual*, with the exception of medical students, clergymen, and theology students. Third, the value scale being an "ipsative" measure, a high score on one value necessarily entails a correspondingly low score on another value. But the low scores of the art students that complement their high aesthetic value are not distributed randomly among the remaining five values. They tend to affect only two of the other values, the economic and the social. Finally, the range of values from the greatest acceptance of a particular value to the greatest rejection of another value is greater than for any group except clergymen and theology students.

This pattern points clearly to a significant conclusion: Art students are committed to the values of their work single-mindedly. Persons planning to devote their life to art—like those devoting themselves to religion —must be completely identified with their calling; other professions for which there is greater societal support do not require the same exclusive value commitment.

In addition to the extremely high aesthetic value, art students also have very low economic and social values, the latter being lower than those for all the 29 student and professional groups cited in the *Manual*. This may be interpreted at two separate levels. At a behavioral level, low economic value is adaptive to artists, who are risking careers in which the only thing they can count on is economic insecurity, and low social value is a necessity for working in the loneliness of a studio in this age of togetherness. At an ideological level, low economic and social values represent a rejection of two predominant values of our time, materialism and the cult of sociability—a rejection that helps establish the artist's identity.

It is enlightening to compare the value profile of future artists with that of people of established creative achievement, as represented by highly creative scientists and architects for whom data are available on the same value scale. The comparison is shown in Figure A1.1. The value pattern of creative scientists and architects is remarkably parallel to that of art students. Despite the diversity of specific fields, the three groups are united by creative endeavor, and the similarity of values reflects this unity. The two highest values of the three groups are theoretical and aesthetic, although there is an understandable reversal in the first and second value of the scientists. The lower economic and social values of the three groups are also noteworthy, the only substantial difference being the additional low religious value of the scientists.

The value system of artists is a pivotal aspect of their personality. It is tempting to say that the strength of their value commitments, already well-formed for these students, is more important than their cognitive characteristics—especially if by the latter we mean only standard intelligence. The value profile reflects their will to achieve aesthetic goals; how strongly they are prepared to hold them may determine whether they will survive the severe pressures that eliminate all but a few from the approaches to a creative career.

Personality.   Most people do not have a high opinion of the personality and emotional maturity of artists. Artists are supposed to be moody, extravagant, unreliable, promiscuous, and altogether a bad match for one's daughter. To call someone "artistic" often implies not so much a given set of skills but a personality that is disreputable, or at least unconventional. The notion that the personality of artists is somehow disordered obtained "scientific" credence in the late nineteenth century when Lombroso published his influential *The Man of Genius,* in which it was argued that genius is a morbid condition resembling many forms of mental disorder. Freud was believed to have lent support to this line of thought by postulating that the common neuroses and the creativity of a Leonardo da Vinci both have their sources in unconscious conflict. The relationship between creativity and psychic malfunctioning is still a lively topic of debate, as the recent works of Andreasen and Powers (1975), Komarik (1972), and others show.

It has not always been so. Throughout most of history, artists were craftsmen and women similar to, say, wool dyers or ironsmiths. They were expected to be reliable, steady, and sober workers. No one paid enough attention to notice whether they lived up to these expectations, any more than other groups of craftsmen did. But since the role of the artist and expectations for the artist's behavior have changed over time, we cannot consider the artist's personality without taking into account the social environment of his or her time.

In ancient Egypt, most art was mass-produced by craftsmen who were obliged to respect an aesthetic tradition that was a tool for preserving the stability of the social and political systems. The artist was akin to a bureaucrat working for the government, perhaps not unlike an officially-approved Soviet artist of our time. There is no reason then to believe that Egyptian artists were temperamental; more likely they behaved like proper civil servants.

In Greece and Rome artists were respected, but only with rare exceptions were they accorded a substantially greater status than other skilled craftsmen. Hauser describes the situation as follows: "The plastic or graphic artist is and remains a *banausic* artisan who, with his wages, gets all that he is entitled to" (Hauser, 1951, I, 113). Poets, dramatists, and musicians were held in higher esteem, partly because they did not work manually on material substances, partly because their medium was freer than that of the visual artist. Painters or sculptors were not expected to be "creative" or "original" in the sense that we conceive of them today; the main requirement was that they portray beauty and depict historic events. Their function was conservative, and their status decidedly below the first rank.

There were exceptions to the general rule. During the reigns of Alexander the Great and his successors, for instance, artists seemed to enjoy fame and affluence. Hauser attributes this change of status to Alexander's need to impose Greek culture on the occupied territories; hence artists became powerful instruments of political conquest. Paradoxically, it was during this period that tales about the eccentric personality of artists came into vogue. A similar rise in the artist's status also occurred in the late stages of the Roman empire. But by and large, antiquity seems to have held the opinion attributed to Seneca: "We offer prayers and sacrifices before the statues of the Gods, but we despise the sculptors who make them" (Lactantius, quoted in Hauser, 1951, I, 119).

In Medieval civilization, artists were again supposed to be chiefly concerned with the maintenance of the social order. Their task was to illustrate the events and symbols of the religious system, often for the benefit of the illiterate masses who had to be instructed in the verities on which the culture rested. If an artist represented a saint in too relaxed a pose, or if he painted an angel without the customary halo, the abbott who commissioned the work might refuse to pay for it, and there would be no private collector to buy it as an "original." Moreover, artistic production was more a collective than an individual enterprise. As Hauser describes it, "The artist's studio in the early Renaissance is still dominated by the communal spirit of the mason's lodge and the guild workshop; the work of art is not yet the expression of an independent personality" (Hauser, 1951, II, 54–55).

The Renaissance changed this. New techniques and expanded demand projected the individual artist to the forefront of society as a figure of public interest. In 1550 Vasari published the first collection of biographies of artists, many of whom he knew personally. It is in this work that qualms began to be expressed about the distinctive "artistic personality." As Vasari said of the Florentine artists:

> . . . in truth . . . the greater part of the craftsmen who had lived up to that time had received from nature a certain element of savagery and madness, which, besides making them strange and eccentric, had brought it about that very often there was revealed in them rather the obscure darkness of vice than the brightness and splendor of those virtues that make men immortal . . . (Vasari, 1959, 232)

It is difficult to see from Vasari's own evidence why he should have attributed "savagery" and "madness" to the personality of the artists he describes. They were certainly asocial, independent, and nonconforming; apparently these traits were enough to provoke derogatory labels even from a sympathetic chronicler like Vasari. Here, as one instance, is a short sketch of Tommaso di Ser Giovanni di Simon Guido, which is fairly typical of others:

> He was a very absent-minded and careless person, as one who, having fixed his whole mind and will on the matters of art, cared little about himself, and still less about others. And since he would never give any manner of thought to the cares and concerns of the world, or even to clothing himself, and was not wont to recover his money from his debtors, save only when he was in the greatest of straits, his name was therefore changed from Tommaso to Masaccio ["Oafish Tom"], not, indeed, because he was vicious, for he was goodness itself, but by reason of his great carelessness . . . (Vasari, 1959, 42–43)

A man who is so dedicated to his art that he forgets to ask for the money that is due him, neglects to dress himself properly, and ignores the concerns of the world would have indeed seemed mad to his contemporaries—as he would to us.

The image on which the modern conception of the "lonely, demonically impelled artist" has chiefly been built is that of Michelangelo. Perhaps more than any other artist, the "divine Michelangelo" was able to establish the idea that artists are entitled to abundant material support and at the same time to independence to work out their own creative vision. But independence and freedom from cultural traditions also deprived Renaissance painters of the firm guidelines of the guild, and the assured moral support of the community that their predecessors had enjoyed. Perhaps this psychological isolation is the root of the "savagery" and "madness" of which Vasari spoke. Or perhaps artists were always like that, but being less noteworthy, the oddities of their personality were not recorded.

The conditions in which the artist worked continued to change. The large shop where the master painted surrounded by apprentices with whom he lived a communal existence gave way to an increasingly independent and individualistic practice. At the same time, the unifying themes and tastes of the church-centered culture broke down into segregated, often contradictory, symbols and values. By the nineteenth century, when the ideology of Romanticism enjoined nonconformity as the conformity of the day, artists were ready to assume the alienated personality that they still hold in the public eye.

This question about the nature of the artist's personality and how it fits (or conflicts with) the social forces of a given time, is inseparable from the question about the sources of creative thinking. Time and again, men and women of genius have stated that their work issues from the very depths of their being; in the words of D. H. Lawrence, "Art is . . . at-oneness, the state of being at one with the object" (Lawrence, 1955, 71). Therefore, an inquiry into the personality of artists is a necessary backdrop against which the more purely cognitive processes of artistic creativity may be more clearly perceived.

Systematic evidence bearing on the accuracy of the stereotype for the artistic temperament that has been built up through the centuries does not exist in any quantity. This is at least partly due to the serious conceptual and methodological difficulties that plague the study of personality, even more than the study of intelligence, perception, and values. A catalogue of personality tests developed over the past 40 years contains more than 500 instruments, of which more than three-quarters are still in use. The diversity of tests reflects the lack of a generally accepted theoretical position or the validity of any given test. As the editor of the catalogue notes ruefully, "The vast literature on personality testing has failed to produce a body of knowledge generally acceptable to psychologists. In fact, all personality instruments may be described as controversial, each with its own following and devotees" (Buros, 1970, 25–26).

Faced with this awkward state of the art, we had to choose among three alternatives: ignore the psychometric personality dimension completely; develop a new instrument especially for this study; or use an existing instrument despite its lack of universal acceptance. We chose the third alternative for obvious reasons. We did not wish to exclude the objective observation of personality out of hand, and we had no desire to add yet another to the 500 instruments already available.

One of the most widely used omnibus measures of personality is the *Sixteen Personality Factors Questionnaire* (16 PF). As the name implies, the 16 PF was designed to measure sixteen fundamental behavioral predispositions which, when taken together, yield a comprehensive profile of personality. The sixteen factors, each reflecting a basic trait, have portentous names like "cyclothymia" or "premsia," corresponding to readily identifiable characteristics like "aloofness" or "sensitivity."

Table 3.1 shows how future artists perform in relation to pertinent norms. It is readily apparent that male and female art students differ significantly from average students of their age on no fewer than 11 of the factors, and that on six of these *both* males and females differ from their respective norms in the same direction.

The six factors that show a consistent pattern for students of both sexes point to the following portrait: future artists are socially reserved and aloof (Factor A–). They are serious and introspective (F–). Accepted standards of behavior and morality have little hold on them—they score low in "superego strength" (G–). They are intensely subjective, unconventional in outlook, and imaginative (M). They tend to be radical and experimental (Q1). They are resolute and make their own decisions—they score high in "self-sufficiency" (Q2).

On each of these factors art students of both sexes were significantly different from "normal" college students. Apparently, the image of the artist as socially withdrawn, introspective, independent, imaginative, unpredictable, and alienated from community expectations is not far off

Table 3.1. Sixteen Personality Factors: Comparison of Art Students with College Norms [a]

Factor	Art School Males (N = 94)	College Males (N = 535)	Significance Level of t	Art School Females (N = 111)	College Females (N = 559)	Significance Level of t
A. Cyclothymia (reserved: low; outgoing: high)	7.63	9.79	.001	8.89	12.06	.001
B. Intelligence (dull: low; bright: high)	8.04	7.92	n.s.	8.08	7.57	.05
C. Ego-strength (emotional: low; stable: high)	13.99	15.35	.01	14.06	14.58	n.s.
E. Dominance (humble: low; assertive: high)	14.17	13.78	n.s.	12.96	10.61	.001
F. Surgency (serious: low; frivolous: high)	12.70	16.00	.001	13.19	16.09	.001
G. Superego (nonconforming: low; conscientious: high)	11.24	12.64	.01	9.68	13.14	.001
H. Parmia (timid: low; venturesome: high)	11.41	12.99	.01	12.27	12.20	n.s.
I. Premsia (tough-minded: low; sensitive: high)	9.95	8.65	.01	11.88	11.95	n.s.
L. Protension (trusting: low; suspicious: high)	10.16	9.76	n.s.	9.45	8.00	.01
M. Autia (conventional: low; imaginative: high)	14.34	11.49	.001	15.65	12.71	.001
N. Shrewdness (naive: low; worldly: high)	10.46	10.96	n.s.	9.43	10.56	.01
O. Guilt (confident: low; apprehensive: high)	11.38	10.14	.01	11.33	11.24	n.s.
Q1. Radicalism (conservative: low; experimenting: high)	10.36	9.65	.05	10.34	8.74	.001
Q2. Self-sufficiency (dependent: low; autonomous: high)	13.33	9.86	.001	13.49	9.66	.001
Q3. Self-sentiment (norm free: low; norm bound: high)	9.72	10.08	n.s.	9.38	10.81	.01
Q4. Ergic tension (relaxed: low; tense: high)	14.02	12.26	.01	13.86	13.51	n.s.

[a] IPAT Preliminary Normative Tables, November 1963. Sample: 535 males, 559 females.

the mark. The artistic personality described by Vasari more than four centuries ago applies remarkably well to young artists today.

It is possible that these traits are necessary for pursuing a creative activity, at least under the historical conditions that have prevailed in Western civilization since the Renaissance. The cognitive task of restructuring old problems or discovering new ones is apparently embedded in a set of personality traits that facilitate this potentially deviant task. It takes a person who is cut off from others, who has an intense inner life, who does not depend on outside direction and support, to break away from the premises on which the majority bases its thinking.

In addition to this general finding, an important set of differences appears between male and female art students. The latter are significantly more dominant (E) than other women of their age, while male art students are significantly more sensitive and "effeminate in feeling" (I) than is usual for males. That is, future artists possess traits that our culture traditionally associates with the opposite sex.

This reversal may be explained in at least two ways. Artists, whose function is to express universal truths about human existence, must be exposed to as broad a range of experience as possible. A person who is too "masculine" or too "feminine" would not be in touch with modalities that did not fit his or her restricted outlook. The one would not be familiar with emotion, sensitivity, and harmony, which in our culture are considered feminine traits; the other would not be exposed to the use of logic, toughness, or dominance, which in our culture are considered to be masculine. Artists cannot afford this kind of limitation, for strict sex-typing would cut them off from half the range of human experience, and thereby reduce the scope of their art.

Carl Jung wrote that "the psychology of the creative is really a feminine psychology" (Jung, 1930a, 43). What he seems to have meant was that the thought processes and feelings of creative persons resemble more those of women than of men. But he must have arrived at this generalization by studying only creative men. If he had studied only creative women, he would probably have arrived at the opposite conclusion: "The psychology of the creative is really a masculine psychology." A more nearly true, although more cumbersome generalization, would run something like this: "The psychology of creative men is a feminine psychology by comparison with less creative men; the psychology of creative women is a masculine psychology by comparison with less creative women."

Another explanation of the reversal may also be proposed. In our culture art does not enjoy a high prestige. Fathers tend to become upset if they discover their sons taking art seriously; not only is art unlikely to lead to riches, it also has effete connotations. Yet throughout history, all first-ranked artists we know of have been men. There have been famous women heroes, saints, monarchs, poets, novelists, scientists—even great warriors. But there is no record of a woman painter of the very first rank. Here then is the paradox: On the one hand, it is unlikely that a young man with a strong "masculine" personality will identify with a vocation that is considered inappropriate for strong males; on the other hand, a young woman who wishes to be an artist must have rather strong masculine traits to have any hope of success in such a traditionally male profession.

There is no way of ascertaining which, if either, of the explanations accounts for the reversals. The data and circumstantial evidence from other sources suggests that both explanations might be true. Empirical work by Torrance (1959, 1961), for instance, has indicated that overemphasis on sexual stereotypes in socialization has a negative effect on the expressiveness and creativity of children. Rau (1963) has found that ability in spatial visualization is associated with imaginativeness in boys and with aggressiveness in girls. These and similar findings point to an intrinsic relationship between visual aptitude and creativity on the one hand, and reversals of sex-typed behavior on the other. However, the explanation based on cultural factors cannot be dismissed either. Whatever the explanation, there is some tendency for personality traits of male art students to be typical of traits generally found in females, and vice versa.

One other result derived from the personality data presented in Table 3.1 merits report at this point. In work with people of demonstrated creative achievement, Cattell and his associates (IPAT, 1963) found that a certain combination of weighted scores on the 16 PF clearly differentiated creative from noncreative persons in the same occupational field. This "creative personality" measure includes such factors as aloofness (A−), imaginativeness (M), and sensitivity (I). By applying this index to large groups of subjects, it was possible to establish norms for general creativity, including norms for college students—that is, a group of young men and women of approximately the same age and educational level as our sample.

When this index was computed, the average score of the 205 students who took the test was higher than that of 89 percent of the college population. That is, only one college student in 10 can be expected to have such a high score. The high score is not likely to be due to the slightly greater age and educational level of the art students, since neither variable is correlated with the creativity score. To get more than 200 people in one school with a personalistic creativity score in the top 10 percent is remarkable, and points as perhaps no other single datum can to the unique personality configuration of art students. No sex differences were found—male and female young artists scored equally high relative to their respective comparison groups.

Values and Personality.   Since we see, then, that future artists have distinctive value and personality patterns, we must ask whether the two are related. One might expect, for example, that a person with high aesthetic value on the values scale would show high sensitivity on the 16 PF. If scores on the two scales are in fact related, the emerging portrait would acquire that much more substance and credibility.

Table 3.2 shows what happens when two of the crucial values for artists—the aesthetic and the economic—are correlated with the 16 personality factors. Part A of the table displays correlations between the two values and the six "core" artistic factors—that is, those on which art students of both sexes differed significantly from their respective norms. Part B displays the correlations with the remaining 10 factors, which are presumably less important in defining artistic temperament.

Ninety percent of the correlations in Part A are in the expected direction, and 40 percent are statistically significant. Since art students score low in economic value and low in personality factors A (sociability), F (cheerfulness), and G (superego strength), the correlations should be positive; and since they score high in factors M (imaginativeness), Q1 (radicalism), and Q2 (self-sufficiency), the correlations should be negative. This is in fact the case for 12 of the 12 correlations. The opposite is expected for correlations between aesthetic value and the six personality factors. Again, this is the case in 10 of the 12 correlations. To be sure, the values scale is an *ipsative* instrument, and scores on aesthetic and economic values are not entirely independent. Nonetheless, the consistency is strong, suggesting that for our students values and personality are meaningfully integrated.

Table 3.2.   Correlation Between Art Student Main Value and Personality Traits[a]

Personality Traits	Factor	Values			
		Economic		Aesthetic	
		Males (N = 86)	Females (N = 93)	Males (N = 86)	Females (N = 93)
A. "Core" personality variables					
Cyclothymia (−)[b]	A	.16	.16	−.26*	−.15
Surgency (−)	F	.16	.06	−.12	.05
Superego (−)	G	.11	.24*	−.24*	−.28**
Autia	M	−.40***	−.19	.42***	.30**
Radicalism	Q1	−.12	−.13	.06	−.04
Self-sufficiency	Q2	−.25*	−.36***	.18	.23*
B. Remaining Variables					
Intelligence	B	−.17	−.11	.14	.16
Ego-strength	C	.21	.04	−.13	−.16
Dominance	E	.07	−.06	.05	.25*
Parmia	H	.20	.03	−.18	.11
Premsia	I	−.45***	−.33**	.46***	.27**
Protension	L	−.12	−.09	.19	.06
Shrewdness	N	.30**	.36***	−.25*	−.26*
Guilt	O	−.04	.05	.14	−.03
Self-sentiment	Q3	.22*	.26*	−.20	−.29**
Id tension	Q4	−.14	−.06	.30**	.19

[a] Correlation coefficients based only on the "core sample" of 179 art students.
[b] For the meaning of factor scores see Table 3.1.
*$p < .05$.
**$p < .01$.
***$p < .001$.

Part B of the table shows that 32 percent of the correlations between the two values and the remaining personality traits are also significant, and in the expected direction. A closer look shows that 8 of the 13 significant correlations are due to two factors: I (sensitivity) and N (shrewdness). That is, each of the possible correlations of economic and aesthetic values with the traits of "sensitivity" and "shrewdness" is significant.

It is easy to see why high sensitivity (I) should be related to high aesthetic value and to low economic value. It is also clear why worldly shrewdness (N) should be related to high economic value. But why should it be inversely related to aesthetic value?

According to the constructors of the test, the low end of the shrewdness factor measures naivete, not in the sense of credulousness, but in the sense of spontaneity, ingenuousness, and freedom from the conventional and contrived. It calls to mind Goethe's remark that naivete is the greatest asset of the creative person, and Matisse's admonition: "Naivete is the chief cause of every artist's suffering. It is also the source of anything good that he may do. Remember that. Study as hard as you like, but guard your naivete. It will be all you've got, some day" (Eliot, 1972, 104).

Naivete is presumably required for that open problem-finding attitude that is an essential part of artistic creativity. To be able to reject the givens—the perceptual and cognitive customs—of their time, artists must be unspoiled, spontaneous, and free from what is conventional. Only naive persons risk questioning phenomena everyone else takes for granted, or dare impose their own interpretations on percepts that have established meaning. Nor is the need for this kind of naivete confined to creativity in the arts. Einstein, for example, implied the same function of naivete in science when he remarked that he had to discover new laws because he could not understand the old ones. He seems to have meant that he could not understand why the existing problems and formulations in physics must be accepted as definitive. The naive "not understanding" led to the posing of new problems, which is the precondition for all forms of creativity.

In any case, the pattern of relationships in Table 3.2 confirms that the values and personality traits of art students are not randomly distributed, but form an interlocking cluster of characteristics significant for understanding their activities and distinguishing them from other people.

To define a thing means to relate it to a broader class to which it belongs, and then describe how the particular thing differs in specific ways from other things in its class. In this chapter we have examined the ways in which young artists resemble and the ways in which they differ from college students in general.

If one defines artists in terms of a larger class of nonartists, however, the dimensions on which the resulting description is based may be restricted to traits that apply only to nonartists. There is a danger of missing the very characteristics that might be singular to the people one wants to describe. For instance, in examining intellectual processes, IQ-type tests were used, because these are the only tests with enough general currency to permit quantitative comparisons between art students and the general population. But if the thought processes peculiar to artistic creativity are not measured by these tests, any effort to define the thought of artists in terms of conventional thinking will obscure rather than illuminate the issue.

In view of this possibility, we resorted increasingly to a more direct phenomenological approach. In subsequent chapters we explore the thoughts and feelings of young artists in their own terms, letting their behavior suggest analytic categories rather than imposing existing categories on their behavior.

Nevertheless, the observations based on standardized tests must also be taken into account. They begin to outline a recognizable profile, one that in many ways resembles the portrait of the artist that has been developing ever since the Renaissance. Young artists, while still students, already tend to be reserved, amoral, introspective, imaginative, radical, and self-sufficient, and tend to possess attitudes usually associated with the opposite sex. They hold aesthetic values in high regard, and neglect economic and social values—a pattern that contradicts the ethos of the culture in which they live. They do not differ substantially from college students in intelligence as measured by conventional tests, but are far superior to them in spatial and aesthetic perception.

As our inquiry becomes more idiographic, more concerned with the specific character of young artists and the conditions of their task, we shall increasingly abandon the convenient generalizations and global comparisons permitted by the application of standardized tests. In exchange, we hope to gain deeper and more detailed insights into the unique nature of the artist and of the creative process.

CHAPTER 4

■

The Choice of Artistic Careers

The creative process cannot be explored without describing the people involved in it—in this case, young artists. But studying future artists soon leads to an impasse; we cannot assume that everyone who is called an "artist" today is involved in doing the same things, or is equally creative.

The increasing fragmentation and refinement of skills ushered in by the Industrial Age has not bypassed artists. The age of industrial specialization is also an age of artistic specialization. Throughout the Middle Ages and until quite late in the Renaissance, artists had had to use their skills in a broad variety of ways. The same person painted murals and decorated altarpieces, carved stone and cast gold, planned buildings and designed furniture (Hauser, 1951, II, 78 ff.). It is probable that the versatility of earlier artists was at least in part due to the restricted demand for works of art. Even the most renowned master could not survive economically by painting or by sculpting alone. Botticelli, for example, did not consider it demeaning to paint flags for the Florentine weavers' guilds, which in contemporary terms would be akin to producing posters for the Teamsters Union. Perugino gladly accepted commissions to decorate furniture, and the great Leonardo designed comic costumes for his patrons' parties. Whatever the causes of their versatility, artists of past centuries were able to use the full gamut of creative expression available in their culture.

The Specialization of Talent.   Modern artists are rarely so flexible. For one thing, their training is not as broad as was that of artists living four or five centuries ago. The division of labor has affected them along with members of other occupations and professions. The early Renaissance artist was usually the only aesthetic worker in his community, and accepted any job his compatriots were willing to give him. In a typical workshop, apprentices might be setting jewels, forging a sign for a nearby inn, preparing the cartoon for a tapestry, and designing a saltcellar, as well as painting and sculpting—all under the vigilant eye of a master who owned the shop and might do parts of each task himself. Now these tasks, or their equivalents, are done by different specialists in separate locations. Quite early in their training contemporary art students must decide whether they will become illustrators or architectural designers, painters or weavers, go into advertising art or fine art, into industrial art or art education; and they rarely acquire great competence in more than one specialty.

But it is not only a question of training. What is perhaps more decisive is the change in attitudes toward what artists should be and do. Whereas in the past even the greatest artists were not making objects purely for beauty, but justified their work also in terms of usefulness, in more recent times aesthetic values have been emphasized at the expense of other considerations. As the Industrial Revolution progressed, destroying old values and symbols, people increasingly needed reassurance that some values were permanent—and beauty seemed to qualify. Art promised to perform a stabilizing function, and thus was divided into "fine" and "applied" branches. The only real artist became the fine artist, who was bid to make objects of abstract beauty unsullied by practical concerns. At the same time, he was expected to be a bohemian; it helped if he were sickly, alcoholic, and dissolute. It is as if the bourgeoisie had given the fine artist a double role: to demonstrate that in this materialistic world it was possible for some to devote their lives to work motivated by the most refined aesthetic values, and simultaneously to show that those who were imprudent enough to live by this rule would come to a bad end. Thus the patrons of art could at once be uplifted and warned by the fine artist's example (Hauser, 1951, II; 72, Read, 1969; Lukács, 1975).

To be sure, all along objections were raised to this specialization and fragmentation in art. In the last century, for example, Ruskin and the Arts and Crafts movement advocated a return to medieval craft as a healthier form of artistic expression. In this century, the Bauhaus movement encouraged artists to engage in an active transformation of the human environment. Instead of caging human experience in a frame and delivering it to be hung on the walls of the wealthy, the artist was told to reshape everyday objects so that art could infiltrate the life of the masses. The many communal workshops that have sprung up recently across the country, in which artists are working in clay, textiles, prints, and so on, are reflections of this same sensibility.

But these sporadic movements only point up the predominance of specialization. The estrangement of fine artists from any real object or event seems lately to have reached its extreme in the advent of "conceptual art." The proponents of this artistic ideology contend that the essence of the work of art lies in its conception; hence the actual execution is unnecessary. All the artist needs to do is to imagine the work of art (and presumably alert friends and critics to his or her act of imagination). To carry through with the actual work would cheapen the beauty of the idea. Many artists who are not themselves identified with this ideology feel its influence; for example, some may draw scale plans of paintings or sculptures and, if they can afford it, commission someone else to make the objects that they will eventually sign and sell. In a sense, thinking up artistic ideas and putting together artistic objects seem to have become specializations in themselves.

Applied artists are also becoming more and more specialized. To be an illustrator is not specific enough any longer. One may specialize in children's book illustration, women's journal illustration, or medical illustration, for example. Advertising artists specialize in one or another sector of the mass media. Industrial artists specialize in smaller and smaller fragments of the technical domain.

The most important consequence of this fragmentation, so far as our study is concerned, is that creativity has become more and more a central issue for fine artists, while it has decreased in relevance for applied artists. Free-lance painters and sculptors are expected to find their own style, their own subject matter; they have to be original to a degree that artists of previous generations could hardly have conceived. Applied artists, on the other hand, are increasingly expected to subordinate their personal vision to the requirements of production techniques, new materials, economic considerations, or public taste as reconstructed by computers fed on polling data. Compared to artists of past centuries, contemporary fine artists must work in a vacuum under enormous pressures to be original, while contemporary applied artists must be responsive to an array of narrow demands that frustrate their autonomy and imagination.

Specialization in Art School. The art schools, responsive to developments in technology and the demands of the marketplace, have institutionalized the divisions in art through specialized training. At the time of our study, individuals with graphic talent could enroll in the School of the Art Institute in one of four "majors," encompassing nine specializations. Fine art included (1) drawing, painting, and printmaking, (2) sculpture and architectural sculpture, and (3) ceramics. Industrial art included (4) industrial design, (5) interior design, (6) dress design, and (7) flat pattern and weaving. The third major was (8) advertising art, and the fourth was (9) art education.

In the first year, all students took a common core of studio and academic courses. It was only in the second year that they began to diverge toward what would presumably become their career. According to admissions officers, administrators, and teachers, the students do not differ in artistic skills and preparation when they enter the school, or during the first year of common courses. A student who later selects a fine art major is neither more talented nor better equipped technically than a student who majors in advertising art.

Yet the fine artist and the advertising artist, the art educator and the industrial artist have dramatically distinct tasks, career lines, job markets, and reward structures. They are expected to do such widely different things, often for diametrically opposed reasons, that individuals who specialize in any of the four artistic fields might be expected to differ considerably from those in the other three. Since this difference does not lie in technical skill and early training, in what does it lie?

The information at our disposal was almost ideal for attempting to answer this question. A comparison of the cognitive, perceptual, values, and personality measures for the four groups might identify what traits, if any, differentiate one group from another, and thus point to the grounds on which the choice of artistic specialization is made. In addition, the analysis might speak to the function of art in society, since it is likely that the choices and artistic divisions are not arbitrary, but reflect social needs for different kinds of artistic contribution.

When performance on the standard tests was compared for students in fine art, advertising art, industrial art, and art education, two salient results appeared. The four groups did not differ on any of the cognitive or perceptual measures. Stated most simply, none of the scores for the 14 cognitive-perceptual instruments showed any significant differences among the groups. Clearly, whatever accounts for choice of specialization does not lie in the areas of intelligence, cognitive style, or perceptual ability.

But when we analyzed values, unmistakable differences emerged. The data can be seen in Table 4.1.

The differences among the groups are in the same three values that differentiate the total group of art students from college students in general, and this despite the already extreme scores on those values for the entire sample. The findings may be summarized as follows: Relative to the other groups, fine art majors have low economic values and high aesthetic values. Conversely, advertising and industrial art majors have high economic values and low aesthetic values. The art education majors have low economic and aesthetic values but high social values.

The pattern is congruent with the specialization each group has selected. Advertising and industrial artists are almost indistinguishable from each other. In a manner consistent with their future roles, they accept the value of material gains and sociability more than do the other groups. In light of the theoretical analysis to follow, it is also relevant that advertising artists have the highest political values. Art education students, whose task it will be to teach, outscore the other groups in social value. Finally, the fine art students have the low economic–high aesthetic value pattern, which makes them the most "artistic" subgroup within the total group of young artists. They reflect to an extreme degree the value pattern that differentiates art students from college norms.

Here, then, is a first indication of what might be involved in the choice of one artistic career over another. Acquired values affect how young persons will apply their graphic talent. Those who value social goals highly will tend to utilize their talent in a teaching capacity. If they value material goals highly, they will tend to utilize their talent in the more remunerative applied occupations: advertising and industrial art. Only students who hold the highest aesthetic values will have the courage—or

Table 4.1. Differences in the Values of Students in the Four Fields of Artistic Specialization

Specialization	N	Theoretical	Economic	Aesthetic	Social	Political	Religious
Males							
Fine arts	35	45.06	34.08	54.60	31.63	38.40	36.83
Art education	12	44.67	36.50	50.17	35.00	36.83	37.08
Advertising	16	41.87	36.44	51.56	30.13	40.12	39.31
Industrial arts	23	43.48	37.69	53.00	31.74	38.65	35.04
Females							
Fine arts	44	44.16	31.27	57.16	33.48	35.64	38.25
Art education	15	40.47	30.67	52.67	37.73	38.20	39.47
Advertising	7	37.57	38.00	48.28	33.00	40.00	43.00
Industrial arts	27	41.37	37.55	52.78	32.15	39.48	37.15
F Value effects	Degrees of Freedom						
Sex	1,171	4.46	3.40	.95	2.57	.87	2.36
Major	3,171	2.71	6.19***	4.89**	3.36*	2.75	1.34
Interaction	3,171	.61	1.38	1.02	.23	1.46	.09

$*p < .05.$
$**p < .01.$
$***p < .001.$

will be driven by their values—to risk specialization in fine art, where creativity is encouraged, but material success is rare and unpredictable.

This pattern of values is not only sensible in terms of the fields of specialization a student chooses in art school. Perhaps more significantly, it is also related to the kinds of problems that the fine artist works on. Persons with graphic talent may apply their talent to problems that are assigned by others, primarily to achieve extrinsic economic goals—for example to create an illustration for a cornflake box that will increase sales. Or they may devote their talent to problems that they themselves find and formulate, primarily to achieve an intrinsic creative expression, without concern for economic or social consequences. In this sense, the self-initiated creation of problems is the essential characteristic of fine artists. It is perhaps not too much to say that they must necessarily reject economic values in order to have the widest freedom to find and formulate aesthetic problems allowing the widest range of individual creative expression.

The personality data show a pattern similar to that found for values. Again, the between-group differences are all the more meaningful in view of the already extreme scores attained by the entire sample. Six of the 15 personality factors on the 16 PF (intelligence is excluded from this analysis) show significant variation by field of specialization. In some cases the difference among the four subgroups is as large as that between the whole art student group and the norms. This is particularly so for the fine art subgroup. (The data are presented in Table A 1.4).

On each of the six factors that show significant differences, male and female fine art majors score at the "artistic" end of the distribution. For instance, Factor A (cyclothymia) differentiates art students as a whole from college students; the former are significantly less sociable than the latter. This factor also differentiates students specializing in fine art from those in other areas of specialization. Future advertising artists are almost as sociable as the average college student.

The same pattern recurs on each factor for which there are differences. If the art student sample as a whole scored significantly higher than the norms on a given factor (see Table 3.1), the young fine artists will score higher than other art students, and the advertising and industrial artists will score closer to the norms. If the art student sample as a whole scored significantly lower than the norms on a factor, the young fine artists will score lower than the other art groups, and the advertising and industrial artists will be closer to the norms. In general, the art education group falls between the fine art and the advertising and industrial arts groups.

The mean scores of the fine art students are significantly different in the expected direction from at least one of the other groups on factors A (sociability), G (conscientiousness), I (sensitivity), M (imaginativeness), N (shrewdness), and Q3 (self-sentiment); on factor A, the fine artists are significantly different from each of the other groups for both sexes. In other words, future fine artists are less sociable, less conscientious, more imaginative, more naive, and less conforming than other art students. In most cases, the advertising artists are at the opposite end in these traits.

In values and personality, then, future fine artists show an extreme, almost exaggerated intensification of the basic artistic profile: advertising and industrial artists show a blurring of these traits, a dilution of artistic values and attitudes. These sharp differences between majors confirm the reality of polarization between the fine and applied arts. The data show that such differences do not lie along the dimension of conventional intellectual and perceptual skills. What distinguishes the future fine artist from the advertising and industrial artist, or the art educator, is a difference in attributes of temperament, attitudes, values, and personality traits. Presumably the pattern of such traits suggests the type of person who is ready to become involved with creative problem finding, as opposed to the solution of assigned problems.

Inner Structure of Artistic Attributes.   In some cases, even though the four groups were similar on certain measures, strong differences still appeared in terms of how the traits were related to each other within a group. A full description of such differences is technical and cumbersome, and need not detain us now; it has been reported in detail elsewhere (Getzels and Csikszentmihalyi, 1966a). Here it will be enough to present two short examples.

When scores on the Wonderlic Intelligence Test are correlated with perceptual tests separately for male fine and applied artists, the correlations are much larger for the latter group (see Table A1.5 in Appendix 1). The pattern suggests that intellectual and perceptual abilities overlap more for applied than for fine artists. This does not mean that one group is superior in intelligence or in perception—the two groups do not differ significantly on these variables. The results do suggest that despite the similarity in the separate attributes, there are differences in the way they are patterned within each of the two groups of students. A highly intelligent applied artist will have strong perceptual skills; one less intelligent will be perceptually less fluent. The same is far less true of a fine artist. Having noted this pattern, we are at a loss to explain it. Perhaps perceptual and cognitive sophistication are both needed to function as an applied artist, but just one of these is sufficient for a fine artist. If this were so, however, the applied artists' scores on these variables should cluster around the mean, and the fine artists' should have a wider range. This not being the case, we can only say that intellect and perception are more integrated in future applied artists than in future fine artists; what this signifies for the way the two groups function remains unknown.

An even more complex pattern emerges when one inspects the correlations between the personality factor "ego-strength" and the cognitive variables (see Table A1.6). Briefly, male fine artists high on factor C (ego-strength) do better on cognitive tasks than do those who score low. The same is not true for female fine artists, nor for applied artists of either sex. In five of the nine possible relationships, male fine artists differ significantly in this respect from at least one of the other three groups—in one case from each of the others. Cognitive abilities and stability of the ego are relatively interlocked for people who plan to enter a more creative artistic career. The same is less true for those who plan to devote their skills to problem solving rather than to problem finding. Whatever else these results may mean, they indicate that there is variation between students in the several fields of specialization that go beyond simple differences in mean scores. It seems we are dealing here with a discrete organization of personality and cognitive traits, as well as with differences in absolute magnitude.

The Functions of Artistic Roles. In considering the reasons for the emergence of four specialized forms in which artistic skills are expressed, we were struck by the similarity between the aims of the four fields and those of the four role-clusters that social theorists have identified as necessary for the existence of social systems.

Most sociologists accept as axiomatic that a group of interacting individuals, whatever its size, must solve four main problems if it is to survive as a group. Energy must be transformed from the environment to keep its members alive; cooperation must be established; efficient means for attaining individual and collective goals must be found; and mechanisms for transmitting experiences from one generation to the next must be designed. Talcott Parsons (1951; 1966) called these the adaptive, integrative, goal attainment, and pattern maintenance functions.

Whenever an efficient procedure for fulfilling one of these four functions is found, it tends to be preserved and to become one of the institutions of society. Technology, industry, and commerce are all essentially adaptive institutions; forms of association based on kinship or status relations are integrative; political and administrative entities serve goal-attainment; religious, cultural, and educational organizations which conserve and communicate values and knowledge are pattern maintenance institutions. If one adopts this functional model of social systems, the development of four specialized artistic roles is clearly not a historical accident, but the reflection of a more general social phenomenon.

Industrial artists use their talent and learned skills within the adaptive subsystem. Their work advances the process of production. By creating more aerodynamic car bodies, more comfortable luggage handles, more refreshing office interiors, industrial designers help make adaptation to the environment smoother and more efficient. To identify with this role, they must have, in addition to technical skills, the values and personality traits that make them sensitive to the material well-being of people.

Students who choose a career in art education fulfill a role that contributes to the integration of art as a system of action. The task of art teachers is to socialize recruits into artistic roles, and to mediate between artists and nonartists, helping the latter to relate to the symbolic heritage of the culture. They are not expected to contribute anything new to art or to the environment; their task is the more social one of introducing others to ways of seeing, feeling, and acting that are prized in the culture. Art teachers have control over who will or will not become an artist. They are expected to make sure that the right people take their right positions in the structure of art; hence they contribute to the integration of the system. Students entering this field of specialization possess the high social values and personality characteristics required by their future role.

The role of advertising artists is a curious one. They are paid to motivate people to want certain things, whether merchandise, political candidates, or the prevention of disease—in short, their task is to guide people toward certain ends. In this sense, their work accomplishes a goal attainment function. Whether we like it or not, the social system does depend, to a certain extent, on the unifying direction provided by advertisers.

Advertising students are most similar in their personal characteristics to the general population, and they possess relatively high political values, reflecting interest in power and persuasion, consistent with their role.

Fine artists produce objects supposedly devoid of use or social purpose. But this presumed lack of function is more apparent than real because objects created by fine artists become part of the symbolic culture, shaping the ways people perceive and interpret their lives. The acts of fine artists record the inarticulate hopes and despairs of their fellowmen, and preserve experiences that cannot be expressed by other means. As Hannah Arendt has said, "The whole factual world of human affairs depends for its reality and its continued existence, first upon the presence of others who have seen and heard and will remember, and, second, on the transformation [by the artist] of the intangible into the tangibility of things" (Arendt, 1958, 95). This is the main function of fine artists: to maintain and create patterns of meaning, in their own time and through the gaps of generations.

This tidy functional scheme is of course only an analytic framework; it is not intended to be more than that. In reality things are not so simple and clear-cut. There have been times when the main activity of those whom now we would call fine artists was closer to the work of present-day advertisers. Much of Western art had its roots in ecclesiastical propaganda, nouveau-riche status seeking, or the raising of political consciousness as was the case with the revolutionary Latin American painters. Art education, whose function is presumably integration, contributes at the same time to pattern maintenance since it keeps alive the artistic traditions of the culture.

One may also disagree with the notion that Western art has been serving any pattern maintenance functions for the past few generations. Quite the contrary seems to be the case: Art in the recent past has been ruled by an obsession to reject cultural patterns. To say that fine art serves a pattern maintenance function, however, does not imply that it always will do so, or that it does so within any given span of time. There are periods when art fails to accomplish its purpose, thereby contributing to a cultural disintegration whose severity depends on the health of all other institutions. This is the sense in which the lay person's charge of incomprehensibility and degeneracy in modern art can be understood. It is an opinion shared by art historians like Lalo and Ligeti, historians like Spengler and Toynbee, or sociologists like Pitirim Sorokin, and more recently the art critic Harold Rosenberg, all of whom insist that modern art reflects a dissolving civilization, whose patterns of meaning are no longer capable of being maintained.

There is no need here, nor is it within our competence, to expand on this subject. It is enough to say that, paradoxically, the artist's apparent rejection of culture is not in itself a denial of the artist's pattern maintenance role. Despite their comments to the contrary, most contemporary artists are just as eager to have their work survive as any artist of the past was. They believe their work expresses their experience of the times, and they hope it will become part of the canon of art and of the record of civilization.

If not reified and applied mechanically, the functional scheme helps to combine within a single set of related concepts the questions raised initially regarding the emergence of artistic specialization, the curricula of the art school, and the values and personality characteristics of students entering different fields of specialization. The fields of specialization are not arbitrary administrative divisions but correspond to the functional prerequisites of social systems: industrial art serves the purpose of adaptation; art education promotes integration; advertising art is concerned with goal attainment; and the task of fine art is pattern maintenance, both in its conservative and reconstitutive aspects. Formerly all these functions were performed by individual artists. Today the simple role has been fragmented into segregated roles, each demanding specialized attitudes and providing different rewards—and, as we have seen, each attracting talented young people with distinctive patterns of values and personality traits.

CHAPTER 5

■

Performance in Art School

T he first real test of whether an art student will become an artist is confronted in the school itself. A substantial proportion of the young people who had high hopes for a career in art will be discouraged by low grades, the teachers' lack of enthusiasm concerning their potential, or by disillusionment with their experiences in the school.

Like other institutions of learning, art school grooms its students for their future status in many subtle ways. How to mix paints, how to make a print, how to carve or weld a sculpture are only the most obvious, and probably not the most important, skills taught at the school. Much of what is conveyed is not described in the curriculum. It is in the school that most students first learn how artists look, what they talk about, how they dress, what kinds of places they live in, what kind of spouses they marry if they do marry, and how they earn a livelihood. Students usually enter art school holding popular, superficially glamorous impressions of the lives of artists. Now they find themselves in a setting where for four years they not only draw and paint, but learn to behave like artists. During this period they must find out if this is actually what they want to do the rest of their lives. At the same time, the teachers at the school will find out whether the student has the skills and the temperament necessary for success in the field.

The decision to continue in art depends on students' experiences in the school. If they are successful, if they have the values and personality traits that make full concentration on artistic creativity possible, then they will probably go on. The teachers play an important role in determining who will become part of the next generation of artists and who will not. Like teachers everywhere, they perform their selective function almost unconsciously, and often against their will. When they give a low grade, they are expressing a negative judgment not only of what a student has done, but of what that student is likely to do. There is "nothing personal" about it, and it may even be for the student's "own good." After a number of low grades, however, the students get the message that their work is incompetent, that their teachers—artists themselves—will not accept them as peers. They might begin to think of other, more congenial, careers.

Indices of Achievement in Art School.   Since performance in school is one of the earliest determinants in the selection of artists, we wanted to know more about what was being rewarded in school, and what traits were associated with success. Fortunately, the school files contained two straightforward measures of student performance. One was grade point average for studio courses. Grades are a serious matter even in art school. They determine, as they do in other schools, professional credentials and opportunities for further study or employment. No one expects a one-to-one correspondence between grades in school and later success, or even with achievement inside the school. Nonetheless, grades are perhaps the most valid criterion of artistic accomplishment at this stage in a young artist's development.

Also available in the files was a second and in some ways more interesting measure. In addition to course grades, teachers also rated their students on originality and artistic potential. By averaging these ratings for the students' first year, and then for the second year, two originality and artistic potential scores were derived. Each rating is based on the teacher's familiarity with the student's performance in at least one studio course, and each composite score includes the judgment of several teachers. These ratings are made seriously since they become part of the student's permanent record; they were not made at our request.

The grades and ratings, in short, have a convincing face validity as measures of performance in art school. We expected the two measures to be largely redundant; indeed, initially it seemed sensible to use grades and ratings interchangeably, since they were given by the same teachers at the same time. But as soon as we began to analyze the data a number of surprising relationships emerged, suggesting that the overlap between grades and rating was less than had been expected. Table 5.1 presents the correlations among the three primary criteria of achievement—that is, ratings in originality and artistic potential and art grades, as well as academic grades, first for the entire group of students, and then for the groups divided by sex and field of specialization.

We turn first to the relationships among the originality and artistic potential (OAP) measures and the art grades for the entire group. The correlation between the two OAP ratings is .32 ($p < .001$) and the correlation between the ratings for each of the two years and the art grades are .41 and .31 ($p < .001$)—relationships that are statistically reliable but far from redundant. Although some inconsistency in the OAP ratings over the two years is to be anticipated, the dimensions on which the ratings were made could be expected to have a more common meaning than the correlation of .32 suggests. On second thought, however, differences of opinion among the raters, and perhaps genuine changes in the students themselves, may well account for the lack of a stronger relationship. Is it more reasonable to be disappointed that the agreement over the years is not greater, or to be gratified to attain any agreement over the years on so subjective a criterion as originality and artistic potential? Indeed, in view of the character of the judgments, how much agreement *should* there be?

The correlations of .41 and .31 between the ratings and the grades are at first sight perhaps more surprising than the correlation between the ratings themselves. The correlations are surely not as high as might be expected if one considers that the same instructors rated the students at the same time that they graded their work. But of course one of the reasons for the difference between the grades and ratings is precisely what led the school to institute this double system of judgment in the first place. Class performance often does not represent what the instructors might feel to be the latent creativity of a student, and latent creativity is often not expressed in classwork.

Apparently some students approach a studio course as if it were an academic course in which fulfillment of assignments is the main goal. Others treat a studio course as a workshop—their own studio, as it were—in which assignments are less important than experimentation and enjoyment of the work itself. The first kind of student might do all the assignments and produce work that is good enough without being truly original, and the second kind might not complete the assignments and yet produce a single work of true originality.

We should note in this respect that the correlation between studio and academic grades is .45, while the correlations between OAP ratings and

Table 5.1. Correlations Between Achievement Criteria in Art School: Teachers' Ratings of Originality and Artistic Potential (OAP-1, OAP-2), Art Grades, and Academic Grades

Correlatiodns Between	For the Core Sample (N = 179)	For the Core Sample Divided by Sex		For the Core Sample Divided by Sex and Field of Specialization (27 Art Education Students Excluded)			
				Male		Female	
		Males (N = 86)	Females (N = 93)	Fine Arts (N = 35)	Applied Arts (N = 39)	Fine Arts (N = 44)	Applied Arts (N = 34)
OAP-1 and OAP-2	.32***	.33**	.32**	.35*	.20	.52***	.23
OAP-1 and art grades	.41***	.35**	.48***	.29	.27	.60***	.25
OAP-2 and art grades	.31***	.18	.42***	.22	−.09	.49***	.49**
OAP-1 and academic grades	.11	.08	.17	−.11	.07	.26	−.06
OAP-2 and academic grades	.10	.05	.13	−.08	.04	.19	.25
Art and academic grades	.45***	.35**	.53***	.24	.38*	.51***	.62***

*p < .05.
**p < .01.
***p < .001.

academic grades are only .10 and .11. That is, although there is significant overlap between teachers' grades in art and academic classes, there is no overlap between their ratings of the students' originality and academic performance. The intriguing question of whether grades or ratings are predictive of success after leaving school is reserved for our section on the follow-up phase of the study.

The dynamics among indicators of success provide insight into the forces affecting performance in art school. One example is the relationships among the OAP ratings, art grades, and academic grades when the total group is divided by sex and field of specialization. Although the correlation between art and academic grades for the total group is a substantial .45, the subgroup correlations range from a not significant .24 for male fine art students to an extremely significant .62 ($p < .001$) for female applied art students. And although the correlation between the two OAP ratings is .35 ($p < .05$) and .52 ($p < .001$) for male and female fine art students respectively, it is only .20 (n.s.) and .23 (n.s.) for male and female applied art students. The most striking and significant differences are those between the two ratings and the art grades for female as opposed to male fine art students. For women, the correlations are .60 ($p < .001$) and .49 ($p < .001$); for men the correlations are only .29 (n.s.) and .22 (n.s.).

Evidently there are critical differences either in the way the art instructors view male and female art students, or in the way male and female students actually perform. Either instructors make a distinction between originality and class performance in the case of male students but not in the case of female students, or the classwork of female fine art students is actually more representative of their potential than the work of males, although it is not obvious why this should be so. Perhaps female students treat a studio course more like an academic course, and male students treat it more like a workshop. One datum lends support to this interpretation: The correlations between art grades and academic grades for female fine arts students is .51 ($p < .001$); for males it is .24 (n.s.).

The criteria of success in art school are clearly enormously complex and dependent on a variety of factors, including whether the students are rated or their work graded, whether they are male or female, and whether they are in one field of specialization or another.

Characteristics of Art Students and Achievement in Art School. Since the relationships both among the descriptive variables and the criteria of success in school vary so much depending on the sex and specialization of the students, few generalizations are possible. To get at a set of relationships with any precision, we must focus on each subgroup separately.

Table 5.2 presents the descriptive variables that correlated significantly with either rating, or with art grades when the sample was divided by sex. The data were extracted from a matrix which contained the 39 original variables. Of these, the 14 in the table correlated significantly ($p < .05$) with one or another of the achievement criteria.

A number of patterns are worth noting. For male students 12 of the 45 possible relationships between the 16 PF personality factors (excluding factor B, intelligence) and the three criteria of achievement are significant; for females none is. Conversely, for female students 5 of 6 possible relationships between the two main perceptual tests and the criteria of achievement are significant; for male students not one is. For male students, 6 of a possible 18 relationships between values and the criteria of achievement are significant, 3 at the .05 level, 2 at the .01 level, 1 at the .001 level; for female students only 2 of the possible 18 relationships are significant, both at the .05 level. For male students, the correlation between economic value and the three criteria of achievement are $-.32$ ($p < .01$), $-.23$ ($p < .05$), and $-.40$ ($p < .001$); for female students the respective correlations are $-.03, .02, -.04$. Conversely, for male students the correlations between perceptual memory (error) and the three criteria of achievement are $-.09, -.07$, and $.03$; for female students the respective correlations are $-.25$ ($p < .05$), $-.36$ ($p < .01$), and $-.33$ ($p < .01$).

Evidently male and female students reach success in art school by different routes. For males success is related to a constellation of values and personality factors. The most successful male students—those who are rated high in originality and artistic potential and/or receive high grades in studio courses—are characterized by traits of personality such as aloofness (A−), low ego-strength (C−), introspection (F−), sensitivity (I), imaginativeness (M), self-sufficiency (Q2), and lack of conformity to social norms (Q3−). The relationships may hold significantly for one of the ratings and not the other, or for the grades and not the ratings. But even when not significant, the trend is always in the expected direction across the three criteria; in not a single instance is the sign of the relationship inconsistent. The case is similar with values. Most striking is the very strong and consistent relationship between low economic value and high achievement. What must be also noted is that the variables showing significant relationships with achievement are the same ones that differentiated the entire art student group from the general college student

Table 5.2. *Variables Correlating Significantly with the Three Criteria of Achievement: Teachers' Ratings in Originality and Artistic Potential (OAP-1, OAP-2), and Art Grades*

Variables	16 PF Factor	Males (N = 86)			Females (N = 93)		
		OAP-1	OAP-2	Art Grades	OAP-1	OAP-2	Art Grades
Academic grades		.08	.05	.35**	.17	.13	.53***
Spatial visualization		-.04	.10	-.20	.06	.22*	.27**
Perceptual memory (error)		-.09	-.07	.03	-.25*	-.36**	-.33**
Theoretical value		.27*	.05	.35**	.18	.25*	-.08
Aesthetic value		.09	.26*	.20	.08	.14	.20*
Economic value		-.32**	-.23*	-.40***	-.03	.02	-.04
Cyclothymia	A	-.23*	-.02	-.29**	-.11	.01	-.18
Ego strength	C	-.33**	-.15	-.24*	.02	.10	.07
Surgency	F	-.28*	-.19	-.26*	-.01	.00	-.14
Parmia	H	-.34**	-.19	-.15	-.11	.01	-.09
Premsia	I	-.18	.33**	.25*	-.08	.08	-.02
Autia	M	.03	.26*	.05	-.05	.09	.05
Self-sufficiency	Q2	.28*	.18	.15	.06	-.02	.05
Self-sentiment	Q3	-.27*	-.13	-.07	.14	-.06	.09

*$p < .05$.
**$p < .01$.
***$p < .001$.

group, and differentiated students in one field of specialization from those in another.

The contrast with female students could hardly be greater. Not one of the personality variables has any connection with the criteria of achievement, nor is there even a consistency in the direction of the relationships. Economic value is also unrelated to the criteria of achievement. Success for women seems almost exclusively a matter of perceptual abilities, which play no part in the achievement of men.

These differences are real and substantial; they are not due to statistical artifacts in the range and distribution of the variables. Art teachers seem to appraise a male student on the basis of long-range possibilities suggested by his personality, rather than on his perceptual aptitudes; they seem to appraise a female student on the basis of the perceptual skills she actually displays. This may reflect a tacit belief that a male student will develop his aptitudes with time, while a female student who does not have them to begin with will abandon her aspirations and settle for more traditional pursuits. Other explanations are also possible. It might be, for example, that male students, whose perceptual skills are already significantly higher than those of female students, do not gain an additional advantage by having even greater perceptual abilities. Female students, having lower perceptual abilities than males to begin with, might need higher abilities to compete successfully with males. When the groups are subdivided by field of specialization, the following pattern is observed: The correlations between spatial visualization and art grades for male and female fine art students are $-.32$ and $.18$, a statistically reliable difference; and for male and female applied art students they are $-.02$ and $.52$, again statistically different.

Indeed, when the samples are subdivided by field of specialization, other results come to light that are not apparent when the students are classified only by sex. When the group is divided by sex alone, there are 14 descriptive variables significantly related to at least one criterion of success (Table 5.2). When the sample is now further divided by fine and applied fields of specialization, the number of different variables showing such relationships increases to 27, despite the smaller number of cases in each cell.

Among the cognitive and perceptual variables, in addition to spatial visualization and perceptual memory, significant relationships now appear also in ideational fluency, TAT novelty, object question, 16 PF intelligence, and Welsh art judgment—relationships that in the analysis reported in Table 5.2 had been attenuated through reversals by field of specialization within sex groups. For example, the Object Question Test, which tests for a questioning attitude shows a significant *positive* relation with art grades for male fine art students, but a *negative* relation for male applied art students. That is, the more prone to a questioning attitude the former are, the better their grades; the more prone to a questioning attitude the latter are, the worse their grades will be.

Similarly, social values have a significant negative relationship with art grades for male fine art students, and a positive, albeit insignificant, relationship for male applied art students. Analogous effects are found in the personality variables; for example, dominance has a significant negative relationship to performance for male fine art students, but a positive one for male applied art students. It is clear that such relationships tend to be obscured when fine and applied art students are combined into "male art student" and "female art student" categories.

On the whole, the impression from the patterning of results is that for fine art as opposed to applied art students success depends more on emotional rather than on cognitive or perceptual factors, especially if the student is a male. Teachers encourage and reward men who hold values and personality traits that are adaptive to problem finding. Women, on the other hand, and men who are in applied art are evaluated more in relation to skills that are useful for problem solving. This difference may mean that the various subgroups of artists indeed do need different qualities to succeed, because the kind of work they do requires a questioning, independent personality on the one hand, or because it requires certain cognitive skills on the other. Or the difference may reflect a biased reward structure on the part of faculty members who reward only male fine artists for the temperamental qualities conducive to discovery. In either case, male fine art students are reinforced for displaying personality characteristics consistent with the questioning approach that must underlie the cognitive process of problem finding.

The Performance of Fine Art Students. The foregoing analysis led to a central conclusion: Although success in art school can be to some extent predicted from knowing a student's traits, this prediction cannot be generalized from one subgroup of students to another. To examine artistic performance in depth, both in school and afterward, it was necessary to focus on a single group of students of the same sex and the same field of specialization. An alternative—to select a few students from each subgroup—would have so fragmented the data that any generalization would have been impossible.

We decided to choose for more intense study the fine art students, those whose role is critical to the existence of art, who find and formulate new artistic problems. It is the fine art student who is the most "artistic," who owns to the highest degree those traits that make art students different from other students, and who most resemble already recognized artists.

But there was no way to study in depth all 79 fine art students, or to follow them up after they left school; resources for such an undertaking were not available. (Since no foundation or government support was obtained for the follow-up study, we did it on our own, helped by the freedom the University of Chicago granted to pursue our interests.) To study half the male and half the female group would have excessively reduced each sample. And the results would not have been additive; the evidence had shown that differences between male and female students might cancel out findings that held for one group separately.

Given these circumstances, we limited the intensive study to the male fine art students on the ground that historically the vast majority of painters and sculptors have been men, making a knowledge of male fine arts students more relevant to the understanding of the process of becoming a creative artist, and of creativity itself, at least in our society. Needless to say, a detailed study of women students and artists will be an important addition to knowledge in this field, especially in terms of what art *could* become if its practice were not so generally restricted to males. We might add parenthetically that in the last years several studies have focused on creativity in women (see, for instance, Bruch and Morse, 1972; Torrance, 1972) and in women artists in particular (Bachtold and Werner, 1973). This last study is particularly relevant because it used the 16 PF personality test, and its findings were in line with the results reported here.

Of all the criteria of success in art school, the most telling is the student's grade point average. Grades reflect on the record what art instructors think of the student's competence. More than any other measure, they determine his future credentials, and although we may wish it were not so, his opportunity for further study and the likelihood of his obtaining a foothold in the art world.

Accordingly, it seemed crucial to examine in greater detail the relationship between the male fine art students' personal traits, and their performance in school. For this purpose, from the total group of 35 the 10 with the highest and the 10 with the lowest art grades were compared. Each of the 10 "high" students had an average art grade of "B" or better, with a group average of "B+." Each of the 10 "low" students had an average of "C+" or worse, with a group average of "C." The high students also received better ratings in originality and artistic potential, the difference between the two groups being .64 standard deviations on the first year's rating and .57 standard deviations on the second year's rating in terms of the distribution for all male students. They also had somewhat better academic grades. The central question of the analysis then was: Do successful fine art students differ on any measurable trait from those who are unsuccessful in art school?

The first finding is that although the groups are of approximately the same age (the highs are .8 years older), eight of the high students had attended college before entering art school, but none of the low students had any prior college experience ($p < .003$ by Fisher's Exact Test)—an observation that does not support those who believe that all one needs to be a good artist is a set of healthy artistic instincts. Previous exposure to academic subjects such as English or mathematics is not likely to give a direct advantage to those who had been to college, since written require-ments and theoretical knowledge play an insignificant role in studio courses. Nonetheless, the data are clear: Students who have been to college elsewhere—transfer students or, by a different definition, college dropouts—receive higher grades in studio courses than students who have never attended another college.

The difference cannot be attributed to greater maturity by age or, as we shall see, to higher intelligence. Nor is it due to an earlier interest in art. If anything, the reverse is true: Five of the more successful students report that it was only after leaving high school that they became seriously interested in art as a career, while all but one of the less less successful students report considering a career in art before leaving high school ($p < .06$). Two other explanations for this difference are likely. One is that experience in institutions of higher education is itself salutary: The college student has learned the ropes of survival in school, and this gives him an advantage over recent high school graduates. Another possibility—and one we favor—is that students who have left college to attend art school are more highly motivated to succeed; they have tried another way of life and found it wanting.

Contrary to stereotype, the family background of the high students seems more stable than that of the lows: Five of the latter report that their parents were either separated, divorced, or widowed; all of the former report that their parents are living together ($p < .01$). The fathers of the highs were of superior occupational status than those of the lows: Five of the former held positions of junior executive or higher in the status scale; only one of the latter held such a position ($p < .06$).

In sum, successful fine art students have more extensive academic backgrounds, come from more stable families, and are of somewhat higher socioeconomic status than the less successful students. It is apparent that early life and family background have an effect on success in school; whether their infiuence extends beyond graduation is another matter, to which we shall come in due course.

The next issue to be examined is whether the more successful fine art student also differs from the less successful one in cognitive and perceptual characteristics measured by conventional tests. The results show that highs are no better at these tasks than are lows (see Table A1.7). In fact, on 6 of the 10 tests their performance is inferior, in two cases by almost half a standard deviation. Only on the Object Question Test did the more successful students score measurably better, with a difference in the order of a standard deviation ($p < .01$).

There is a good reason why the difference should have appeared on the Object Question Test. This is the least structured of the 10 instruments, the one that provides the greatest opportunity for free responses. It requires the ability and inclination to ask novel questions about common objects. To ask unexpected questions about common objects may reflect a more general talent for seeing unusual possibilities in what others take for granted—a talent that may be a condition for problem finding, and hence for success in settings that require creative performance, such as studio courses.

The difference in quality between the responses of the two groups may be illustrated by comparing two protocols. To the stimulus word *sea shell*, a student from the more successful group asks: "Is it the sea really inside a sea shell, or is it a sea shell that is the sea?" To the same stimulus a less successful student asks: "In what kind of shells does one hear the sound of the ocean?" Again, to the stimulus *grass*, the high student asks: "Why. does grass grow up and not down, and tickles your feet and bend?" To the same stimulus word, the low student asks: "How much of the earth is covered with grass?" One asks imaginative, playful, fantasy-provoking questions that cannot be answered with facts; the other asks concrete, pedantic questions that could be answered by looking up the appropriate reference.

One other cognitive task was found to differentiate the two groups. This too was not a standard test of intelligence or cognition. It was the Production of Novelty score derived from responses written to TAT pictures; the ability to produce unusual responses to TAT-type stimuli may be considered a cognitive function. The average standard score of the high group was 55.0 and that of the low group 48.1, a difference of .69 standard deviations.

To illustrate the difference, we cite from two representative protocols. A student from the low group writes in response to the slide showing a man carrying an attache case:

1. An unimpressive person is presented in an unimpressive manner doing nothing very exciting.

2. One may have wanted to present such an atmosphere and chosen this situation to do so.

3. It is just a man walking down the street with an attache case in his hand.

4. Nothing of much significance will happen.

A student from the high group writes in response to the same slide:

1. The man drawn is walking to work. Will he make it on time? The drawing is pretty poor. What will his boss say?

2. He overslept because it was too cold to get up.

3. He wishes he could be a real man instead of just a drawing.

4. He will be late because he is such a poor drawing.

The two responses reflect a similar initial reaction: Both students are unimpressed—as artists well might be—with the aesthetic quality of the stimulus picture. But the content and the style of the two subsequent stories are quite different; the second is more playful and imaginative than the first.

It should be stressed again that the only two "mental" tests on which reliable differences were found are those allowing respondents to give the freest rein to richness in cognitive style. On the more standard and restricted instruments, no significant differences between the two groups were present. The implications are difficult to avoid. Whatever intellectual process might be relevant to the creative process, it is not the kind that is measured by standard tests. The thinking that leads to successful artistic performance is a far more questioning, more uninhibited form of thought. The outlines of this distinctive cognitive process, which we examine in detail in the next chapter, continue to emerge.

Turning to the value and personality tests, the situation changes dramatically. As we have seen, art students have an extreme set of values, and within the total group the values of male fine art students are especially extreme. Such extreme means made us suspect that no further differences could be found between the less and the more successful students. Yet precisely the same three values—aesthetic, economic, and social—that differentiated the art students from other college students, and fine art students from other art students, also separate the more from the less successful male fine art students (see Table A1.8). For each of the three values in question, the difference between the means of the two groups is of the order of a standard deviation, and in the expected direction.

Again, the data suggest that the basic attitude toward life measured by the value scale is a prerequisite for the problem-finding cognitive approach that leads to creativity. The artist has a better chance of success in art school the more he rejects the goals of financial and social achievement our culture values so highly, and if he concentrates all his energies on the pursuit of aesthetic goals.

A similar effect holds true for personality variables. Notwithstanding the extreme mean scores for the group as a whole, marked differences between the more and the less successful students still appear. On five factors—A (sociability), C (ego strength), F (cheerfulness), G (conscientiousness), and Q3 (conformity)—the highs have a mean *sten* of 3, corresponding to the 11th percentile of the norms. On the same five factors, the less successful have a mean *sten* score of 4 or more. On two factors—M (imaginativeness) and Q2 (self-sufficiency)—the *sten* scores of successful students are 8 (89th percentile) and 7.6. The respective scores of the less successful ones are 7 and 6.8. The high and the low groups differ by about two *sten* scores on C (ego-strength), Q3 (conformity), and G (conscientiousness), with the more successful students scoring lower on these traits.

No profile of any of the 28 occupations reported in the 16 PF Manual contains as many extreme scores as does that of the more successful fine art students. The closest is that of 300 eminent researchers in physics, psychology, and biology, chosen for their creative achievements. Common to the two profiles are extremely low scores in sociability, cheerfulness, conscientiousness, and high scores in sensitivity. The main differences between creative scientific researchers and the more successful fine art students are that the latter have lower scores in ego-strength, adventurousness, and conformity, and higher scores in imagination and self-sufficiency. The comparison is shown in Figure 5.1.

The successful students are extremely aloof and reserved (A−), serious and introspective (F−), lacking in rigid internal standard (G−), and sensitive (I)—characteristics also found in creative researchers. In addition, they are also very emotional (C−), imaginative (M), self-sufficient (Q2), and have very little concern for conforming to socially accepted standards (Q3).

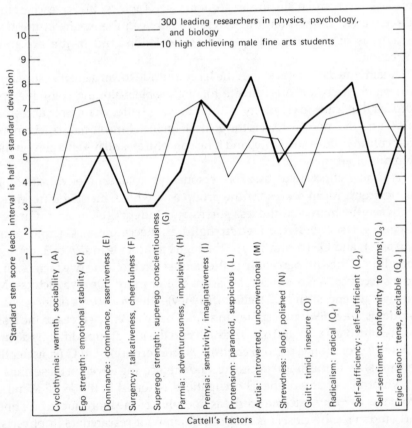

Figure 5.1. *Comparison of the personality profile (16 PFQ) of fine art students successful in studio art courses and of leading researchers in science.*

Some years ago Cattell derived what he called a "Composite Creativity Score" from the 16 PF profiles of creative people (IPAT, 1963). When this composite creativity score is applied to the *entire* group of male fine art students, their mean is 101 (corresponding to the 9th *sten*); for the subsample of the *less* successful students the score is 97.4 (8th *sten*); and for the subsample of *more* successful students it is 103.6 (10th *sten*), or higher than the composite score of about 99 percent of the male college population. Again, the relatively small difference between the two subgroups is undoubtedly due to the extremely high score of the entire group of future fine artists, whose mean composite score was superior to 96 percent of the male college norms, and thus was already at the upper limit.

Everything points to the conclusion that successful fine art students have the attributes of creative individuals. They possess to an extreme degree the values and personality traits that make art students different from other college students and from art students in other fields of specialization. They are also more questioning and subjective in cognitive style, although no different in standard tests of intelligence and mental functioning. They enter art school with a more diversified past experience, and come from more stable and higher socioeconomic class families.

It should be remembered, however, that these concomitants of success apply only to male fine art students. The evidence suggests that values and personality factors are less related to the performance of female students, while intelligence and perceptual abilities count more toward success for them and for applied artists.

The development of an artist is contingent on a complex interplay of many factors. All the resources of a person are involved in this process. Talent, intelligence, values, and personality traits are dedicated to the goal of becoming an artist. Teachers at the art school evaluate the behavior of students, and support those who possess the qualities prized by the institution. Through the formal encouragement of grades, and many informal signs of approval, some students are confirmed in their purpose, while others are discouraged from it. But because the artistic role is so fragmented, the teachers' criteria of selection vary depending on the specialized function that the student intends to pursue after graduation. Therefore to succeed in each major a student needs a different blend of personal resources.

In terms of surviving formal training, the best resource for a male fine art major is to be provided with the appropriate set of value and personality traits. These will allow him to bend his purpose to the creative tasks expected of him. How his art will be evaluated will not depend on intelligence or perceptual ability, but on a general attitude toward life that leads to questioning and problem finding. It would be fascinating to know whether this way of selecting future artists is functional or not. Perhaps teachers are guilty of preserving a sterile status quo by helping to admit only a narrow range of people to the artistic status, those who conform to the stereotype of what artists should be like. Or perhaps there is wisdom in their choice, because only a questioning, lonely person disconnected from the values of his culture will be motivated to pursue that hard task of posing new problems necessary for the creation of real works of art.

PART 2

■

The Making of Art

CHAPTER 6

■

Problem Finding and the Creative Process

The results of the first phase of the study were initially exhilarating. We had a reasonably consistent picture of individuals committed to the field of art, and of how they differed from other people of the same sex, age, and educational level; we began to see how these differences were associated with the pursuit of various specializations within the field of art; and how they related to creative achievement, at least as defined in art school.

These descriptive results, however, only gave us indirect information about the creative process itself. From characteristics of people involved in a creative activity, it is possible to infer some characteristics of the creative process. It seems clear, for instance, that creativity in the fine arts requires a questioning approach quite different from the usual problem-solving steps measured by intelligence tests. This approach is based on a very strong value system and an extreme set of personality traits. Only people who are willing to reject the goals that are valued in the culture seem to have the required motivation to challenge accepted artistic forms and contribute truly new ones. Instead of predefined formulations, the creative process in art appears to be inspired by personally felt problems of an existential nature which the artist tries to confront on his own terms. The sensitivity and openness to experience that are required of a successful artist imply that he or she must not be excessively stereotyped in a masculine or feminine role.

But although such inferences about what the creative process must be like are useful, they still fail to give direct evidence as to how one goes about making something creative. We wanted to know exactly what artists do when they attempt to produce a work of art.

We expected that it would not be too difficult to observe what art students do in their studio courses. Thinking that one needs but look at them and their actions, we watched art students at work, and we talked to them about what they were doing.

But the first observations and conversations were bewildering. Some students brushed oil on canvas, others bent wire or poured concrete, chipped blocks of granite and carved wood; some made huge constructions and others fastidious line drawings. Some worked rapidly, others slowly; some daubed flecks of color on the canvas with a light brush, others smeared gobs of paint with a heavy trowel. One artist claimed that what he enjoyed most about painting was the smell of pigments; another claimed to enjoy squeezing the tubes of paint more than anything else. One declared that what he wanted most was to develop a "new image of universal man," while another admitted that he painted simply because he could do nothing else.

We saw students in advertising art begin with assignments—problems as specific as problems in mathematics; and we saw students in fine art begin with only a blank canvas for a guideline. We recognized some solutions as resembling reality, and others as having no likeness to anything imaginable. Some products we thought to be highly original and creative, others trite and pedestrian.

There appeared to be no connection between the activity and the quality of the outcome. We looked at everything and recognized the truth in the ancient adage: one who looks at everything might end up seeing nothing.

What we needed to move forward in this phase of the exploration was a set of explicit categories, a conceptual scheme to guide our selection of what *should* be observed and recorded of the plethora of activities in which art students at work are engaged.

This procedure has its own dangers: A rigid framework may restrict attention and direct it to marginal activities while excluding the most relevant phenomena. Nonetheless, we felt we had gone as far as we could without a theoretical point of view and an explicit definition of what was to be looked for. Instead of looking *at* a featureless totality, a point of view had to be adopted that would permit us to look *for* a defined something.

Remote Request Form

Date: _____

Time: _____

Patron Name: Stephanie Whiting

Patron Telephone: 861 441 0118

Patron Email: Stephanie.whiting@students.

Requested Title: The creative vision: a longitudinal
study of problem finding in art

Call Number: N 71 . G4

Author (Book): Getzels,Jacob

Date (Periodical): 1976

Situations That Require Problem Finding.   Artistic creativity has not been widely studied as a cognitive process amenable to empirical examination. Although researchers have collected reports from artists and other creative people, relating the thoughts and feelings they had while they were working, these are unique case studies rather than evidence for a theory about the mental processes underlying creative work.

Yet there are suggestions in the literature that should have encouraged research into artistic creation along cognitive and empirical lines. Dewey (1910), for instance, describes the problem-solving process in five stages, the first of which is the feeling that there is somewhere a problem that needs to be formulated. The process of problem solving from the recognition of a problem to the verification of the solution is essentially that of the creative act: The solution of a problem that had not existed before. More recently Ecker (1963) reworked Dewey's formulation and applied it to the artistic process. But the promise of such theoretical suggestions have for the most part gone unheeded.

In the tentative conceptual framework we adopted the creative process is seen as a response to a problematic situation. Therefore the main elements of creativity, as of other problem situations, are the formulation of a problem, the adoption of a method of solution, and the reaching of a solution. But while all problem situations are similar in that these three structural elements are present, they differ from one another depending on whether the person confronted with the problem has to discover a formulation, a method, and a correct solution, or simply adopt already available formulations, methods, and solutions (see Getzels, 1964).

At one extreme there are *presented problem situations* where the problem has a known formulation, a routine method of solution, and a recognized solution; here a person need only follow established steps to meet the requirements of the situation. At the other extreme there are *discovered problem situations* where the problem does not yet have a known formulation, a routine method of solution, or a recognized solution; here the person must identify the problem itself, and there are no established steps for satisfying the requirements of the situation.

Within these extremes it is possible to differentiate systematically a number of problem situations varying in what is known and unknown, and to infer the corresponding mental processes typical of each situation, ranging from rote memory to creative imagination. The elements of the analytical model are summarized in Table 6.1.

In type-case 1, the problem is generally known, and it is also known to

Table 6.1. Types of Problem Situations and Cognitive Functions

Problem Situation	Problem		Method of Solution		Solution		Cognitive Functions Primarily Engaged
	Others	Individual	Others	Individual	Others	Individual	
Type-case 1	+	+	+	+	+	–	Memory
Type-case 2	+	+	+	–	+	–	Reason
TYpe-case 3	–	–	–	–	–	–	Imagination

Note: + known; – unknown.

the individual (that is, the problem solver). The method of solution is also known to both; only the solution needs to be found by the individual. To illustrate with Wertheimer's example of the task involved in finding the area of a rectangle, the "others" (experimenter, teacher, etc.) assert that the area of a rectangle is side *a* multiplied by side *b*, and the individual is required to solve the problem: What is the area of a rectangle when *a* is 3 and *b* is 4? The problem is given—it is presented—and there is a standard method of solution known to others and presumably to the individual as well. All the problem solver has to do is plug the given data into a known formula to find the solution that is also already known and permits of no deviation. The mode of thought required is primarily memory and retrieval. This process has been well investigated both theoretically and empirically.

To continue with the illustration, in type-case 2 the "others" do not begin by giving a formula for solution. Instead, as in Wertheimer's classic instance, they begin by posing the problem: How would you go about finding the area of a rectangle? Here the problem is still presented, but no standard method for solving it is known to the problem solver, although it is known to others. The primary mode of thought is no longer memory and retrieval. The individual must reflect upon the presented problem until he reaches a solution, a solution that matches the one already known to others. The primary mode of thought required is reasoning and rationality, although of course not to the exclusion of other modes of thought. A substantial amount of theoretical and empirical work has been devoted to this type of thinking as well.

In type-case 3, at the other extreme, the "others" may say: How many important questions can be asked about a rectangle? Or, Formulate a problem about a rectangle and solve it. Here it is the general task—the dilemma—that is presented, but the specific question or problem must be discovered by the problem solver. In contrast to the preceding presented problem situations, this is a discovered problem situation. *The problem solver must become a problem finder.* And the problem he finds may range all the way from "How would one determine the distance around a rectangle?" or "What is the area of a rectangle?" to "Are there dimensions of a rectangle that make it more pleasing to the eye than other dimensions?"

To turn from a problem solver into a problem finder one must feel that there is a challenge needing resolution in the environment, one must formulate this feeling as a problem, and then attempt to devise appropriate methods for solving it. That is, the problem solver himself must pose the problem before he can begin to think of a way of solving it, and when he reaches a solution—if he reaches it—he has no way of knowing whether it is right or wrong. Not only the solution but the problem itself must be discovered, and when the solution is found, it cannot be compared against a predetermined standard. It can be accepted or rejected only on the basis of a critical, relativistic analysis—as is the case with works of art. The primary mode of thought required is usually called imagination or creativity, although of course memory and reason also play their part. About this kind of mental process we know next to nothing. Little theoretical and almost no empirical work exists to guide our understanding.

Problem solving and problem finding are not as discontinuous as the schematic representation of the model implies. Nonetheless, it is clear that finding a problem, that is, functioning effectively in a discovered problem situation, may be a more important aspect of creative thinking and creative performance than is solving a problem once the problem has been found and formulated. As Wertheimer (1945, 123) observed, "The function of thinking is not just solving an actual problem but discovering, envisaging, going into deeper questions. Often in great discoveries the most important thing is that a certain question is found. Envisaging the productive question is often more important, a greater achievement than solving a set question." Or as Einstein and Infeld (1938, 92) have put it, "The formulation of a problem is often more essential than its solution, which may be merely a matter of mathematical or experimental skill. To raise new questions, new possibilities, to regard old problems from a new angle, requires creative imagination and marks real advance in science." And, we would add, in art.

Some individuals, such as pure scientists and fine artists, prefer—and of course it is not only a matter of conscious preference—to work in discovered rather than presented problem situations. They do not wait for others to assign them a task; they cannot help being constantly sensitive to previously unidentified problems. Indeed, this may be the essential difference between the scientist and the technician; the difference is not that the one is more technically proficient or better informed than the other. Similarly, this may be the essential difference between the original artist and the copyist; the difference is not in the ability to draw, in graphic talent or craftmanship per se. Many copyists are more "talented" than fine artists. Rather, it is that one applies his talent in a discovered, the other in a presented problem situation. The latter's work may be judged for accuracy—whether it matches the original or not. The former's work cannot be judged by this criterion, but is appraised by the very criterion that is automatically a defect in the other's case —originality.

Problem Finding and the Artistic Process.   The work of a fine art student is structured around discovered problem situations. The difference between applied and fine art students does not lie in graphic skill; many of the former have superior technical abilities. The difference, which becomes clear in terms of the model, is that although the applied art student may legitimately work in a presented problem situation—say, accept an assignment to draw a replica of a cornflake box—the fine artist typically works in a discovered problem situation where he must create his own problem as well as his own solution.

In general, the fine artist must find a problem to work on, then he must discover a method appropriate to its solution, and afterward he has no clear way of knowing whether what he did was "right" or "wrong." Not only the solution but the problem itself must be found, and when he reaches a solution, it is *his* solution, and it cannot be compared to a predetermined standard of objective correctness or error. This is the problem situation at once permitting and calling for a maximum of imagination and creativity.

Our initial observations had been fruitless because we had been attempting to observe only one phase of the artistic process, and perhaps not even the crucial phase. We, like others, had been looking at the students' activity as they went about solving problems *after* the problem had already been found and formulated. We neglected to look at how the problem had been found. The model suggested that we investigate not only what artists do at their easel but how they conceive of a problem before they begin working as well as while they are working. In fact, the work at the easel may itself be seen, at least in part, as a continuation of the problem-finding process.

As an abstract proposition all this seems tenable, or at least worthy of exploration. But how is it to be translated into a set of empirical variables for observation?

It is possible to observe how a problem is *solved*. But it is difficult to see how one can observe the finding of a problem. At first glance it seemed nonsensical to think that a problematic or potentially creative situation can be approached without having a problem already in mind. On second thought, however, this is in fact the situation in which a fine art student (and the artist) often works. He wishes to do a drawing; this is the problematic thing—from cornflake boxes to the depths of the human soul. How should it be done? When is it complete? When, in effect, is it finally "correct"? And how wrong the term "correct" sounds in this context. It is like asking when Cezanne's half-dozen paintings of the same mountain were finally correct.

These questions—what is the work to be about (i.e., what is the problem); how is it to be done (i.e., what is the method); when is it completed (i.e., what is the solution)—represent genuine variables. Sometimes the problem, the method, or even the solution itself are predetermined; at other times they are almost completely open. In the first case, we have a presented problem situation; in the second a discovered one.

Discovered problems are common not only in fine art, but in all fields where creativity is at issue, from physics to politics, and from mathematics to poetics. Einstein and Infeld worded the distinction between ordinary scientists (whom they likened to detectives), and creative scientists as follows: "For the detective the crime is given, the problem formulated: Who killed Cock Robin? The scientist must commit his own crime [formulate his own problem] as well as carry out the investigation" (1938, 76).

In all such cases, whether in science or in art, the process that might lead to a creative solution begins with a diffuse feeling about things not fitting into place, and the first step—probably the crucial one—is an effort to *find*, that is, pose and formulate, the problem itself.

It follows that differences in *problem finding* attitudes and activities should play a crucial part in the work of fine art students. Individuals who approach potentially creative situations with a high concern for discovery—determined to commit their own crime, as it were—should arrive at more original results than individuals who approach the same situation already knowing what needs to be done, how it is to be done, what the outcome must be, and what criteria of rightness and wrongness apply to their work. The central question in this phase of the inquiry then becomes: Is there a significant relationship between the problem-finding behavior of fine art students and the aesthetic value, more especially the *originality*, of the drawings they produce?

Once we formulated *our* problem in these terms the rest of the task was relatively straightforward. To answer the question we had posed, a setting that met two essential requirements had to be provided. First, an indeterminate situation where a person could find and formulate an artistic problem of his own choosing and work toward its solution—that is, a situation conforming to the characteristics of a discovered problem situation—was needed. And second, it had to be a situation in which the steps taken to formulate and solve the problem were open to observation.

Classroom studios had several obvious disadvantages. Too many students worked together at the same time, making observation of an individual student difficult; the conditions in the different classrooms, or even for different students in the same classroom, were not constant. Hence comparisons among students were compromised as a function of different conditions.

Instead of using classrooms, we set up an experimental studio. We took over an empty room at the school, furnished it with two tables, several chairs, bristol boards, drawing paper, and a variety of dry media of the sort the art students customarily use. In effect, the room was a reasonably realistic replica of an artist's studio.

A constant arrangement of 27 objects of the sort students use to construct still-life problems was placed on one of the tables. Among the objects were a small manikin, a bunch of grapes, a steel gearshift, a woman's velvet hat, a brass horn, an antique book, and a glass prism. The objects were selected to give the greatest possible variety for simple and complex, human and mechanical, abstract and concrete choices. The second table was left empty. Each of the 31 male fine art students* came to the studio by himself, and was given the following instructions:

> There is a variety of objects on this table. I am asking you to choose some of them, rearrange them in any way you please on this other table, and draw them with the material provided over there. The important thing is that the drawing should be pleasing to you.
>
> You may choose as many objects as you want. You may spend as much time as you want selecting the objects and drawing them. However, it would be best if you could finish this task in an hour or so. Are there any questions?

If any questions were asked, they were answered by emphasizing the freedom of the situation. We said, for example, "You may do whatever you want so long as the drawing will be pleasing to you." Some students asked for more precise indications of the time they should take to do the

---

*By this stage of the study 4 of the original 35 male fine art students had dropped from the sample—2 had switched majors and 2 had left the school.

drawing. Such questions were answered by saying, "You may take five minutes or five hours so long as you are pleased with the drawing." Throughout, the main concern was to make the student feel at ease and to duplicate as closely as possible a free work situation. The observer had coffee with almost every student before the experiment began, and an informal relationship was maintained throughout the experimental period.

When the student was ready, the observer (the same one for all 31 students) began to keep a running record of the student's behavior. The record focused on the following items: the number, kind, and sequence of objects handled or manipulated; type of handling and manipulation (e.g., feeling the texture or weight of the objects, moving their parts, changing their shape, etc.); number and kind of objects finally selected; procedures used in arranging the objects selected; behavior during drawing (e.g., changes in the type of media, rearrangement of the objects, etc.); and any unusual or unanticipated behavior. In addition, photographs were taken three, six, and nine minutes after the drawing was begun and at six-minute intervals thereafter until the drawing was completed. (The photographs were taken with available light to avoid disturbing the artist with the glare of flashbulbs.)

After the drawing was completed, students were interviewed in the studio where they had worked. The purpose of the interview was twofold. First, although the situation seemed to us reasonably close to the students' usual working conditions, we wanted to find out what each artist thought of the situation in which he had worked. Second, we wanted to get a subjective account of what the artist experienced while he was working, to compare with the behavioral record. Among the 15 questions asked were the following: "In what ways were your thoughts and working methods different in this experiment from your thoughts and methods when you work on your own?" "Why did you pick up these objects?" "Why did you arrange the objects as you did?" "What were you thinking while you were choosing the objects?" "What meaning does the drawing have for you?" Any additional comments volunteered by the students were also recorded.

Before we look at the results, we should consider whether the experiment did in fact replicate the artistic process to a useful degree. Despite its apparent artificiality, three lines of evidence suggest that the setting was not very different from the ones in which young artists often work.

The first is based on the students' own reports. One of the interview questions was: "In what ways were your thoughts and working methods different in this experiment from your thoughts and methods when you work on your own?" Most students answered that they saw the situation as we had hoped they would.

Twenty-three of the 31 students, or 72 percent, stated that it was not different from free creative settings to which they were accustomed. If there was a difference, it was minimal, they said. Once they began working, they proceeded as usual. For example, one student said simply, "Not a bit different"; another replied, "If I had been painting, I would have come up with the same thing—I was expressing myself." Other comments were: "I felt free, freer than in the classrooms"; "Not different at all . . . sort of thing I would have done normally"; "I enjoyed the freedom of doing what I wanted, there was no pressure as in class"; "I would have done the same thing, the same way."

Four students, or 14 percent, said that although the experiment was unconstraining it resembled a studio classroom in the art school more closely than a free drawing situation. The remaining four students said they felt some degree of unusual constraint in the situation: "The paper was working against me"; "Usually I get more involved with the subject matter, but I didn't like to work with pastels"; "I would use different material, different paper, I wouldn't have done a still life"; "When I am free, I do five to seven sketches before really finishing . . . starting is always difficult." In fact, some of the students did make several sketches.

The second line of evidence rests on the quality of the drawings produced in the situation. If the setting had been unduly restrictive, presumably there would have been little variation in behavior and in the type of drawings. Had the students viewed the situation as a presented rather than a discovered one, they would have confined themselves to copying the available objects. The resulting processes and products would have been similar to each other. Yet, there was a very wide variety in the way each student approached the task, in the way he went about solving it, and among the solutions themselves, that is, the drawings produced.

The third line of evidence is based on the judgment of five artist-critics whom we asked to evaluate the drawings. Four of these well-known experts expressed spontaneous surprise and pleasure at the high quality of the drawings, although they had no knowledge of the conditions under which the drawings had been made.

We are confident, then, that the majority of students found the experimental setting familiar, that they engaged in a wide range of problem-finding and problem-solving behaviors, and that many of the drawings were of a high caliber. The procedures did reproduce the real situation to the extent that any quasi-realistic experimental setting can. Perhaps the major difference is that the process of making a work of art had been telescoped into a single session. Although some students changed their drawing considerably before settling on its final form, changes from one sketch to another through a period of days or weeks could not be observed. This appears to be the chief restriction that the experiment imposed on the free drawing process.

First Step in Problem Finding: The Problem Formulation Stage.   After the instructions were given, each student had to decide where to begin and what to do. He had to find and formulate a problem to work on. This process can be divided into a predrawing stage in which the artist tries to determine what to do, a drawing stage in which he actually works at the drawing board, and a retrospective stage in which he evaluates what he has done.

Perhaps the basic difference between presented and discovered problem situations is that in the former both task and specific problem are given, while in the latter the task is given but the specific problem must be found. Therefore in describing the discovered problem-solving process, we must first describe the manner in which the problem itself begins to take form, even though later it may be altered—as it often is—in the actual drawing.

The discovery of a problem can be described in at least two ways: the thought processes of the person engaged in the activity may be reconstructed and classified, or his manifest behaviors may be observed, recorded, and classified. This section deals with observed behavior; in a later section, introspective reports on the same behavior are analyzed.

The young artists acted differently from one another right after they walked into the studio. Three sets of differences at this stage were especially notable: the *number* of objects manipulated, the *interaction* of the artists with the objects, and the *uniqueness* of the objects selected for the final arrangement of the still life.

The number of objects handled ranged widely. Some students touched or manipulated as many as 19 of the 27 objects; others no more than 2. The *interaction* of the artists with the objects varied too. Some students picked up only a few objects from the first table and immediately placed them on the second table. Others explored the objects as if intent on discovering something not given in their immediate appearance; they changed the position of the manikin's limbs, felt the texture of the velvet hat, moved the levers of the gearshift, looked through the prism, and so on. As for the uniqueness of what was chosen for the arrangement, some artists selected only very popular objects—that is, items many others had also chosen; some selected objects almost no one else had chosen. For example, the antique book was used by 12, or 38 percent, of the students; the glass prism by only two (7 percent) of the students.

These differences in behavior seem on a priori grounds to be related to the quality of problem finding. The more objects one manipulates, the more likely it is that one will discover among them new relationships, contrasting features—unanticipated bisociations, to use Koestler's term (1964). Similarly, a thorough exploration through different sensory channels may lead to the discovery of previously hidden possibilities in even the most familiar objects, and hence result in the formulation of more original problems. And the selection of unusual items may facilitate the discovery of original problems by suggesting unique themes. A great artist can create an original drawing from the most hackneyed objects, but other things being equal, we assumed that attraction to a more unique stimulus reflects a greater potential toward originality.

Whether these overt behaviors reflect parallel covert mental processes is a moot question. In normal practice artists do not necessarily touch and move objects around as they did in the experimental setting. But they always have to weigh visual stimuli, emotions, or ideas in their minds. We assumed, since it is impossible to look into the "black box" itself, that the behavior in the experiment reflected mental operations involved in considering inner stimuli during problem finding, quite as the manifest behavior in the Vigotsky test or the Kohs Blocks is taken to reflect underlying mental operations during problem solving. A person who considers many objects, who selects stimuli after an intensive exploration, and who chooses unconventional objects, is also likely to utilize inner stimuli —thoughts, feelings, perceptions—only after probing their deeper, more diverse, and more idiosyncratic qualities.

Many scholars who have studied creativity have argued that the distinctive feature of genius is the ability to produce a greater than usual number of "blind" or random association of ideas (see the brief but excellent reviews in Campbell, 1960 and 1974; for an opposing view see Henle, 1975). This ability, however, has never been operationally measured in real-life situations. We expected that the first two categories (number of objects manipulated and extent of interaction), and perhaps the third as well (uniqueness of objects chosen), would reflect the degree to which a person generates, or is responsive to, ideas and other stimuli.

Variation in these three categories suggested that while all the students were required by the experiment to engage in problem finding—all had to formulate a problem to work on—some tried to maximize the discovered nature of the task, and others acted as if they were in a presented problem situation. The difference is crucial because what one does *before* starting to draw determines to a large extent what may or may not happen *after* one starts. The drawing might be changed later and its form altered beyond recognition, but the starting point is the selection and arrangement of objects made during the problem formulation stage. The empirical question we hoped to answer is whether drawings that started as discovered problems are in some ways "better"—more original, of greater aesthetic value—than those that were approached as presented problems.

Problem Finding at the Problem Solution Stage.   From the moment a person begins to draw to the time he has completed a drawing, he is involved in what our model calls "solution of the problem." A student described what this might mean: "The representation on paper . . . of a group of objects that I adapted to an emotional and visual experience."

This part of the process again consists of measurable activities that reflect the presence or absence of problem-finding behavior. Three dimensions of behavior seemed pertinent: *openness* of the initial structure and content of the problem; *exploratory* activity shown during the solution of the problem; and *changes* introduced in the structure and content of the problem. At first glance "problem finding at the problem solution stage" seems to involve a contradiction in terms. Does a problem not have to be found before it can be solved? But our model helped reject this conventional distinction. In a creative process, stages of problem definition and problem solution need not be compartmentalized. In fact, one would expect that a discovered problem does not become clearly formulated until several attempts at solving it are carried out. Hence problem finding continues throughout the creative process, and may continue even after the work is completed and the problem ostensibly "solved."

The first dimension along which the students varied was the *length of time the problem remained open* for alteration. This was reflected in the successive photographs taken while the drawing was in progress. We wanted to know when the essential form of the finished drawing could first be recognized. One student worked for 55 minutes, but the structure of the final composition, and the elements of the finished drawing, were already present in a frame taken 6 minutes after he had begun. Another student worked for 49 minutes, but the gestalt of his drawing was not recognizable until a frame taken 36 minutes after the start. In the first case, only 11 percent of the total drawing time had elapsed before the problem had been structured in its final form; in effect, the problem was "closed" almost at once. In the second case, the student used 74 percent of the time to structure the problem on paper; the problem remained "open" almost to the end. The median time at which the problem was structured, as rated from the photographs by two persons unconnected with the study, was 35 percent of the total drawing time.

Another dimension on which students differed was the extent to which they used *exploratory* activities while drawing. Some began drawing in one medium and kept on working without interruption until the picture was completed. Others began with pencil and moved to charcoal, or moved from one kind of paper to another. Some students made a single sketch; others made several sketches on paper varying in size and texture. Still others interrupted their work to change the position of an object, to alter the initial arrangement, to discard an item or look for additional ones. They seemed to be engaged in discovery-oriented behavior by restating the problem even while they were in the process of solving it.

Perhaps the most striking differences were in a third dimension measured: amount of *change* from still-life arrangement on the table to finished drawing. Some were almost exact renderings of the assembly of objects. Others included changes in perspective; the arrangement was purposely flattened or foreshortened on the paper. A few students introduced changes in the relative magnitude of the objects. Others changed the position of the objects, omitting some and adding new ones. And there were drawings that seemed to have lost all connection with the still-life arrangement.

These three dimensions—openness of the problem, exploratory behavior while drawing, and changes in the structure and content of the initial problem—were thought to indicate whether a person continues to be involved in problem finding even during the solution stage of the artistic task. We assumed that closure of the problem must be delayed if a creative solution is to emerge; that a person who does not explore different methods of solution might transform a new idea into an old routine; and that changing elements and introducing new combinations—that is, going beyond the information given—is more likely to contribute to an original solution.

Problem Finding as a Personal Attitude.   The six dimensions of problem finding just described were based on what students did before and while they drew. In addition to these "objective" indications, we also wanted to know whether the students were consciously aware of searching for a problem as they worked, or whether they had purposely adopted a predetermined problem on which to base their drawing.

To this effect each person was asked a set of questions after he finished working. Twelve questions dealt with art in general, and three with the artist's subjective experience while working in the experimental situation. The responses were examined in relation to four sets of attitudes: concern with problem finding mentioned by the student in the *general context* of his art work, in the *problem formulation* stage of the experiment, in the *problem solution* stage, and at the *evaluation of the solution* stage after the drawing was completed.

Concern with Problem Finding in General.   First the interview protocols were examined as a whole, excluding the three questions dealing specifically with the experimental situation. We looked for statements that mentioned problem finding as a general goal for the artists' work. Remarkable differences among students emerged. Some viewed their work explicitly as a seeking for understanding, a literal search and discovery experience; others spoke of the expression of emotions or ideas; still others thought of their work as a rendering or representation of reality that involved transformation from one spatial dimension to another.

The question "Why do you paint?" was answered by students in the first group as follows:

> I want to paint because it is necessary to me. . . . I want to say something, but don't know what. It's a basic questioning of what one wants.

> I want to know what I am doing. . . . I like to look at people once removed, to understand and enjoy them, to interpret, probe their characters.

> I guess I don't know. I like, I like to do it. Not knowing is part of why I do

it. . . . My intention is to discover what my intentions are, formulate my opinions. I get a logical satisfaction in seeing the work conform to intentions or develop into new things.

To the question "What do you paint usually?" a student in this group replies:

I am interested in portraits more than anything else. In the universal context of man: *The* man rather than *a* man. I don't know what this is, that's why I am searching for it. . . . Which is real, the concept or the object? [In my drawings] visual pleasure, emotions are subordinated to the intellectual quest for reality.

We could cite many similar statements by these and other students who share a questioning attitude, an awareness that meaningful but as yet unresolved problems exist, a desire to identify such problems, and then use their talent to state the problem and seek answers. In one or more answers, 19 students, or 61 percent, expressed concern with problem finding and discovery as a central purpose of their work.

The remaining students gave different responses. Some saw their main purpose in art as the expression of known or felt things—almost an opposite orientation from searching for the unknown; some simply wanted to reproduce aspects of reality in pleasing ways.

The following are typical answers from this group to the question "Why do you paint?":

I do it for the satisfaction of being able to do it. To transfer onto canvas my view of reality. . . . I transform the object so that it expresses my personal feelings about textures, colors, and such.

I don't have anything special to say in my work. I just want it to be enjoyable to look at. . . . Anything that is well done is enjoyable; I don't look for content, just concern with how it looks, how it was done.

The function of the artist is the betterment of human beings. Art must improve society, its benefits are on the emotional, not the intellectual level.

To the question "What do you paint usually?" a student in this group gives a typical answer: "What I do is simple. I combine groups of forms that are pleasing to the eye. There is no meaning, relation between them. I would like to work with large geometrical forms—they cannot be improved upon." In contrast to the questing of the first group, what lacks in these statements, and in the protocols from which they were drawn, is a recognition that the work might lead to the discovery of problematic relations, insights, or feelings.

Concern for Problem Finding at the Formulation Stage. The interviews were next examined for evidence of concern with problem finding in the experimental situation itself. First of all, we looked for statements reflecting these attitudes during the predrawing stage of the activity. The pertinent interview question was: "Why did you arrange the objects as you did?" The responses again revealed a great variety of approaches. At one extreme were students who said they arranged the objects according to an a priori principle, in order that they might represent it or its resulting effect. They used the objects to fit a predetermined idea, the still-life arrangement being merely a concrete example of an already known problem. In effect, these people immediately altered the discovered problem situation into a presented one. At the other extreme were students who said that the arrangement emerged out of the process of interacting with the objects, and was not a reflection of a preconceived problem; indeed, the ultimate structure of both problem and solution were to be worked out in the drawing and did not depend on the concerete arrangement of objects.

Typical of the former group is this statement: "I arranged [the objects] so that they produce a sense of pleasing harmony. The book has a regular shape, in pleasing contrast with the irregularities of the bunch of grapes. The same contrast exists between the book and the brass pitcher." People in the second group tended to answer in this way: "The arrangement on the table did not make any difference. I arranged the work on the paper . . . [but] I liked [the arrangement's] pattern, its subtle rhythm—not obvious, though strong."

Those in the first group were inspired by the visual clues in the objects to represent a standard aesthetic problem, and thus arranged the still life to illustrate "a pleasing harmony," "a startling vanishing point," "a tall-centered axis," or "a pleasing contrast." The second group of students did not feel that the objects were merely a means for structuring an already formulated problem. The responses of 15 students, or 48 percent, fell largely into the first group; those of 11 students, or 35 percent, into the second. Five students, or 17 percent, gave neutral or indeterminate responses.

Concern-for Problem Finding at the Problem Solution Stage. The second measure of the student's attitudes in the experimental situation dealt with their concern for problem finding while they were drawing. The pertinent interview question was: "What were you thinking of while you were drawing—what was your major concern?" Some artists answered that it was to "draw a likeness" or to "reproduce" the arrangement on the table. Others said that although their drawing was inspired by the still life, they were not bound by it; the arrangement was integrated with other ideas as they worked on the paper.

The contrasts between these two approaches are illustrated by the following statements. One student in the first group replied: "I was drawing likeness. The feeling was there already in the arrangement—I had no need to put it in." Another said: "I tried to get as close as possible to reproducing the objects." In the second group, one student said: "I wasn't worried about the drawing. The work was corrected and developed in terms of what was in the mind." A second said : "The objects are real as far as the world is concerned, but I can abstract some parts, and present them as just as real."

Some artists saw their task as doing a mechanical rendering of the still life they had assembled. In terms of our model, they were routinely applying a technical solution. If the arrangement reflected a "startling vanishing point," the student felt bound to reproduce it on paper no matter what else the developing drawing suggested. Others, however, were aware that the meaning of their work changed as they took into account the feedback provided by the colors and shapes unfolding before their eyes. They felt their drawing grew by incorporating new syntheses of external and, perhaps more important, internal reality. Fifteen students, or 48 percent, fell into the first group; 11, or 35 percent, into the second. Five, or 17 percent, gave neutral or indeterminate responses.

Concern for Problem Finding at the Problem Evaluation Stage. The last analysis of the interviews dealt with the students' explanation of their work. The relevant question was: "Could any of the elements in your drawing be eliminated or altered without destroying its character?" Our assumption was that a student who could imagine his drawing changed had worked toward discovering a solution to an emergent problem instead of producing a single "right" solution to an already set problem.

Since the drawing was not intended to conform to an established criterion of "rightness," it could be altered without losing its character as a satisfactory drawing. By contrast, if a student had adopted a known problem entailing a solution with a predetermined form, say, according to accepted rules of composition, then changing the drawing after it had reached that form would be unthinkable; it would make the drawing wrong as a solution.

This expectation is confirmed by the attitude of many famous artists toward their work. Picasso has been quoted as saying: "The picture is not thought out and determinted beforehand, rather while it is being made it follows the mobility of thought. Finished, it changes further, according to the condition of him who looks at it" (Zervos, 1955, 57). Or in the words of Robert Motherwell: "All my life I've been working on the work—every canvas a sentence or paragraph of it. Each picture is only an approximation of what you want. That's the beauty of being an artist—you can never make the absolute statement. . . ."*

The responses given to the interview question distinguished two groups of students. Typical of the responses of one group was:"I don't know. It would *change* the drawing, not *destroy* it. I don't believe in the conventional rules of composition." Typical of the responses of the second group was: "No. If you cut out part of it you *kill* it. It's a living thing. It's a valid statement, even if parts of it are wrong." An openness to change, a recognition of possibilities for further development both in the problem and in the solution contrast with a belief that the drawing cannot be altered without "killing" it. For the first group, the drawing is not a copy of an external arrangement. There is no *external* reference point—a known problem with a known solution—by which to assess its validity. For the second group, the drawing could not be changed without destroying its character. For them there *is* an external reference point—the accepted aesthetic solution by which to assess the validity of the drawing. The drawing is either "it" or nothing. The groups split almost down the middle of this variable—13 students, or 42 percent, said elements in their drawing could be changed or eliminated; 18 students, or 58 percent, said they could not.

Quantification, Reliability, and Interrelation of Problem-Finding Process Variables.   After the creative process in art had been analyzed in terms of

*The New York Times, February 3, 1976, p. 33.

the distinction between discovered and presented problems, the six behavioral and four attitudinal variables were quantified so that we might examine systematically their reliability, the interrelation among the variables, and finally the crucial substantive question: What is the relationship between the problem-finding variables and the originality of the products, that is, the finished drawings?

The rest of this chapter presents the operational description of how the problem-finding scores were obtained. Readers who are not interested in these technical details may skip to Chapter 7 and then to Chapter 8, which examines the relation between these process variables and the quality of the works produced, without losing the thread of the argument.

Quantification of Problem-Finding Behavior at the Problem Formulation Stage. The three kinds of problem-finding behavior observed before the students began to draw—the number of objects manipulated, the uniqueness of the objects chosen for the arrangement, and the exploratory behavior during the selection and arrangment—were categorized and quantified as follows.

A1. *Number of objects manipulated.* How many of the 27 objects were handled by a student before beginning to draw, based on the record taken by the observer.

A2. *Uniqueness of the objects chosen.* A count of the objects selected and actually transferred from the first to the second table. Each object was given a score corresponding to the rank order frequency with which it had been used by the sample as a whole. Thus the book, the most frequently chosen object, was given a score of 1; the lens, which was chosen least frequently, had a score of 25.5. An artist's score on this variable was the averaged rank score of all the objects he selected.

A3. *Exploratory behavior during selection and arrangement.* A score of 1 was given if the artist just picked up objects from the first table and placed them on the second table. A score of 2 was given if he was observed holding an object up to his eyes, assessing its weight, feeling its texture, and so on. A score of 3 was given for active experimentation with the objects—folding the hat into different shapes, changing the position of the legs on the manikin, and working the mechanical parts of the gearshift, for example. A score of 5 was given when actions for both scores 2 and 3 applied.

AA. *Total problem-finding score at the problem formulation stage.*

Whenever an artist was above the median for the sample on one of the three preceding variables he was given a score of 1. By adding these scores, the total score was obtained. A constant of 1 was added to give a numerical value to artists who otherwise would have had a score of zero. The total score therefore ranged from 1 to 4.

Quantification of Problem-Finding Behavior at the Problem Solution Stage. The three kinds of behavior observed while the student was drawing were openness of the problem structure, discovery-oriented behavior, and changes in problem structure and content. These variables were measured as follows.

B1. *Openness of problem structure.* To score this variable, the sequence of photographs taken at the three-minute and six-minute intervals during the experiment was examined. For each artist, that photograph was selected which for the first time revealed the final structure of the drawing in all its essential elements. The score consisted of the number of minutes elapsed between the beginning of the drawing and the taking of the given picture, divided by the minutes taken for the drawing as a whole. The score is therefore the percentage of the total drawing time elapsed before the final structure of the drawing was essentially completed.

B2. *Discovery-oriented behavior.* The subject received a score of 1 if he drew without interruption. He received a score of 2 if he changed paper or switched from one medium to another. A score of 3 was given for change in the arrangement of objects and for substitutions or manipulations of objects. A score of 5 obtained if both 2 and 3 applied.

B3. *Changes in problem structure and content* A score of 1 was given if the artist simply copied the still-life arrangement on paper. A score of 2 was given if he introduced changes in perspective. A score of 3 was given if he changed the relative magnitude of objects, or left one or more of them out. A score of 4 was given if he changed the position of objects on the paper. A score of 5 was given if there was an addition of nonexistent objects or major visual elements. A score of 9 was given if both actions for scores 4 and 5 applied.

BB. *Total problem-finding score at the drawing stage.* Whenever an artist was above the median for the sample on one of the three preceding variables, he was given a score of 1. By adding these scores, the total score was obtained. A constant of 1 was added to give a numerical value to artists who otherwise would have a score of zero. The total score therefore ranged from 1 to 4.

Quantification of Concern for Problem Finding. The four sets of attitudes derived from the interviews—that is, concern for problem finding within the general context of art, concern for this while formulating the problem, while solving the problem, and while evaluating the solution after the drawing was completed—were quantified as follows.

C1. *Concern for problem finding in general.* This was scored on the basis of the whole interview excluding the responses to the three questions to be dealt with separately below. A score of 1 was given to each theme in the protocol that mentioned the student's interest in "discovery," "seeking for understanding," "quest for reality," "curiosity," "wanting to know," and so forth. The scores ranged from 0 to 4.

C2. *Concern with problem finding at the problem formulation stage.* Scored on the basis of answers to the question, "Why did you arrange the objects as you did?" Answers suggesting that the student came with an a priori principle and arranged the objects to reflect this principle in order to make an exact representation of it in the drawing were scored low; answers suggesting that the student did not have an a priori principle in mind but that the arrangement emerged from the objects, and that the real structure was to be worked out in the drawing itself, were scored high. The range of scores was from 1 (low) to 5 (high).

C3. *Concern for problem finding at the problem solution stage.* Scored on the basis of answers to the question, "What were you thinking while you were drawing—what was your major concern?" Answers suggesting that the major concern was to "reproduce" the objects in the still life were scored low; those suggesting that although the drawing started from the arrangement, the major concern was to develop it beyond what was given were scored high. The range of scores was from 1 (low) to 6 (high).

C4. Concern for problem finding at the evaluation stage. This was scored on the basis of answers to the question, "Could any of the elements in your drawing be eliminated or altered without destroying its character?" An affirmative answer was scored 1, a negative answer 0.

CC. *Total concern with problem-finding score.* When a student was above the median on one of the four preceding variables, he was given a score of 1. By adding these scores the total score was obtained. A constant of 1 was added to give a numerical value to students who otherwise would have a score of zero. The total score therefore ranged from 1 to 5.

ABC.   *Total problem-finding score.*   This score was the sum of the three preceding total scores (AA, BB, CC). It is therefore the global indicator of all the process variables measured. The highest score obtained was 13, indicating that the particular student was above the median on all 10 process variables (13 − 3 = 10). The lowest score obtained was 3, by a student who was below the median on all 10 process variables. Figures 6.1 to 6.4. provide examples of how the scoring system was applied.

Reliability of Scoring the Process Variables.   After the variables had been scored by one of us, the records were given to an independent rater (or raters) for rescoring. Reliabilities in general were very high; all correlations were significant at the .005 level or beyond (see Table A1.9 in Appendix 1). It must be noted, however, that three variables (A1, A3, B2) were not based on "primary sources," but on the record kept by the observer, the accuracy of which is unknown. It was unfeasible to have more than one observer at a time in the experimental studio, since this would have interfered with the natural situation we wished to maintain; more than one observer was bound to disturb the artist at his task. But these variables—the count of the items handled, for example—were of such evident nature that it is unlikely serious errors were made in the recordings. Moreover, the process variables were only a few of the many observations recorded, and the protocols were coded at random over a period of time to decrease experimenter bias. In light of these factors it seems fair to say that the experimental setting allowed reliable observations of the problem-finding variables as these were defined.

Relations Among the Process Variables.   The three clusters of measures with which we are dealing were drawn from sources independent from one another. The problem formulation variables are based on behavior that took place *before* the actual drawing was begun. The problem solution variables are based on behavior observed *during* the actual drawing. And the attitudinal variables are based on an interview conducted *after* the drawing was completed. The variables were scored independently of one another over a period of time.

(a)

(b)

Figure 6.1 S.01. (a) *The arrangement of objects.* (b) *The drawing halfway through the drawing process. Examples of the scoring system: this artist's work was scored above average in the uniqueness of the objects chosen (A2), very high on "exploratory behavior" before starting to draw (A3), and high in the amount of "change in problem content and structure" (B3). Compare the changes introduced in this work with those in Figure 6.2.*

101

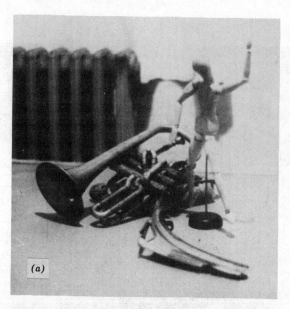

(a)

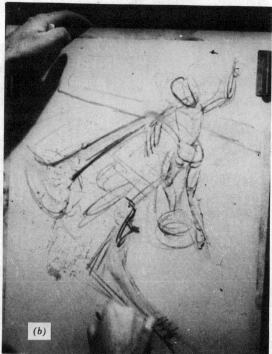

(b)

Figure 6.2 S.15. (a) *The arrangement of objects.* (b) *The drawing about one-third through the drawing process. Examples of the scoring system: this artist's work received the lowest A2 score because he selected the least unusual objects, a low B1 score because the basic structure of the finished drawing was completed very early, and a low B3 score because he did not introduce any change in problem content or structure (B3).*

102

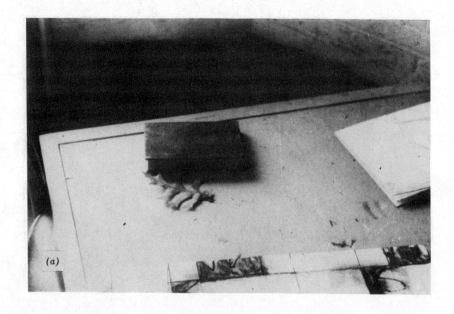

Figure 6.3   S.31. (a) The arrangement of objects. (b) The completed drawing. Example of the scoring system: this artist took the book and a leaf from a branch, and with these two objects created a serial modular pattern. His work was scored very high on "exploratory approach to drawing" (B2) and on the amount of change in problem content and structure (B3).

Figure 6.4 S.09. (a) The arrangement of objects. (b) The drawing about one-fifth into the drawing process. Examples of the scoring system: this artist's work received one of the lowest A2 scores because none of the objects he chose were unique, a very low B1 score because the final structure of his drawing was completed very early, and very low B2 and B3 scores because his approach to drawing was not exploratory and no changes were introduced in the drawing.

If the theory and method are tenable, then behavior at the predrawing stage, at the drawing stage, and the attitudes expressed in the interviews should not be entirely random; a person who approaches the task as a discovered problem ought to show the same concern throughout his work.

The three sets of measures are in fact correlated (see Table A1.10). The coefficients are not high, suggesting that problem-finding behavior at one stage and at one level does not necessarily carry over in its entirety to another. Nonetheless, there are systematic relations between discovery behavior in the predrawing stage and in the drawing stage, and between attitudes expressed in the interviews and behavior observed in the experimental situation.

A more detailed view of the correlations between the 10 process variables, the 3 subtotals, and the grand total is shown in Table A1.11. Since there might have been a question as to whether the data satisfied the assumptions of the correlational statistic, the contigency coefficient (C) and the index of association (H), which do not require these assumptions, were also applied. The three methods provided essentially the same results. Since the correlation metric is the most familiar, it is the one that is reported in the tables.

It is clear from Table A1.11 that all 10 variables are significantly correlated with the total score. Although several correlations, that is, between A2, B1, B2, and ABC, are barely above what would occur as a consequence of "spurious overlap," most of the correlations are fairly high. The relevant conclusion is that the total score represents a substantial number of its subscores. It is also clear that some variables are far more highly related to the overall pattern than others. Variable B3 (amount of change introduced during the drawing stage) correlates significantly with seven of the remaining nine variables, variable A1 (number of objects manipulated during the predrawing stage) correlates with six of the other nine variables. By contrast, variable B1 (openness of problem structure during the drawing stage) shows only one significant correlation. Some variables derived from the interview also show very high correlations with measures of behavior. Variable C2 (concern with problem finding at the predrawing stage) is correlated .68 with variable A3 (exploratory behavior during the predrawing stage) and .55 with variable B3 (change in problem structure and content at the drawing stage); it is also correlated .39 with subtotal AA (total problem-finding behavior at the predrawing stage) and .34 with subtotal BB (total problem-finding behavior at the drawing stage).

The evidence suggests that making a work of art is an open-ended, problematic task that can be approached either as a discovered or as a presented problem. The attitude of the artist presumably determines which it will be. A person who has learned to be concerned with problem finding will not approach a situation like the experiment with a ready-made picture in his mind. He will not let past experience completely determine what he will do, but will let the new challenge suggest new forms of visual expression.

Reliable measurement of problem-finding behaviors and attitudes is a considerable methodological advance. The creative process in art has been described with some objectivity, and young artists who practiced problem finding were distinguished from those who did not. Moreover, the model and the method are in principle applicable to the study of creativity in fields other than art.

But the test of the real usefulness of the model and method depends on whether artists who use problem finding make "better" works of art than those who do not. The following chapters examine this question.

■

CHAPTER 7

The Evaluation of Works of Art

The theory that we began considering in the preceding chapter made it possible to advance this hypothesis: There will be a positive relationship between problem finding and the quality of art products. A method of recording behavior and attitudes reflecting discovery orientation was developed and applied in a true-to-life setting where problem-finding and problem-solving activities could be recorded with some fidelity.

But a major obstacle remained. How could we measure the dependent variable, that is, the quality of the drawing completed in the experiment? The theoretical model itself suggests that this is no easy task. The correct solution to a presented problem is either known or could be found out by turning to an accepted criterion, but in a discovered problem situation there is no way to tell whether a given solution is "correct" or not; nor is it possible to adopt objective criteria.

People have tried often enough to develop "scientific" methods for evaluating art. Some of these attempts are interesting but, at least so far, not very useful. The judgment of art involves so many variables in shifting combinations that a formula for assessing the worth of a drawing would necessarily be a simplification deserving the label of "vulgar scientism." Not the least of the obstacles is the fact that aesthetic taste changes considerably over time, especially in our culture.

In the absence of absolute standards, expert opinion provided a more modest but more realistic means for evaluating the drawings produced in the experiment. Experts are often used to make the same kinds of judgments that were needed in our experiment. Expert juries determine, for instance, which paintings are worth a fellowship, a prize, or a place in a museum.

Therefore panels of judges were asked to evaluate the drawings. This also provided a possibility to study the degree of agreement between judges. Little is known about the reliability of aesthetic judgments, and something could be learned from analyzing the judges' opinions.

The procedure for getting evaluations was simple. Four groups of five judges each were selected. The first group, which we called the "artist-critics," consisted of established artists whose work is represented in museums and galleries across the nation. Several had also "juried" competitive exhibitions. The second group was also made up of practicing artists, all of whom taught full-time at the art school. This group was called "artist-teachers." The third group was made up of doctoral students in theoretical mathematics at the University of Chicago; the fourth, of graduate business students in the Executive Training Program, also at the University of Chicago. The first two groups are referred to as "expert" judges; the second two, which were not involved in art other than as viewers and perhaps potential buyers, are referred to as "lay" judges.

The drawings made in the experiment were hung as for an exhibit. Each judge, working alone, was asked to rate each drawing on three aspects: first on the *craftsmanship* or technical skill of the work, second on its *originality* or imaginativeness, and finally on its *overall aesthetic value*. No attempt was made to define these dimensions; we felt that definitions might have made it possible to obtain a high degree of agreement among judges, but such an agreement would have been illusory since precision in the definition of nebulous concepts is bought at the expense of credibility. Instead of agreement on artificially narrow, a priori criteria established by experimenters, we wanted to use as a measure the judges' own interpretations of what constitutes technical skill, originality, and overall aesthetic value. Such evaluation reflects personal conviction and is not made merely for the purpose of our research. Presumably not all the judges would share the same criteria. But a certain amount of disagreement might be an advantage, since the sum of multiple opinions is likely to reflect a complex idea better than a single definition. After all, this is the way artist-critics operate in "real" situations where aesthetic judgments are made.

Only one restriction was placed on the judges' choices. To systematize evaluations, they were requested to rate the drawings on a 1 to 9 point scale with a "prenormalized" distribution. That is, one drawing was to be rated 1 (the lowest on the given dimension) and one was to be rated 9 (the highest on the dimension); two drawings were to be rated 2 and 8 each; four were rated 3 and 7 each; five were rated 4 and 6; the remaining seven were given the "average" rating, 5. Although more formalized, this kind of choice is not very different from what art judges usually do: select some paintings and reject others; among those selected separate out the better ones from the worse; among the better ones choose the best, the second best, and so on. By applying correlational methods to the preset distribution, estimates of relative agreement were obtained within each group, between groups, and between the several types of ratings.

Consistency of Aesthetic Evaluation Within Groups of Judges. We first wanted to explore the extent of agreement within each group of judges, and especially among the group of "expert" artist-critics. The results were straightforward; artist-critics agree to a moderate but statistically significant degree in their evaluation of the quality of the drawings produced in the experimental setting (see Table A1.12 in Appendix 1). The overlap of opinion appears to be no less than in the judgments of "real" exhibitions; in a review of a dozen prizes given in the 1972 Biennial Exhibition of American Art, the critic for the *New York Times* said that he agreed with only two of the prizes awarded.

As might be expected, agreement among artists teaching at the same school is substantially higher. That they should have been more consistent than any other group, at least in the overall ratings of the drawings, is not surprising. Although they did not know it, they were rating the work of their own students. If anything, the consistency should have been greater, especially in the craftsmanship rating. The comparison of the artist-critics with the two lay groups, however, is both surprising and revealing. The mathematics and business groups tended to agree among themselves more about what was good or bad in the drawings than did the artist-critics.

Two other trends are brought to light by the data. The consistency of ratings in craftsmanship seems to increase the less expert the judges are in art, or at least the further they are from commitment to artistic endeavor. The five artist-critics, familiar with the techniques of producing art, agreed significantly less among themselves as to which work was done more skillfully than did the five business students, who presumably are least familiar with art. And second, artist-critics and art teachers agree among themselves more on the overall value of a drawing than on its craftsmanship; conversely, mathematics and business students agree more on the craftsmanship of a drawing than on its overall value. The less viewers know about art, the more they agree on what technical skill is and, if we may anticipate ourselves somewhat, the larger technical skill looms as a determinant of their overall aesthetic preference.

What is at issue here is the *consistency* of aesthetic preferences, not their validity. Nothing has been said so far about what lay judges were evaluating when they agreed on the relative craftsmanship of the drawings, or what expert judges were responding to when they disagreed on the same issue. It may very well be that the two groups defined craftsmanship differently from each other. Yet all the judges believed they were rating technical skill, and the independent ratings of nonexperts were in greater agreement than those of experts.

Since the criterion of quality for experimental drawings is the artist-critics' judgments, a more detailed account of their ratings is in order. The correlations among the ratings of the five artist-critics are all positive. Two-thirds of all the nonsignificant correlations involved rater B (see Table A1.13). He was the youngest of the five, and when asked to define the dimensions, he gave the most idiosyncratic responses. Where, for example, C's definition of originality emphasized "the introduction of unusual shapes, of unusual relationships of color and form," and A's "freedom from the influence of another painter or school of painting," B's definition hinged on work "which did not try to impress with gimmicks" and was "basically honest and naive."

The reliability could have been higher, were aesthetic quality not purposely left undefined so that we could approximate the usual conditions under which such judgments are made in real life. The "total" score based on the sum for the group, however, did correlate quite highly ($p < .005$) with each of the separate ratings, and is therefore a representative measure of the group's judgment. However, in view of the low correlations between rater B and the others, a "total" score omitting his ratings was also used to compute the relationship between process variables and the quality of the products. The results were almost identical, and so the score based on all five raters was retained throughout.

Relationship Among Originality, Craftsmanship, and Overall Value in Aesthetic Judgments. A second question concerns the relationship among the three dimensions on which the judgments were made—originality, craftsmanship, and overall aesthetic value. The issue is whether a drawing rated very high in originality or in craftsmanship could be rated low in overall value, or whether a high rating in one dimension automatically carries with it a high rating in the others.

The relevant results, presented in Table 7.1, suggest that the dimensions are highly interrelated. But again a distinction must be made between expert and lay judges: the further the judges are from involvement in art, the more independent are their evaluations. Thus the correlation between originality and overall value for artists was .90, but for business students only .64 (the difference between the two correlations is significant at the .05 level). The correlation between craftsmanship and originality for artists was .76, while for business students it was .53. For all intents and purposes, the artists hardly differentiated at all between originality and overall aesthetic value, and only a little more between originality and craftsmanship. These observations support the claim sometimes voiced by artists that it is impossible to analyze a work of art in terms of separate criteria such as technical excellence, originality, and so on. The nonexperts seem to have less difficulty in making such distinctions.

A possible reason for the great overlap in judgment is that the artists were too involved in the drawings as aesthetic wholes to be able to differentiate the separate dimensions of analysis. Or perhaps the lay judges were differentiating between dimensions that artists consider spurious abstractions. Is there really no distinction between the conceptual originality of a drawing and the quality of its technical execution? The artists never suggested that they could not make the required distinction. On the contrary, they made each rating as if they were discriminating between the dimensions; they were genuinely surprised when the similarity between their ratings was pointed out.

Table 7.1. *Correlations Between Dimensions of Evaluation* [a]

Judges	Correlations Between		
	Overall Value-Originality	Overall Value-Craftsmanship	Originality-Craftsmanship
Artists	.90	.82	.76
Art teachers	.86	.79	.65
Mathematics students	.75	.89	.58
Business students	.64	.80	.53

[a] For all correlations in this table $p < .005$.

This issue was pursued through a more refined analysis of the trends in Table 7.1. The relationship between overall aesthetic value and originality, and between originality and craftsmanship, was highest for artists, and tended to decline steadily with declining involvement in art. But the relationship between overall value and craftsmanship remained the same for all four groups. When partial correlation is applied, the distinctive judgmental patterns of artist and lay groups becomes clearer. The data are presented in Table 7.2. With the ratings in craftsmanship partialed out, the relation of overall value to originality remains highest for the two expert groups and lowest for the two lay groups, as in Table 7.1. But with the ratings in originality partialed out, the relation between overall value and craftsmanship is lowest for the expert groups and highest for the lay groups.

This suggests that for the nonartist the overall value of a drawing depends on craftsmanship rather than originality. Not only is there a clearer consensus among lay persons about what constitutes technical skill—which of course does not imply that their consensus is valid—but technique is held by them as a more important determinant of the overall aesthetic value of a drawing.

Experts, however, appear to base their global evaluation of a work of art more on its originality than on its technical skill. This discrepancy is probably a symptom of a larger misunderstanding between artists and the public about values in art. For the public, a valuable piece of work is one that is technically accomplished. But experts take skill for granted, and must look for other qualities; in our times the foremost of these is "originality."

This simple difference in ratings introduces us to a central problem for

Table 7.2.   Partial Correlations Between Dimensions of Evaluation [a]

Judges	First-Order Partial Correlations Between	
	Overall Value-Originality (Craftsmanship Held Constant)	Overall Value-Craftsmanship (Originality Held Constant)
Artists	.76	.49
Art teachers	.74	.59
Mathematics students	.62	.85
Business students	.43	.71

[a] For all correlations in this table, $p < .01$.

the practicing artist. His teachers expect him to be original above all else. He shares with his peers and teachers the belief that originality is what gives value to a work of art. He will strive to perfect the approach that leads to the finding of original problems. But the great public, the potential customers for his work on whom his economic survival depends, is by and large not impressed by true originality. From the finding just reported we see that if a painting conforms to his definition of skill, the potential customer will think it valuable, and presumably will be prepared to support the artist who painted it. Thus the artistic subculture rewards the young artist for problem finding, while the broader culture tends to give its rewards to problem solvers. As we shall see later, these contradictory expectations lead to many conflicts and frustrations when students try to establish themselves as professional artists.

Agreement Between the Four Groups of Judges. Another aspect of this question is to what extent artists and art teachers agree with business and mathematics students on the quality of works of art. In general, the data are in line with what common sense suggests: there is high agreement between the two expert groups, high agreement between the lay groups, and less agreement across the line of expertise (see Table A1.14).

But two observations are surprising and deserve further thought. First, of the three dimensions of rating, the one on which there is greatest agreement is originality. It seems that artists and nonartists agree with one another more on what is imaginative than on what is skillful or on what has overall aesthetic value.

This could mean that in our culture the ambiguous concept of "originality" has become so well defined that it is easier to agree on it than on the concept of craftsmanship. Or it could simply be that craftsmanship, being based on objective criteria, is more difficult to evaluate than the fashionable dimension of "originality." These alternatives should be pursued, since they deal with crucial issues of the culture. In any case, the finding suggests that if lay persons place less value on originality, it is not because they cannot recognize it. They do agree with experts on which works are original, and which are not. In deciding whether originality or craftsmanship is to be given greater value, however, they tend to opt for the latter.

Second, despite the lack of strong agreement among artist-critics, when the judgments of these same artists are averaged, the resulting composite judgment is fairly similar to that of art teachers, who had agreed quite substantially among themselves. One way of accounting for this pattern is to assume that while each artist-critic has a personal criterion of evaluation, one that is quite unlike that of the other artists, these criteria are complementary. When they are combined, they add up to a composite judgment that is similar to the judgment of the more consistent art teachers. It is as if each artist-critic was using a single dimension of the criterion of evaluation, while each art teacher was using all the dimensions; but when the judgments of the two groups are added up, the rankings that result are very similar.

Aesthetic Judgment: "Realism" versus "Abstraction." Despite occasional vagaries of judgment, there is one issue on which all groups without exception agreed. The data on whether "abstract" or "realistic" drawings are preferable are unequivocal, and the result somewhat unexpected.

The 31 experimental drawings had been previously rated with high reliability by two nonartists on a continuum from "very realistic" to "very abstract." The evaluations given by the four groups of judges to the five drawings in the "very realistic" category and to the five drawings in the "very abstract" category were then examined.

The abstract drawings were judged better on each dimension of evaluation: They were held by all groups to be not only more original but more technically skillful, and of higher overall aesthetic value. The differences between the mean ratings of the abstract and of the realistic drawings are all highly significant ($p < .01$), in each case the ratings of the abstract drawings being more positive (Getzels and Csikszentmihalyi, 1969).

Under prevailing cultural standards the fact that a drawing is nonrepresentational tends to raise its value in the eye of the viewer, whether he is an artist or not, at least when the viewer is of a high educational level as were our judges. This interpretation is in line with similar conclusions reached by other investigators (Zavalloni and Giordani, 1958; Marchal, 1958). But there may be another explanation: The more able young artists of our time work in abstract styles, so that the higher evaluations placed on their drawings reflects not style per se but the artists' ability. In either case, the virtual unanimity of preference for abstract works is a powerful illustration of one apparent bias in current aesthetic preference.

The "Artist's Artist" and the "Artist of the Hour." The way individual drawings were judged reveals four basic patterns, which are best illustrated by reference to some actual cases. Figure 7.1 shows how four of the drawings were rated by the four groups of judges.

The drawing of artist S.01 was top on the list of the experts; 6 of the 10 gave it first choice and none thought it average or below (see Figure 7.2). Its mean rank on the 1 to 9 scale was 8.2. In contrast, the two lay groups

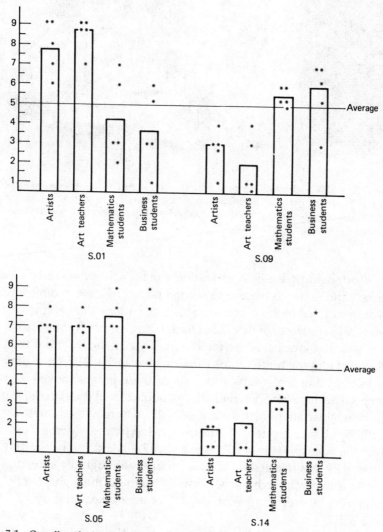

Figure 7.1 *Overall aesthetic ratings of four selected drawings—an illustration of different patterns of consistency. Each asterisk indicates a rating by one judge.*

Figure 7.2   S.01. Completed experimental drawing. The "artist's artist" this student's work was rated first by experts, but generally below average by nonexperts. S.01 sold none of his work and eventually retired from active work in art, whereas S.05 (see Figure 7.4), whose work was appreciated by nonexperts, succeeded as an artist.

gave the drawing a relatively low rating; 6 of these 10 judges rated it below average, and none gave it first or second rank. Their mean rank was 3.9, less than half that of the expert groups. This pattern was reversed for the work of artist S.09 (see Figure 7.3). His drawing was uniformly disliked by the two expert groups. None rated it average or above, and 4 of the 10 judges put it at the bottom rank. The mean was 2.4. The same drawing was liked by the lay groups; only one of these judges ranked it below average. The mean was 5.5, more than double that of the experts. A third pattern is illustrated by the work of S.05, which was admired almost equally by all four groups. The mean ranking by the expert groups was 7.0, by the nonexpert groups 7.1 (see Figure 7.4). And finally, the drawing of artist S.14 was rejected by all four groups, although the spread in the business group was from the very lowest to almost the highest rank. The mean rank of the expert group was 2.0, of the nonexpert group 3.7 (see Figure 7.5).

There are no unequivocal concepts for describing creative drawings in readily comparable terms. Consequently the characteristics of the four

Figure 7.3 S.09. Completed experimental drawing. This artist's work was rated among the lowest by experts, although nonexperts rated it generally above average.

pictures cannot be related to the patterns of judgments by the various groups in any systematic way. At this point one can only say that drawing S.01 was produced by what may be called an "artist's artist." The picture was a deceptively bland pencil drawing on the borderline between realism and abstraction. In many ways it was a showcase of unobtrusive skill and subtle imagination, which appealed to experts. As one of the artist-critics remarked when he was asked why he had given top rank to the picture, "Look at the wonderful use of space"—a reason that might not readily occur to laypersons, whom the picture left unimpressed, if not disturbed. Drawing S.09 was the opposite of S.01. It tried to attract attention with a showy exhibition of bold relief, strong contrast, sweeping movement. And it did impress the nonexperts, but not those with artistic experience, several of whom remarked that the picture was a skillfully executed cliché. The student who executed drawing S.05 may be called the "artist of the hour," and the drawing can be seen as a combination or a purposeful compromise of S.01 and S.09. It has sophisticated flair to please the artists, yet is within the bounds of popular expectation for skill in rendering.

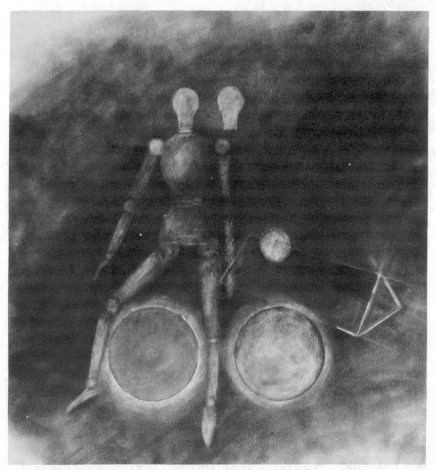

Figure 7.4   S.05. Completed experimental drawing. The "artist of the hour"–this student's drawing was rated highest by nonexperts and second highest by experts on every dimension of evaluation.

How pictures S.01 and S.05 were evaluated closely reflected the actual status of the two students. Student 05, whose drawing received high ratings from all four groups of judges, was, at least while in art school, the most successful of the 31 young artists. He had won prizes at several competitive exhibitions, had two one-man shows, and at the time of the experiment a fashionable gallery was entirely devoted to his work. He was very much the "artist of the hour." Student 01's life was also accurately reflected by the ratings of his work. His drawing had been rated

Figure 7.5 S.14. Completed experimental drawing. This artist's work was rated lowest by experts and nonexperts alike.

higher by experts than that of Student 05 (they gave drawing S.01 six top ratings, S.05 none). But his drawing lacked the popular appeal of the other work and was rated far lower by laypersons. Student 01 had not sold any of his work, nor had he had an opportunity to show it; he was not sought after by fashionable galleries. Although he was an "artist's artist," as the ratings show, he worked in obscurity and lived in financial straits.

The follow-up study showed that the positions of the two artists were the same seven years later. The former was still the most successful artist in the sample, while the latter has stopped doing art entirely, discouraged by the lack of appreciation on the part of lay audiences. In these cases at least, public opinion seems to have been a more important determinant of success than the judgment of experts.

Aesthetic judgments are based on vague and subjective criteria, yet they are consistent and predictable. Pooled judgments by a group of artist-critics, for instance, closely duplicate the same ranking by a group of art teachers; and when groups of mathematics and business students are asked to rate a set of drawings, their choices will also be very similar. However, and here artistic judgment may differ from evaluations in other fields, the rankings by experts and laypersons have little in common. On one thing everyone agrees: Drawings done in an abstract style are in every way better than realistic drawings. But artists and nonartists have different definitions of technical virtuosity and overall value. Originality, which would seem to be the most vague of the dimensions of evaluation, is the only one on which the ratings of expert and lay groups agree. Although the judges concur on which drawings rank low, their interpretation of what originality means clearly differs. For experts, the originality and the overall artistic value of a drawing are almost the same; the overlap in the variance of the two ratings is more than 80 percent. For laypersons, originality enters much less in judgments of overall value; the variance of the two ratings overlap only 52 percent. The opposite trend holds for evaluation of technical skill: Laypersons esteem it as a far more important component of overall value than do experts.

There are also indications that the judgment of educated laypersons is crucial in determining the success of an artist. Favorable judgment by experts appears to be necessary, but not sufficient, to ensure that an artist's works will be noticed, exhibited, and sold. If the work fails to appeal to the public, the opinion of other artists is not enough to assure professional success.

The reason for examining patterns of aesthetic judgment was to develop a criterion to validate our problem-finding measures. We expected that drawings created as a result of a discovered problem-finding approach would be of a higher quality than those that were the outcome of a presented problem-solving process. The different criteria used by the laypersons in judging the quality of art works presents a problem. Which opinion should be used as a benchmark? Despite the limitations inherent in the judgment of experts, our decision was to go along with their opinion. Problem finding is related more to originality than to technical skill, and the artist-critics seem to respond more to originality as the essential ingredient of artistic quality. In the short run, their judgment may not coincide with success; but in terms of approximating a measure of absolute creativity in art, we felt it was safer to heed the word of experts. The following chapter reports the relationships between our measures of problem finding, and the ratings made by the group of artist-critics of the quality of finished drawings.

CHAPTER 8

■

Problem Finding and the Quality of Works of Art

We now reached the crucial point in this phase of the investigation. Having devised a method for observing the artistic process in terms of a model of creativity, and having established the value of the artistic products, we were ready to test a hypothesis. If the model of creativity was valid, then there should be a systematic relationship between the extent of problem finding and the quality of the drawings as evaluated by experts.

The originality of the drawings was expected to correlate most highly with the problem-finding score. No matter how one defines "originality," the concept must include a restructuring of elements, which in turn implies finding a new problem. But restructuring alone may lead to a sterile exercise in novelty, or result in merely bizarre rather than creative products. For an idea or object to be called creative, originality is not sufficient; it must also be adaptive. Therefore, overall aesthetic value ratings were expected to correlate with the problem-finding score as well. Finally, it was predicted that technical skill would not be correlated with problem finding, or at least substantially less than the other two ratings. In theory, a person's craftsmanship need not be highly related to his ability to discover new problems; the skillful copyist, who can reproduce a drawing so that it cannot be distinguished from the original, is not necessarily able to conceive of an original drawing.

The Relationship Between Process and Product Variables. Table 8.1 presents the correlations between what students did in the experiment and said in the interview, and what the artist-critics thought of the resulting drawings. The data confirm the theoretical predictions. The total problem-finding score (ABC) correlates at a very high level of significance ($p <$ .0005) with the originality of the products, quite highly ($p <$ .005) with

Table 8.1. Correlations Between the Ratings by Five Artists on Three Dimensions of Evaluation, and the Problem-Finding Variables Observed in the Experiment (N = 31)

Process Variables	Overall Aesthetic Value (five raters)	Originality (five raters)	Craftsmanship (five raters)
Problem formulation			
A1. Manipulation	.46[b]	.52[b]	.17
A2. Unusualness	.35[e]	.42[c]	.22
A3. Exploration	.44[c]	.58[a]	.34[e]
AA. Total	.40[d]	.54[b]	.28
Problem solution			
B1. Structure time	.09	.08	−.18
B2. Exploration	.23	.37[d]	.01
B3. Changes	.44[c]	.61[a]	.37[d]
BB. Total	.26	.38[d]	.12
Concern with problem finding			
C1. In general	.22	.27	.15
C2. In problem formulation	.41[d]	.60[a]	.26
C3. In problem solution	.31[e]	.31[e]	.24
C4. In problem evaluation	.36[d]	.45[b]	.33[d]
CC. Total	.41[d]	.56[b]	.31[e]
Total problem-finding score			
ABC: Grand total	.47[b]	.65[a]	.31[e]

The columns fall under: **Dimensions of Evaluation (Product Variables)**

[a] $p <$ .0005.
[b] $p <$ .005.
[c] $p <$ .01.
[d] $p <$ .025.
[e] $p <$ .05.

their overall aesthetic value, and less highly though still significantly ($p <$ .05) with their craftsmanship. The predrawing (AA), drawing (BB), and postdrawing (CC) subscores are also significantly related to the product variables, although in somewhat differing patterns.

The relationships involving single variables merit consideration in their own right. But before we turn to these, a problem of interpretation must be dealt with. As we already know (Table 7.1), the ratings in originality, craftsmanship, and overall aesthetic value overlap with one another a great deal. Consequently the meaning of the positive correlations between the three product ratings and the process scores is somewhat ambiguous. For example, craftsmanship and problem finding might be correlated only because they both share a common overlap with the ratings in originality or overall aesthetic value.

Table 8.2 shows what happens when the variance held in common by the three ratings is partialed out. With craftsmanship held constant, the relation between overall aesthetic value and problem finding remains essentially the same. But with originality held constant, the relationship becomes negative. In practice it is of course difficult to separate originality from overall aesthetic value for the artist-critics (the two ratings are correlated .90). Yet with either overall aesthetic value or craftsmanship held constant, the rated originality of the drawings is still highly related to problem finding. If one may conceive of the three constructs in an abstract sense as "pure" dimensions of aesthetic evaluation, then the problem-

Table 8.2. *First-Order Partial Correlations Between the Total Problem-Finding Score and the Evaluation of the Products (N = 31)*

Correlations Between the Total Process Score (ABC) and	Zero-Order *rho* (Same as Table 8.1)	Variables Held Constant	First-Order Partial Correlation
Overall value	.47	Originality	−.36*
Overall value	.47	Craftsmanship	.40*
Originality	.65	Overall value	.60**
Originality	.65	Craftsmanship	.67**
Craftsmanship	.31	Overall value	−.15
Craftsmanship	.31	Originality	−.37*

*$p < .025$.
**$p < .001$.

finding process results in drawings that are more original, but not necessarily of a higher aesthetic or technical polish.

This conclusion is strengthened when one applies second-order partial correlations to the data, that is, when the correlations between the total problem-finding score and each dimension of the product are examined with the other two dimensions held constant. As Table 8.3 shows, when overall value and craftsmanship are held constant, the correlation between problem finding and originality remains at .61 ($p < .001$). But the correlation of the other two dimensions of evaluation decreases to a nonsignificant negative value when the overlap with originality is removed. It seems clear that problem-finding activity is of little consequence for the overall value or craftsmanship of a drawing, but that it matters a great deal as an antecedent for its originality. Since for experts today the overall value of a work of art is almost synonymous with its originality, problem finding also contributes indirectly to the overall value of a drawing, and to a lesser extent to its technical value.

Problem-Finding Behavior and the Quality of the Product. Of all the possible relations, the most crucial is that between behavior *before* the drawing started, and the quality of the ensuing product. The most severe test of the theoretical model predicts the highest correlations between scores relating to how the problem was found and formulated, and the quality of the drawing.

Table 8.3. Second-Order Partial Correlations Between the Total Problem-Finding Score and the Evaluation of the Products (N = 31)

Correlations between the Total Process Score (ABC) and	Variables Held Constant	Problem Finding (ABC Total)
Overall aesthetic value	Originality and craftsmanship	−.22
Originality	Overall value and craftsmanship	.61*
Craftsmanship	Overall value and originality	−.23

*$p < .001$.

As Table 8.1 shows, each of the three variables observed at the predrawing stage, that is, at the stage when the problem is initially formulated, is significantly related to the originality and the overall aesthetic value of the drawings, and one is significantly related to the craftsmanship ratings. The relation between problem finding at the drawing or solution stage and the quality of the product is somewhat less systematic. Nonetheless, two of the three variables are significantly related to originality, one to overall aesthetic value, and one to craftsmanship.

Of the six possible correlations between behavioral variables and each product rating, five were significant with originality, four with overall aesthetic value, and two with craftsmanship. That is, the finished work of a student who prior to drawing handled more objects, explored the objects in greater detail, and selected more unique objects, was rated higher by the artist-critics in originality and overall aesthetic value; the work of a student who explored the objects in greater detail was also rated higher in craftsmanship. When a student varied his approach and introduced changes in the still-life arrangement, his drawing was rated higher in originality; the work of a student whose drawing altered the still-life arrangement was also rated higher in overall aesthetic value and in craftsmanship.

Since the three dimensions of evaluation share a substantial amount of common variance, the real relationship between behavior and the quality of the products here too presents some question. Table 8.4 shows that when the overlapping variance is controlled for statistically through partial correlation, problem finding still correlates significantly with originality, but not with overall value or technical skill. This is the same pattern shown earlier for the total score. Problem finding results in works that are rated more original. If the drawings are also judged to be of greater overall value and technical skill, it is because these dimensions are not separable in practice from originality.

In view of the surprisingly consistent relationships between behavior during the process of formulating and solving the problem and the quality of the product, a nagging thought presented itself: The higher quality of the final drawing might not be a function of problem finding, but might be because some students took the task more seriously than others and devoted more time to it. So we posed the question, Do evaluations of the product reflect the amount of time a student put into the drawing?

Table 8.4. *Second-Order Partial Correlations Between the Problem-Finding Subtotals and the Evaluation of the Product (N = 31)*

Problem Finding Subtotals	Overall Aesthetic Value (With Originality and Craftsmanship Held Constant)	Originality (With Overall Aesthetic Value and Craftsmanship Held Constant)	Craftsmanship (With Overall Aesthetic Value and Originality Held Constant)
Problem formulation total (AA)	−.14	.46**	−.15
Problem solution total (BB)	−.10	.38*	−.20
Concern for problem-finding total (CC)	−.17	.48**	−.11

*p < .05.
**p < .01.

The answer is straightforward. Three measures of duration were computed. The first was the amount of time each student used to select the objects that he would draw—the time spent finding or formulating the elements of the problem. The second measure was the amount of time he took to arrange the objects he had selected—the time spent defining the problem by constructing the still-life arrangement. The third measure was the actual drawing time—the time spent solving the problem by producing the drawing itself. (Of course, these distinctions are to be taken as relative rather than absolute. A creative person will find and formulate his problems all through the painting process, not just during the time he chooses the objects. However, it seems reasonable to assume that prior to drawing most of the cognitive activity involves formulating the problem, while the greatest part of the cognitive effort after the drawing has begun is devoted to problem solution.)

Table 8.5 presents the correlations between how long a student took to complete each of the three phases of the process and the quality of the product. The only measure of time significantly related to the quality of the drawings is time spent choosing the objects, or finding the problem. Students who took longer to select objects presumably exerted greater effort in discovering the problem, and produced works that were rated

Table 8.5.   Correlations Between Three Measures of Drawing Time and the Evaluation of the Product (N = 31)

Dimensions of Evaluation (Five Raters)	Time Spent Selecting Objects (Problem Finding)	Time Spent Arranging Objects (Problem Definition)	Time Spent Drawing (Problem Solution)
Overall value	.46*	.06	.28
Originality	.53**	.04	.26
Craftsmanship	.29	.13	.26

*p < .01.
**p < .005.

higher in aesthetic value and originality (but not in craftsmanship) than the works of students who spent less time in this phase of the process.

Again the results confirm that the way one goes about problem finding affects the quality of the ensuing creative product. Time spent working on the drawing does not significantly increase its worth, but time spent on finding and formulating the problem does. The student who comes to the situation with a ready-made or "canned" problem is less likely to produce a drawing that will be rated original. He will spend less time at the problem formulation stage of the process.

Why time devoted to problem formulation should result in higher ratings is suggested by two additional relationships. The correlation beteeen the number of objects a student manipulated (A1 in Table 8.1) and time spent in choosing the objects for the still life is .63 ($p < .0005$); that between the uniqueness of the objects chosen (A2) and time spent in choosing the objects is .50 ($p < .005$). Students who take more time finding the problem give themselves a chance to consider a greater variety of objects and combinations (or a greater number of problematic elements and relations), and to discover more unusual objects (or unique problematic elements), thus providing the conditions for the emergence of problems that are more original.

Problem formulation appears to be of real importance in determining how original a product will be. The question is whether this relationship also obtains in other fields where creativity is at stake, such as mathematics, poetics, the sciences, or politics. Although the present exploration does not shed light directly on this issue, it seems probable that the theory and method can be applied elsewhere, provided that the measurement of problem finding is appropriately adapted to the subject matter of each field.

So far as artistic production is concerned, the model and the method have brought into the open a process that normally goes undetected. Of course touching many objects, choosing unique objects, and so on, does not "cause" originality in a work of art. The only assumption made here is that these behaviors are indicative of internal cognitive processes of a *problem-finding* approach to thinking, just as similar observations have been taken to be indicative of cognitive processes in *problem solving*.

Problem-Finding Attitudes and the Quality of the Product. Immediately after each student completed his drawing, he was interviewed at length, and four sets of attitudes revealed by the responses were later analyzed. We expected that the work of students whose responses showed the greatest concern for problem finding would have high ratings in originality and overall aesthetic value, but not necessarily in craftsmanship.

Table 8.1 shows, however, that concern for "problem finding in general" is not significantly related to any of the evaluations by the artist-critics. But concern for problem finding before beginning to draw, while drawing, and while evaluating the finished drawing are significantly related to overall aesthetic value and originality; and the latter is also related to craftsmanship. The proposition that there is a positive relation between attitudinal concern for problem finding and the quality of the product is supported by the empirical results, although it needs further refinement.

The predicted relation between concern for problem finding at the problem formulation stage and the quality of the product was strongly supported by the data. Artists who stated that when they started to work they had no clear idea as to what they would do, and therefore had to discover a problem, did in fact produce drawings that were rated high in overall value and originality (although not in craftsmanship). The work of students who stated that they already had a problem in mind when they approached the task was rated low on the same dimensions. Correlations between concern with problem finding at the predrawing stage and overall value, originality, and craftsmanship of the product were .40 ($p <$ .025), .60 ($p <$ .0005), and .26 (n.s.) respectively. The expected relationship between concern with problem finding while drawing and the overall value and originality of the product was also supported by the data but not as strongly ($p < .05$). The attitudinal and behavioral data reinforce each other. Both are systematically related to the originality of artistic products, especially during the problem formulation stages of the artistic process.

The predicted relation between problem-finding attitude at the evaluation stage and the quality of the drawing was also supported. Since this variable is dichotomous, its relation to the ratings was determined not only by the correlation as shown in Table 8.1, but by means of the gamma measure of contingency, which gave a coefficient of .35 for overall aesthetic value, .57 for originality, and .34 for craftsmanship. The 57 percent improvement over chance (indicating 78 percent correct prediction from the attitudes of the artist to the originality rating of his drawing) represents fairly strong support for the proposition.

Two conclusions are suggested by the attitudinal data, and they confirm the results obtained from behavioral observations in the experimental setting. First, problem finding that precedes problem solving, an activity thus far neglected in empirical studies of creativity, is crucial to the creative process. Second, a subjective concern for problem finding, especially at the problem formulation stage of a task, enhances the originality of products. Artists who were concerned with discovering a problem in the situation itself produced drawings rated as more original than artists who reported that they began with a known problem that they imposed on the elements in the situation.

Of course, "not knowing what to do" in a problematic situation is not going to produce an original work all by itself. The artist must have the needed technical skill and knowledge. But the students were more or less alike in this; all had the requisite craftsmanship. The artist must also want to resolve the problematic situation. In this too the students were similar; they were volunteers and worked with equal commitment. The amount of time spent drawing, presumably one index of motivation in the experiment, did not differentiate between students who produced work of superior or inferior quality. Given a group of artists with the same training and motivation, those who are concerned with problem finding will produce works of higher originality and overall aesthetic value than will artists who are not so oriented. Concern for discovery measured through interviews can be also independently assessed through observing problem-finding behavior while engaged in the creative process; and when this is done similar relationships are found.

It is possible to find fault with any psychological account of the creative process, from the psychoanalytic one to the behavioristic. In our study, one might object to the application of a cognitive model to the process of artistic creation. Collingwood, for example, expressly denies that the artistic process can be likened to problem solving. He writes, "There is certainly here [in the artistic work] a directional process—an effort, that is, directed upon a certain end, but the end is not something foreseen and preconceived, to which appropriate means can be thought out in light of our knowledge of its special character" (1958, 111). But this objection is relevant only to what we have called presented problems. If this were the only type of problem situation, Collingwood would be right. As soon as we distinguish, however, between presented problem situations and *discovered* problem situations—where the problem is not "foreseen" and "preconceived" but found in the situation itself—the objections to the problem-solving model no longer hold.

On the contrary, when the distinction between presented and discovered problem situations is made, and the artist's work is seen as an example of the latter, then the problem-solving model points to neglected issues, and suggests additional procedures for observation, by calling attention to the importance of problem finding as well as problem solving in creative activity.

The Quality of the Products Assessed by the Other Judges. The results discussed so far were based on the judgment of artist-critics, a group chosen as the arbiter of quality because its judgment seemed the most defensible measure of contemporary artistic worth. But how did problem-finding behaviors or attitudes relate to the evaluation of the drawings made by the other judges—the art teachers, mathematics students, and business students? The data in Table 8.6 consist of correlations between problem-finding subtotals, and the evaluations of the drawings provided by the four groups of judges.

The postulated relationships between the process and the product are even stronger when art teachers rather than artist-critics are used as a criterion. The correlations of the process scores at problem formulation (AA), problem solution (BB), attitudes (CC), and the total problem-finding score (ABC) with each of the teachers' ratings are increased, yet the pattern of the relationships remains essentially the same: the highest correlations are with originality, the next highest with overall aesthetic value, and the lowest with craftsmanship. In effect, these data replicate

Table 8.6. Correlations Between Problem Finding and the Evaluation of the Product by Four Groups of Judges (N = 31)

Problem-Finding Process Variables	Artist-Critics			Art Teachers			Mathematics Students			Business Students		
	Overall	Originality	Crafts-manship	Overall	Origi-nality	Crafts-manship	Overall	Origi-nality	Crafts-manship	Overall	Origi-nality	Crafts-manship
AA	.40[d]	.54[b]	.28	.48[b]	.56[b]	.30	.25	.51[b]	.22	.26	.54[b]	.13
BB	.26	.38[d]	.12	.46[c]	.60[a]	.34[e]	.03	.24	-.09	-.16	.18	-.23
CC	.42[d].	.56[b]	.31[e]	.53[b]	.62[a]	.52[b]	.19	.36[e]	.07	.09	.42[d]	.10
ABC	.47[b]	.65[a]	.31[e]	.64[a]	.78[a]	.51[b]	.22	.50[b]	.11	.09	.50[b]	.02

[a] $p < .0005$.
[b] $p < .005$.
[c] $p < .01$.
[d] $p < .025$.
[e] $p < .05$.

132

the previous findings. But there is also a notable difference between the two sets of relationships. Problem-finding behavior during problem solution, that is, during the actual drawing, is substantially more related to the ratings of art teachers than to those of artist-critics. The correlation with overall aesthetic value, which was .26 (n.s.) for artist-critics, rises to .46 (p < .01) for art teachers; the correlation with originality, which was .38 (*p* < .025), rises to .60 (*p* < .0005); and the correlation with craftsmanship, which was .12 (n.s.), rises to .34 (*p* < .05). These uniform differences cannot be accounted for by a greater overlap of art teachers' ratings among the three dimensions; if anything, the overlap was larger for the artist-critics. Nor can the differences be attributed entirely to the greater reliability of the ratings by art teachers.

The issue raised is more profound. Problem-finding behavior and attitudes were reflected in equally high ratings of aesthetic value, originality, and craftsmanship by both artist-critics and art teachers. This was especially so for behavior at the *problem formulation* stage, where the respective correlations between observed behavior and evaluation by artist-critics were .40, .54, and .28, and by the art teachers .48, .56, and .30. But problem-finding behavior during the *problem solution* stage of the process tended to be reflected more consistently in the ratings of art teachers than in the ratings of artist-critics. The first group tended to recognize the more conceptual, perhaps more basic, kind of originality; the second group responded more favorably to its more concrete forms.

An examination of the data for the lay judges reveals still other patterns. For the entire set of relationships in Table 8.6, the dissimilarities between the expert and the lay groups are greater than the regularities. The two groups of artists resemble each other, and so do the lay groups; but with one exception involving the rating in originality, there is little in common between the two sets.

It is more than likely that these differences are due, at least in part, to the fact that for experts the three dimensions of evaluation overlap far more than for lay people. The mathematics and business students rated drawings that were the result of problem-findings higher in originality, but not in overall value or craftsmanship. The artists and art teachers, however, were more global in their judgments: A drawing rated original was also rated as being of greater overall value and of better craftsmanship.

The similarity between the four groups concerning originality was impressive. Of the eight correlations involving originality, eight are significant for the two expert groups and six are significant for the two lay groups; the respective mean correlations are .59 and .41. Most striking is the uniform relationship between behavior at the problem formulation stage and the ratings in originality. The correlation for the artist-critics is .54, for the art teachers .56, for the mathematics students .51, and for the business students .54. Two of the other three sets of correlations involving originality with problem-finding attitudes (CC) are still remarkably regular in view of the subjective nature of the variables; they are respectively .56 ($p < .005$), .62 ($p < .005$), .36 ($p < .05$), and .42 ($p < .025$). The correlations with the composite total problem-finding score (ABC) are also quite similar: .65 ($p < .005$), .78 ($p < .005$), .50 ($p < .005$), and .50 ($p < .005$). When one turns, however, to the fourth set of correlations, that between behavior during problem solution and originality, the pattern breaks down. Not only is there less similarity between the two expert groups, but also between the two expert groups and the two lay groups; the correlations are respectively .38 ($p < .025$) and .60 ($p < .005$) for the artist-critic and art teachers, and .24 (n.s.) and .18 (n.s.) for the mathematics students and business students.

This set of relationships is intriguing. Behavior during problem formulation, which is furthest removed in time from the finished work of art, apparently affects the drawing in such a way that each of the groups is sensitive to it and results in systematic ratings in originality by all four groups, different as they are in their experience with art. The same holds true for attitudes expressed in the interview. Behavior during problem solution, which is closer to the finished work and leaves concrete marks on the picture, has less consistent effects. The two expert groups are sensitive to it and respond with appropriate ratings in originality, but the two nonexpert groups are not sensitive to whatever it is that problem finding during the stage of solution does to a drawing. The contrast between the mean correlations of originality with behavior at the two stages makes the point. For problem formulation the mean correlations for the expert and lay groups are respectively .55 and .53; for problem solution they are .49 and .21.

One thing can be said with substantial confidence: Discovery orientations during the artistic process and the originality of the creative product are highly correlated. That is, a person who starts drawing without a clearly envisioned, standard aesthetic structure in mind, but lets the problem emerge in the situation will end up making something that will be thought to be original. Of the 16 correlation coefficients that speak to this issue, 14 are statistically significant, and the other two are in the predicted direction. Even more important for the model we are exploring is that each of the four correlations between behavior at the problem formulation stage and the originality of the product is highly significant. This amounts to four partial replications of the results with as many independent groups varying in artistic training and commitment.

The results in Table 8.6 also point toward the difficulties the young artists will encounter after their student days. Their problem-finding ability, which is recognized by other artists as leading to both originality and overall value, is only deemed to lead to originality by laypersons. Future purchasers of art do not think that a work based on problem finding is necessarily of greater value than is a work without problem finding at its base. At least in the short run, public indifference to the value of real originality will clearly cause strain for an artist who tries to insure his livelihood by using a problem-finding approach.

The crucial point made by the experiment is that the process of problem finding can be reliably observed and measured, and that it results in works of higher quality, and more specifically, of higher originality. This conclusion, which was reached through the use of precise but dry group statistics, can now be illustrated with greater immediacy by comparing the quality of the actual drawings and the problem-finding scores of several of the artists.

For example, the two artists whose work was rated highest by experts (see Figures 7.2 and 7.4) also tied for first place in their total problem-finding scores. One of the two artists whose drawings received the lowest evaluations (see Figures 7.3 and 7.5) scored lowest on total problem finding, and the other scored below average. Among the other subjects whose work we have considered, Student 31 (see Figure 6.3) was in the top quartile on both variables, and Student 15 (see Figure 6.2) was in the lowest quartile.

In view of these findings, we offer a tentative conception of creativity. Our conception goes somewhat beyond the observed phenomena but is worth advancing, we feel, for its heuristic value.

The first variable observed in the experimental setting, manipulation of the objects (A1 in Table 8.1) suggests that students who explore more objects produce drawings that professional critics rate as more original and of greater aesthetic value. This does not imply that artists need to manipulate objects in their environment to produce a work of art; the experiment was structured so that students *had* to handle certain objects.

But let us suppose that this experiment had been performed: Students are led into a bare room and asked to make a drawing—any drawing they wish. There are no objects to manipulate, but there is still a problem to formulate. We suggest that in the hypothetical experiment—where the environment contains no stimuli—students who manipulated objects in the real experiment would tend to turn over, to "manipulate" as it were, more ideas, feelings, memories; in short, more internal stimuli, while they decided what to work on. They would not merely restate obvious, predetermined, or canned problems in this situation either. They would continue to function in a *discovered problem situation* and not alter it into a *presented problem situation.*

According to this view, the process observed in the actual experiment was the externalized counterpart of an analogous process that would have occurred internally had the instructions not specified that the problem and the solution were to be formulated with concrete objects. The experiment forced out into the open a problem-finding process that presumably takes place inside the "black box" of the mind. To be sure, no direct proof of this interpretation is possible—we cannot look into the mind to see whether what goes on in fact corresponds to our conjectures—but insofar as the postulated relationship between the process and the quality of the product holds empirically, which it does, the interpretation is worth considering further.

To continue with the black box analogy, selecting unusual objects in the experiment (A2 in Table 8.1) reflects openness to more unusual thoughts, acceptance of idiosyncratic experiences. In the quiet of their studios, these artists formulate problems "inspired" by more personal perceptions, more deeply felt passions, more unique memories and desires. In contrast, students who chose conventional objects, the objects of wider appeal—in a sense, "safer" objects—would formulate problems using tried, less risky subject matter for their work. Similarly, with respect to exploration of the objects (A3 in Table 8.1) one would expect that artists who explored and played with objects, moved parts into new forms, and tried to change them to find possibilities not immediately given to the eye—these artists would also probe and play with ideas, feelings, experiences, and mental images.

Comparable analogies for the other variables can also be drawn. But the implications of the experiment transcend the analogies, which are presented to illustrate the argument and should not be reified; the implications transcend also the few variables and the specific conditions of the experiment itself. The crucial implication is that the envisagement of problems is central to the creative process and that the character of the process at the time of posing the problem is related systematically to the quality of the creative product.

The next task is to examine in greater and more concrete detail how a person's life experience becomes the subject matter out of which aesthetic problems are formulated. The following chapter reports what the artists say about motivation for doing their work, and about the sources of their ideas.

CHAPTER 9

■

The Origins of Artistic Problems

The question of how artistic problems are formulated and solved has been kept so far on a safely abstract plane. We must now be more concrete, and examine in closer detail what is meant by an artistic problem. For it is not obvious that drawing a picture is analagous to dealing with a problem. And one might well want to know how the artist explains what he does, and to what extent his account helps to illuminate the nature of artistic problems.

In mathematics, problems are usually unresolved equations. On one side there is a set of variables whose values are known, as well as some that are unknown. The problem is how to restructure these variables on the other side of the equation, while maintaining the lawful relationships among them and at the same time discovering the values of the unknown variables.

This simple paradigm is in some respects representative of all problematic situations. Every problematic situation involves a gap to be filled between a desired or imagined state of affairs and a prevailing reality that is different. For example, a hunter is hungry, and wishes it were not so; his problem is to find game that will satisfy his desire. A basketball player is slow on the rebound; his problem is to discover the missing element of skill at the boards. A composer hears a melody in his mind that he wishes to communicate; his problem is to capture the inner music and transform it into notations on a stave. The artist experiences an inner state that he wishes to express in graphic terms; his problem is to establish an equation between his inner state and a visual object, the work of art.

But there are really two issues that must be dealt with. One is the apparent problem: for the hunter, how to snare the game; for the basketball player, how to increase his speed; for the composer, how to turn the tune into a notation; for the artist, how to represent the inner state in a drawing. The second issue is the source behind the apparent problem. In the case of the hunter, it is hunger, and in the case of the basketball player, it is the desire to win. In the case of composers or artists, the motivation is not as clear nor as simple.

To continue with the metaphor, the artist wishes to establish an equation between his inner state and an objective reality, the work of art. But if the inner state has already been described by others and translated by them into visual form, there are no unknowns; his work will not be original or creative. To be original, what he experiences must be unique yet recognizable once expressed, and the visual equivalent for that experience must be unprecedented yet recognizable by others. In addition, the work of art must have its source in a significant human experience. A trivial problematic experience produces only a slight tension; to find a visual expression for it is only a trivial problem. Hence the truly creative artist explores universal but never fully mastered dimensions of living: growth and decay, harmony and discord, joy and pain, attraction and revulsion.

In this sense, as several of our students noted, artists and scientists work essentially with the same problems. Bronowski has said: "The discoveries of science, the works of art are explorations—more, are explosions, of hidden likeness. The discoverer or the artist presents in them aspects of nature and fuses them into one. This is the act of creation, in which an original thought is born and it is the same act in original science and original art" (1956, 30–31). Like natural scientists, artists are concerned with finding order in the flux of natural phenomena; like psychologists, they are concerned with the springs of human emotion. Their problems overlap those of philosophers and theologians. But they bring a distinctive perspective and mode of exploration to these problems: aesthetic sensibility and skills of visual representation. To cite Bronowski again:

The exploration of the artist is no less truthful and strenuous than that of the scientist. If science seems to carry conviction and recognition more immediately, this is because here the critics are also those who work at the matter. There is not, as in the arts, a gap between the functions (and therefore between the fashions) of those who comment and those who do.

Nevertheless, the great artist works as devotedly to uncover the implications of his vision as does the great scientist . . .

Whether our work is art or science or the daily work of society, it is only the form in which we explore our experience which is different; the need to explore remains the same. (Bronowski, 1956, 92)

This description, however, is still too abstract. One needs to specify where exactly the artistic problems originate, how they are formulated in the artist's mind, and how artists attempt to solve these equations with many unknowns that they set up. For a start in this direction, we turn to the explanations that the students give of their work. In their glosses one finds the richness and detail that experimental data necessarily lack.

The Artist's View of the Artistic Problem. A good way to begin is with an excerpt from the answer of Student 23 to an interview question following the experiment: "What kinds of objects or feelings do you try to represent when you paint on your own?"

I am very much concerned with time—with life and death. That's why I like to work with films, because they embrace the time dimension: you can develop motion, the tension of opposition. After reading Newton—every action produces a reaction—I saw everything in those terms. I began putting one shape down, then the other similar shapes reflecting other forces which counterbalance the first. The tension between forces is the same as between life and death, the symbols of space and time, light and dark. Like Newton established physical relationships in the universe, music and art reflect a similar kind of universal order. I enjoy the way that in science forces balance each other intricately to hold the universe together. Essentially the structure of the old masters' paintings is the same: ordering space, placing emphasis on different areas to give the effect of movement, of time.

This artist sees his problem as the exploration and representation of forces in tension: life and death, space and time. He tries to bring order into these crucial elements of experience. But how can he accomplish such a difficult and abstract goal?

I have a preference for certain forms: classical curves that remind me of the theater. But I can't say what their real meaning is. I have them in my mind, and I like to put them down so I can look at them. These curves are like the turning of a ballet dancer in slow motion: at a certain point her back jerks for a moment—it might be part of the dance but it suggests something painful, it sends a shiver down your back. This tension is what I want to express: the slow curve of the line, then the sweetly painful jerk. In childhood during the war things were pretty bad, it thrills you now to think back about the unusualness of some of those experiences. . . . I like to make flat things round and vice versa. Or to draw plumes as if they were hard and associate them with mechanical objects. It is like parodies on the stage, making things real in a particular context, which turns out to be only make-believe.

This passage contains specific indications of the kind of problems this artist deals with. For one thing, they are related to his personal history in wartorn Europe. The constant danger, the sudden threats of childhood are relived ("it sends a shiver down your back") in the drawing of slowly curving classical lines that end in a "sweetly painful jerk." Visual qualities in his drawing reflect past experience. But he also tries to pose new problems, to "make things real in a particular context," to create a fictitious world with its own reality, like that of a stage play. We begin now to see both the problematic area specific to this artist, and the means by which he can resolve it. For him the artistic task consists in projecting on the canvas a new reality based on familiar experience. He knows that this reality will be "make-believe," but it is also a model from which he might gain new insights into his experience. This general attitude toward art influenced what he did in the experimental situation.

At the very beginning of the experiment, in the predrawing stage of problem formulation, Student 23 was not merely retrieving a preconceived problem for a predetermined solution. He spent nine minutes selecting and arranging the objects. Here are the experimenter's notes for this period:

[S.23] takes *carburetor* and *manikin* over to table B. Picks up *horn*. Pauses for a while. Takes *doll* and *horn* over to table B, starts arranging. He places a chair on the table, puts *carburetor* on the seat of the chair, then places the *doll* on the *carburetor*. Spends some time arranging the joints of the *manikin*. Then places it next to the *doll* and the *carburetor*. . .

He ends up with eight objects: the manikin, doll, statuette, grapes (white and black), book, horn, and carburetor. When asked why he picked out these particular objects, he said, among other things: "I definitely had to pick these objects because they had a meaning to me. The others didn't." Asked what was the criterion by which he arranged the objects, he answered: "My conscious thought was to arrange them so that they would look good also if you were to photograph the arrangement—like a window display. But also immediately I thought that I wouldn't draw them as a manikin, horn, etc.; just as forms. If I had drawn them as they were, they wouldn't have meaning, and I wouldn't have fun."

The problem was formulated on several levels of experience simultaneously, and, like the play of children, the meaning of any object or the arrangement itself at one level was different from its meaning at another level. The object was a manikin, it was not a manikin; it was a horn, it was not a horn. At a calculated conscious level, the student arranged the objects like a "window display" that would "look good" and could be photographed in exact likeness; at a less conscious level, he transmuted the elements into those of a new problem that he went on formulating throughout the drawing process. Despite the first comment about arranging a window display, he reported that once he began working he did not know how the final design would look until quite late in the experiment.

When asked: "At what point did you have an idea of how the final design would look?" this student answered: "About halfway through. At the beginning I was sketching—like running my hand over the objects. During the first 10 minutes I did not think about meaning, just how they would look. Then halfway through I could think how to abandon objects as objects, how to blend them together . . . birds usually appear in my drawings, usually flying in the opposite direction. [S.23 refers here to the head of a bird he had included in the drawing.]"

This is what the artist says about the meaning that the finished drawing has for him:

> The doll is coming out of the carburetor as if it were a gas—a transition from a solid form to a gaseous one—one form is part of the other. The horn becomes a bird. The book becomes a mirrored crystal form; the manikin is a real man and at one point becomes part of the book. The statuette is an old man, perhaps a parent figure. It's sinking into the earth or it's coming out of it, not quite dead nor living. The man [manikin] doesn't know whether to look at the girl [doll], whether to pursue her or the bird. I think he is undecided—perhaps he was me.

Several aspects of the artist's general problem appear in the experimental drawing (Figure 9.1). The transformation of hard into soft is accomplished by changing the doll into a gas fume, the horn into a bird. The death-life theme is carried out by the statuette sinking into (or emerging from) the earth. The slow curve ending in a painful jerk flows through the

Figure 9.1   S.23. Completed experimental drawing. Upper third in total problem-finding score, among the top five as rated by experts. The drawing appears to reflect the artist's concern with "forces in harmony and tension"; transition from inanimate to living forms (hence from nonlife to life and then to death), and from hard to soft. At a different level, the drawing includes theatrical elements, personal concerns about male/female relations, and the recurrent personal symbol of the bird of prey.

doll's billowing robe. The whole composition has a theatrical quality: The manikin with his mask and plumed helmet seems to be stepping out on a stage. And then in the last sentence, almost as an afterthought, there is a very intimate, personal theme: the manikin-self is undecided whether to pursue the doll-girl or the fierce bird.

To summarize, the artist feels a pervasive problem in his life, a problem that perhaps began to take shape in his childhood. In general terms the problem entails understanding the tension of opposites: life and death, soft and hard, male and female—tensions he has experienced but cannot yet understand. So he is moved to represent the problems on the canvas—"to put them down so I can look at them"—and understand. Whether consciously or not, the artist's general problem influenced his choice of objects, their arrangement, and the drawing itself. The solution—the finished drawing—will permit the artist to make a step forward in the understanding of the problem. But since his problem is essentially a metaphysical one, no solution is likely to be ever final. Each step, however, can help to make the artist understand his experiences within the context of his life.

This artist "finds" the problem halfway through the drawing. It consists in visualizing a specific representation of the general tensions he experiences, in a form that has an internal logic, an internal unity: a representation, one is tempted to say, that is a working functional model of the artist's personal predicament. But at a less conscious level, the problem began to be formulated as soon as the artist perceived that there were similarities between some characteristics of the objects before him, and some aspect of his "general problem"—the hardness of the carburetor, the gaseous quality of the doll, and so on. The objects had "meaning" or were given meaning because he could build with their aid a make-believe reality to serve as an explanatory model for past and future experience.

Other students speak of similar personal problems, and the same relationships between specific artistic problems and the process of painting. Asked what he tries to achieve through his work, S.26 answers:

> I try to define myself in terms of where do I fit. . . . I have opinions about myself and I want to see if they are right. My only conscious theme is amalgamation, attempting to combine the different facets of my life and the lives of others.

Again, there is a vaguely general but strongly felt personal theme at the basis of this artist's work. How can the discovery of the place "where one fits in life" be accomplished through art? This student says of his work:

> I begin painting by putting down on the canvas one or two marks, sometimes taken from the environment. One shape will be put down in relation to the others, and pretty soon all contact with the stimulus objects will be lost. . . . I will put down on the canvas certain things as a result of what went on before it. For instance [in the experiment] I felt exposed by being watched, so I emphasized one color doubly because I felt bothered. Additional meanings are always incorporated into what I am doing; outside stimuli might change the type of stroke, or anything.

The work proceeds as in a discovered problem situation. The problem is not preconceived and the solution is not predetermined; the problem is defined in the process of solution; the process of solution is defined in the problem. Student 26 puts down on paper his feelings, the results of his interactions with the environment, in order to delineate and discover his position in a complex, subjective sociogram. In the experiment, the object that he selected first was the chunk of optical glass. This was the most important element in his composition: "the other objects revolve around it." Asked his reasons for choosing it, he answers: "It's the translucency—like ice. You can see through it, it leaves its influence on what goes through it. Distorts what passes behind it." The student produced a completely abstract drawing in the experiment (Figure 9.2); at the center of the design a transformed image of the glass can be recognized (if one knew that it was there). He says of his drawing:

> There is harmony in it, a smooth flow and radiation, then an abrupt stop. It's like transfer of heat through objects—it moves fast through aluminum and iron, then in glass it encounters a very powerful resistance.

Possibly the experimental drawing was again a "model" of the artist's concern in life: that of amalgamating, combining his several roles in life, or his life with that of others. The glass was selected because "it leaves its influence on what goes through it," and the whole drawing is seen in terms of a flow of colors and lines that pass through the glass and become changed in the process. Thus the drawing is very likely a functional symbol of the artist's own process of experiencing, interpreting, and thereby distorting reality.

To an uninformed viewer, the drawing reproduced in Figure 9.2 may seem just a pleasing abstraction, which was composed purely as a result of formal considerations: form, space, light, color, composition. But the interview reveals a deeper logic at work in the artist's mind as he was drawing the picture. The formal visual elements were used as symbols representing elements of an existential problem, just as mathematical symbols are used to represent quantitative elements in an equation. The chunk of glass "stood for" the artist himself; the unknown question to be settled was how the glass would distort the objects around it, which represented the artist's environment. There is no way to know how consciously the artist was aware of the unfolding of this personal drama as he worked on the formal problems of the abstract composition. Probably not much; yet we expect that the reason he became so involved with his work is that at a preconscious level he was aware that the ordering of shapes and colors had something to do with the ordering of tensions he experienced as a person with unique problems.

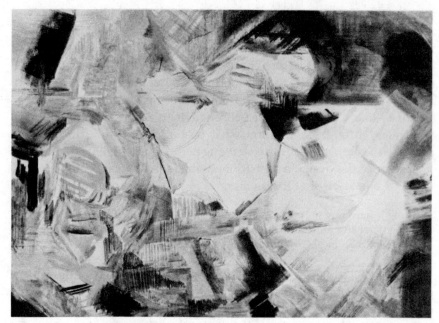

Figure 9.2   S.26. Completed experimental drawing. Upper third in total problem-finding score, average or above in the rating of experts. The work is structured around the central shape derived from the chunk of optical glass which was among the stimulus objects. It seems to reflect the artist's concern with his role in changing, filtering, and distorting human relationships as the piece of glass changes, filters, and distorts the shape of the surrounding objects.

What made it possible for these two students to resolve their general problems with an equation that resulted in the drawings produced in the experiment? Here again the behaviors observed can help us understand the process of artistic problem finding and problem solving. The problematic issues that concern S.23 include unresolved feelings about life and death, and the continuity of matter through changes in form. For these feelings to achieve expression in the experiment (where he was required to structure the problem using concrete objects), he had to explore the stimuli available; had to manipulate objects and observe them closely before he could recognize the "fit" between the statuette of the old man and his feelings about life and death, between the curves of the doll's robes, the hard surface of the carburetor, and his concern for continuity through transformations. All this does not imply that such overt behaviors would usually be needed nor that the "fit" between object and intent is calculated consciously. They are only indications of the process of manipulating ideas and experiences which takes place internally when the artist's subject matter does not issue directly from the environment. Indeed, this artist introduced objects into the developing design that were not part of the still life he was presumably drawing. He added a bird to the available elements, thus making the drawing at once more original and more relevant to his pervasive concern.

The same process is seen in the work of S.26. By manipulating and experimenting with the objects, he discovers in the piece of glass qualities that he recognizes as similar to his own. The glass distorts. It changes the appearance of nearby objects, just as the artist distorts his own environment by evaluating it through his personal lens. So the theme of the drawing (or formulation of the problem) becomes, to a great extent unconsciously, that of the effect of the glass on the surrounding objects: the change in color values, the distortion of forms wrought in the arrangement by the piece of glass. Again, during the process of solution the artist has to change the relationship and form of the objects, to suit them better to the logic of the equation.

On a less rational and more emotional level, the function of painting as a "model" of experience is illustrated by Student 11's answers to the question, "Why do you paint?"

> I like to look at these things, that's why I paint. It's like enjoying dreams, which I do. I like to think, daydream about things I see. The theme of my paintings covers the past, the present, and the future; it has conscious and subconscious elements. I paint only objects with personal significance, those that have meaning for me. With them I create a little world of my own.

> In my paintings, I usually include New York, cats, my uncle; a car, a railroad, or some other sort of transportation, for instance roller skates; addresses, numbers; a dragon coming out of the kitchen. Once I put a boot in a ship to symbolize a trip to Italy; mother, girl friends, myself; organic shapes—trees, plants . . . these things have many different meanings to me, and I enjoy them all. I would like to fly out of the window like the airplane I paint, or be with the person I like and whom I paint.

This artist, unlike S.23, does not seem to be interested in finding universal models for time and death; his art is a means to "a little world of my own" where all the things he likes—mother and girl friends, cats and sportscars—are safely and harmoniously combined. Yet S.11 offers a good example of problem finding in the experimental situation. Before beginning the task, as he and the observer were having coffee together, the student mentioned that lately he had been puzzled by certain aspects of the relationship between the sexes: "Especially this week . . . the male-female symbolism has become a problem I have on my mind."

When confronted with the objects, S.11 at first chose "six objects in two sets of three, males to one side, females to the other." The female objects were the doll ("graceful and corny"), the pewter pitcher ("suggested a Seurat woman in *La Grande Jatte*"), and the carburetor ("it was male, so I put the grapes on top to make it look feminine"). The male objects were the manikin ("he makes a gallant gesture, he's courting the Seurat lady pitcher"), the brass pitcher ("the most obviously male symbol"), and the gear ("I looked for another phallic symbol to balance out the composition"); later he adds the pipe ("in case it wasn't clear enough"). Out of this jumble emerges a drawing (Figure 9.3) that:

> . . . says certain things I think I know what they mean. I decided to put down things that agreed with the idea, the feeling I had. The male figures are protecting, shielding the females. [The thick background lines] exert a

Figure 9.3   S.11. Completed experimental drawing. Tied for second place in total problem finding, rated among the top five by experts. The composition is structured in terms of a group of male figures "protecting" three female figures on the right, and appears to reflect the artist's concern with sexual roles at the time of the experiment.

pressure that pounds down on the figures. . . . The Indian-faced girl is a certain type of female: calm, totally whole individual. Reminds me of a girl I knew who had a schizophrenic personality: very serene on the outside, very beautiful, but very restless inside. Her face was interesting, but inexpressive, always forced to conceal emotions.

We see the great facility with which Student 11 incorporates the objects around him into the "general" problem he has been mulling over. The pitcher, the carburetor, and so forth become problematic elements through their symbolic association with the artist's free-floating problem. With these elements, the artist builds a stage play in which certain aspects of sexual relationships are allowed to develop and resolve themselves. Perhaps the "Indian-faced girl," whose emergence in the drawing had been unplanned, did bring out in the open an insight about a former girl friend which the artist had dimly felt but never fully realized. And once more we hear the admission, as in the preceding two cases, that even after finishing the drawing, it was a work whose meaning he only "thinks" he knows; it may have many meanings depending on the level of experience from which one views it.

These three students were all in the top third of the total problem-finding score distribution (ABC), and their drawings were rated above average by the artist-critics. The richness of personal involvement evident in their reports is conspicuously absent from the protocols of students who were in the bottom third of the total problem-finding score. As an illustration we present S.09—lowest in problem-finding scores, among lowest in product ratings. Asked why he paints, this student answers:

, Consciously I seek beauty, order, and harmony. I want to express order and harmony because I respond most to them. . . . I feel moodiness in things, mood is necessary for my work. Humanity, the human being is the core aspect of nature which revolves around him. . . . I wish to do like Edvard Munch, like Gauguin: to reflect the moody quality of the century, to combine beauty with emotion.

S.09 invokes every appropriate concept: beauty, harmony, order, humanity, emotion, mood. Despite this, or because of it, his answer sounds hollow and impersonal. There is no reference to uniquely felt events as in the case of the other artists, no specific personal involvement with anything but abstractions.

In the experiment, S.09 reacted to the objects by saying that "most of them have structural ugliness." He picked the brass pitcher ("has good

rhythm"), the grapes ("creates harmony"), and the book ("it's charming
. . . almost sentimental-feeling"). Again, no personal involvement or
problematic connections are apparent. The objects are seen as still-life
elements with obvious visual properties to be fitted into a jigsaw puzzle.
About the finished drawing (Figure 7.3), he says: "It has pleasing
harmony—nothing symbolic . . . a sense of design . . . actually it suggests the warmth of the home, the objects are all domestic symbols. But I
didn't realize it when I was drawing, then I only thought about the
harmonic relationship." Here too, S.09 talks in generalities unconnected
with his personal experience. If his drawing is problematic at all, it is in a
learned way of presenting visual relationships, or on a different level, it is
a model of the "warmth of the home," which he states as a stereotyped
problem. At no point in the interview, any more than in the experiment,
did this student convey concern for the problematic, for discovery: what
he wants to do is to express beauty and harmony (implying that he fully
knows what they are), and to imitate precursors like Munch or Gauguin.
In our terms his work consists in "presenting" himself with problems that
are well defined in advance (that is, reproduce the moodiness of Munch,
illustrate the "warmth of the home"), and that are to be solved by tried
methods to the eventual satisfaction of everybody who will recognize in
the drawing the "warmth of the home," say, just as we learned to
recognize it on *Saturday Evening Post* covers. We are still dealing with an
equation between an inner vision and a concrete drawing, but this time it
is an equation with few unknowns.

Aspects of Artistic Problem Formulation.   The four preceding protocols, and
the life histories of artists in general, suggest that the artist discovers
problematic elements in the phenomena of his own experience. In our
experiment, the types of objects students chose reveal the problematic
elements that enter in the formulation of artistic problems.

When one compares the choice of objects made by the 11 students who
have a high total problem-finding score with the choice made by the 14
students who have a low score, omitting the 6 students with middle
scores, the difference displayed in Table 9.1 appears. Nine of the 11
high-scoring students selected a human object for their arrangement,
while only one of the 14 low-scoring students did so. From now on, we
shall call the high-scoring group "problem finders," and the low-scoring
group "problem solvers," although, of course, the first group was also
involved in problem solving.

Table 9.1. Number of Ss Selecting One or More "Human" Objects (Manikin, Doll, Statuette) for Drawing—Ss Divided into High and Low on Total Problem-Finding Score [a]

Subgroups	N	Number Selecting One or More Human Objects	Number Selecting No Human Objects
High problem-finding score (ABC)	11	9	2
Low problem-finding score (ABC)	14	1	13

[a] Fisher's exact contingency test: $p = .0002$.

Some of the problem finders selected more than one human object; in fact the total number of such objects chosen by this group was 14, as against 1 for the other group. In effect, the still-life arrangements of problem finders almost always have a human element in it, although in at least half of the cases human shapes are no longer recognizable in the finished drawings. This suggests that original artists find the elements of their problems in their own feelings: The equation will consist in finding a visual translation for human experience. When the problem begins to be formulated, the artist selects human forms as catalysts for the expression of such experience. The role of the manikin, the doll, and the statuette in S.23's drawing is a clear example of this. Or consider how S.05 explains why he chose the manikin:

> It's a man, but not really one. . . . It's a strange little man that only our culture could produce, the perfect Western man . . . de Chirico and others have made beautiful things with them. I could talk all night about it . . . it could be so many things.

In his drawing, S.05 explores the relationship between the "perfect Western man" and the sphere, which he sees as "the first symbol in all cultures." Again, reality is reinterpreted with reference to human beings. No such attempt is made by the problem solvers, who limit themselves to copying the objects in their "presented" aspect without trying to link them to what they feel; they do not need human objects to stimulate discovery. This does not mean that a painting must have people in it to reflect lived experience; but it seems that in situations such as the experiment, it is easier to do so with the help of human objects that serve to focus the artist's feelings and thoughts on the nature of the problem.

The same argument holds for explanations about the choice of other objects. Here is what two problem solvers say about why they selected the grapes:

The color is pleasing, particularly against the pitcher . . . it creates harmony, blending. Has infinite rhythm, depending on how you place it. . . . I look for beauty in things, I seek beauty and harmony rather than the ugly and sensational. (S.09)

It's a nice, natural form. There is contrast between the shiny horn and the subtle natural form of the grapes. The two objects have similar round shapes, they are variations on the same theme. (S.22)

These are all formal reasons, indicating that the students are dealing with known relationships between presented forms. Compare their responses with what two problem finders say about why they selected the same grapes. These students also mention formal reasons similar to the ones quoted above, but then add:

I like grapes—my mouth waters when I see them. I hung them on the horn so that they would look succulent. (S.23)

I like grapes, I painted them in high school, there are some growing on our building. Fermented, they could provide alcoholic mixture for racing cars [one reason he placed them on the carburetor] and they are associated with French and Italian wine and women [why they are combined with the doll]. (S.11)

The grapes for these two are more than shapes related visually to others on the table. They suggest feelings, evoke real or imagined experience. We can understand how the first two students will structure their problems in terms of a presented formulation, one that involves known rules of composition. But the answers of the second pair cannot be predicted by what is generally known: They discover in the elements of the problem relationships which, although no less "real" (they can be experienced by others), are not entirely determined by the rules of aesthetics.

Another aspect of the problem-finding process is illustrated in Tables 9.2 and 9.3, which report answers to the questions, "At what point did you have an idea of how the final design would look?" According to our model, students who had a clear idea of the final design early in the process were likely to have begun with a preconceived problem and a predetermined solution. Genuine discovery, on the other hand, occurs throughout the process, when the possibilities of the elements have been explored on the drawing surface. As Table 9.2 shows, none of the problem finders claimed to have had a clear idea of how the final design would look *before they began drawing*, but five of the problem solvers did.

Table 9.2.   *Number of Ss Claiming to Have Visualized the Drawing Before and After Drawing Began–Ss Divided into High and Low on Total Problem-Finding Score* [a]

Subgroups	N	Visualized Drawing Before Began Drawing	Visualized Drawing After Began Drawing
High problem-finding score (ABC)	11	0	11
Low problem-finding score (ABC)	14	5	9

[a] Fisher's exact contingency test: $p = .04$.

When the answers were divided according to whether the students said that they clearly saw the final design *before or after half of the drawing time had elapsed*, we find the pattern of responses reported in Table 9.3.

Here are some of the answers typical of the problem solvers: "When I opened the book, I saw the basic composition, the denouement" (S.09). "As soon as I chose the objects" (S.10). "As soon as I saw the objects arranged I had the idea of the final design" (S.15). Typical of the problem finders are these answers: "Not until I finished, the last line I put on. It was growing . . . to get freedom I let it grow. . . . I left it alive until it was done" (S.12). "When I finished; I had no preconceived notion until then" (S.01). "Didn't really have an idea of how the final design would look. I see only segments at a time. I just decided to stop at this point, although I could have gone on and covered the whole wall" (S.11).

These answers illustrate a crucial aspect of problem finding in the artistic process. The student who "sees" the problem and its solution "right away" may do so only because he adopts a known formulation; he does not need to discover anything but simply retrieves a configuration of

Table 9.3.   *Number of Ss Claiming to Have Visualized the Drawing Before and After Half of the Drawing Time Had Elapsed–Ss Divided into High and Low on Total Problem-Finding Score* [a]

Subgroups	N	Visualized Drawing Earlier Than Halfway Through	Visualized Drawing Later Than Halfway Through
High problem-finding score (ABC)	11	3	8
Low problem-finding score (ABC)	14	10	4

[a] Fisher's exact contingency test: $p = .03$.

forms and meanings encountered beforehand and fits the elements presented in the environment into the preconception. The student who holds the problem open, who does not foreclose the emergence of a new pattern by imposing on the elements a retrieved configuration, is attempting, consciously or otherwise, to discover an unknown meaning hidden in the forms. In a sense, the one looks on the problem as familiar, the elements as new; the other looks on the elements as familiar, and the problem as new.

The interviews suggest that the task of the fine artist is to be sensitive to salient life experiences, and to translate these into visual products, thereby preserving as much of the impact of the experience as possible, while at the same time revealing meanings that were not perceived before the work of art was completed. This is the sense in which creating a work of art constitutes a problem-finding process.

If· this is what artists must do, then the various pieces of information that we already have about art students begin to fit into a general pattern. Consider the asocial syndrome that turns up again and again as a component of the artistic personality and value systems. A person whose work involves paying constant attention to idiosyncratic inner events could not do his job if he were extroverted, sociable, and moved by external norms. In effect, what some call the narcissistic element of the artist's personality is an inevitable prerequisite of his role. It is difficult not to take one's own emotions seriously when the work one does depends on being sensitive to inner states.

Rejection of economic values and strong naivete also fit the pattern. A shrewd person interested in material comforts would want to make sure his talent is not going to go unrecognized. Instead of being responsive to his private experiences, he might formulate problems in terms that will please the audience. An artist "sells out" when the results of the visual equation are determined by the known tastes of the marketplace, rather than by the unknown logic of his experiences. Without naivete and a strong disregard for money (probably it matters little whether the latter is "sincere" or just ideological rationalization), it is easy to become reasonable and to do what is rewarded here and now.

The same argument holds for the fine artists' relatively high theoretical values. The artist's role is a form of that search for truth that theoretical values are supposed to reflect. If a person believes in the importance of truth, he will be less likely to modify the accuracy of his experiences for the sake of monetary rewards or social approval. In fact the whole syndrome of values and personality traits observed in earlier chapters —sensitivity, self-sufficiency, aloofness, low superego, and so on —outline an optimal set of attitudes adapted to the artist's problem-finding task.

And finally, it is now clear why conventional intelligence is not greatly involved in the artistic process. The problematic situation in art requires sensitivity, intuition, and holistic evaluation rather than the objectivity, reasoning, and analytical ability required by what we are used to calling "intelligence." The mental process measured by most intelligence tests is, first of all, a *problem-solving* process; secondly, it involves abstract reasoning. The mental process required of a successful artist is, first of all, *problem-finding*. In addition, it is based more on empathy than reason. Although both are responses to problematic situations, it is not surprising that the former is not necessarily an index of the latter.

The students we studied were coping with experiences that included a difficult childhood during World War II, preoccupation with masculine *vs* feminine roles, and difficulty in establishing one's identity. They are young artists, of course, and their experiences are those of youth. As they move through life their experiences will change, and therefore the sources of their inspiration may change, too. Even after only half a decade, the problems they deal with are quite different, as seen in the following chapters. The main themes are similar—the same ones artists are always dealing with—but the concrete expressions will change as life itself changes.

There may even come a time when the medium of art becomes autonomous and detaches itself from other experiences in life. At that point the artist may be motivated to paint solely because a previous canvas had suggested a new technical problem that he feels must be explored, formulated, and solved. Just as in chess, where the rules of the game continuously present new problems without any connection to events in "real" life, art also can become its own source of motivation, and perhaps even of creativity.

Yet it seems possible that when artistic problems are no longer rooted in life situations, but rely solely on tensions generated by the medium itself, the resulting art will be sterile and of limited appeal. The danger of becoming a closed symbolic system is one that art is always exposed to, and the young artists in our sample are very much aware of it. We shall see presently how they manage to avoid this obstacle, and others.

■

PART 3

Who Becomes An Artist?

CHAPTER 10

■

From Student to Artist:
A Longitudinal Study

The person who looks at problematic situations with an open mind, ready to let the issues reveal themselves instead of forcing them into a preconceived mold, increases his or her chances of discovering original responses. This is the implication suggested by the theoretical model and the empirical findings. The results in the experimental situation were unambiguous. But the experimental situation was just that: a small sample of performance in a more or less artificial setting. There is no certainty that behavior in it represents fairly what a person will do in the real world. The data reviewed so far have nothing to say about whether problem finders will become successful artists, or whether they will fail despite their promising performance in the experiment.

It is one thing to show that problem finding results in drawings that are judged original, and another to generalize that it reflects a stable disposition that will lead to artistic success later. The students we have called "problem finders" may not be such outside the experimental situation. And even if they consistently exhibit problem finding in their work, there is no guarantee that it will help them become successful artists.

Many of the obstacles on a student's way to a career in the arts have nothing to do with artistic talent and problem finding. A person must earn enough to survive; he must maintain self-respect, establish a position among his peers, gain recognition from critics, find meaning in what he is doing. Under certain social conditions, these might be accessible only to a very few of those who would like to devote their lives to producing art. If demand for art is limited, few persons will be able to support themselves economically from the making of art. If art is held in low esteem, talented young people will be deterred from taking it up seriously. Or a whole generation of artists may run out of self-confidence; many who normally would be attracted to it will feel that working in art is meaningless.

The case studies in chapters that follow will elaborate in more concrete detail the internal and external obstacles that newly graduated students must overcome before they can function as independent artists. One cannot simply assume that it is the problem finder who will make it. The obstacles often consist in historical forces beyond any one person's control, and the ability to surmount them may have nothing to do with talent or originality. How well a person did in art school or in our experiment may not predict accurately to professional success.

This is why we felt it was crucial to determine what happens to young artists after they leave school, and to see whether problem finding is predictive not only of short-term performance but also of long-term achievement. The initial questions we felt to be significant were of this order: Are any of the family characteristics of the young artists related to later success? Do any of the test scores and school evaluations predict success? And, of course, most important of all from a theoretical viewpoint, Are problem finders more successful than problem solvers?

The Longitudinal Study. To answer these questions we had to follow the careers of the fine art students after they had been graduated from art school. We had to keep in touch with each person over a period of years and record his accomplishment as an artist. In effect, to determine whether anything that had been learned about the students while they were in school had predictive value for later life, a longitudinal study was needed.

Longitudinal research, however, presents many difficulties. Just to keep track of the physical location of the sample is quite a task. As the years pass, the subjects or the researchers, or both, may lose interest in the study; or the concepts and methods with which the research started become obsolete. In any case, the difficulties are severe enough to have discouraged longitudinal studies of artists. Without a precedent to follow, it was not at all clear whether the undertaking was realistic.

Another possibility was that after a few years all 31 former students would give up art as hopeless and settle down in a less demanding career. In this event a longitudinal study would be worthless, or at least not worth the trouble it takes. Not much can be learned about the preconditions of artistic success if none of the subjects achieves it. But even if the former students were still engaged in art after leaving school, it was possible that their achievement could not be evaluated. If they were all working in complete obscurity there would be no way to assess their relative success. And we had no way of knowing how long we would have to wait to obtain a reliable index or artistic success.

Despite these uncertainties, we felt that the chance of getting even meager longitudinal results was worth the risk. All the previous studies with artists had been cross-sectional, near-term, or retrospective. Information obtained from these methods is limited. No matter how many successful artists one interviews, it is impossible to trace back the process of development except through reminiscences, often distorted by hindsight. And it is impossible to compare retrospectively those who achieve success with those who do not.

The opportunity of doing a prospective study of artists was too rare to be missed, so we decided to make the investment of time and effort. With all the detailed data about family background, thought processes, values, personality traits, school performance, and problem-finding behavior at hand, it became almost a duty to find out whether any of this information related to later artistic success.

The 31 former students were contacted again seven years after they had been tested and interviewed (and hence five to six years after they had been graduated from art school, depending on whether they had been sophomores or juniors at the time of the initial testing). The results justified our hopes. Good luck had more to do with it than wisdom; at the time of the follow up the sample was in an almost ideal stage for our purposes. Some of the former students had become artists of repute, some were struggling to succeed, others had already given up the struggle. This varied distribution of achievement permitted a systematic analysis of the correlates of success and failure.

Five or six years after graduation is obviously too soon to tell which artist will succeed in the eyes of posterity. Measures of success taken at various points in an artist's lifetime are not perfectly related with one another, nor with the judgment of following generations. Yet one thing is clear even after a short period of five years. It is possible to tell who is not likely ever to become a successful artist. Those former students who are no longer doing any art work will not be artists; a fortiori, they will not know success. Although it is possible that some will eventually return to serious work, the likelihood is very small.

Among those who have retained a connection with art, further distinctions are evident. Some have exhibited and sold their work, and their names are known to critics and gallery owners. Others have continued to paint, but mainly for their own pleasure and with limited outside recognition. Still others have almost completely discontinued active production but still maintain a foothold in the art world.

There is no way of knowing the permanence of these distinctions. The sensation of today may be forgotten in 10 years; the young artist who secretly accumulates canvasses in the attic may be discovered and hailed as a genius. But it is more probable that the distinctions between more successful and less successful artists will remain pretty much as they are now. Despite dramatic reversals in the fame of some renowned artists, success in art is more stable than romantic myth would have it. Hard work, perseverance, slowly developing competence, and amount of acceptable output are as crucial in art as in any other field. The former student who a few years after graduation from school has not begun "making like an artist" is not likely to "make it as an artist." Again, the prediction that can be made with most confidence is a negative one. Who will be successful in the view of posterity is not as sure as who will not be. Prediction of ultimate fame may be unattainable; in the meantime, knowledge of relative success can be useful.

Three sources of information were used to determine the success of the young artists in our sample: the director of a major art gallery with offices in New York and Chicago; the art critic of a Chicago newspaper and author of books on American art and artists; and the knowledge obtained concerning the young artist's progress in the follow-up study itself, including the judgment of his fellow students.

Whenever one of these sources indicated that a subject on our list was a practicing artist, we recorded a score of 1. If he was reputed to be a good artist, a score of 2 was registered. If he was known as an exceptionally promising artist, a score of 3 was given. The artists' scores could range, therefore, from 0 (given to someone who was unknown to all three sources, or who was known to have left art) to 9 (given to someone considered an exceptional artist by all three sources).

Contrary to our initial fears, some young artists were well known to outside experts. Of the 31 former students, the gallery director was acquainted with 8, and held varying opinions of their work. The art critic knew 7, 4 of whom were also known to the gallery director; and he had written about the work of some of these.

The distribution of artistic achievement from "known to have left art" to "maximum success" is reported in Table A1.15 (see Appendix 1). About half the sample had dropped out of fine art seven years after the last testing. Eight of them had disappeared without a trace; they left no forwarding address, were unknown to their former fellow students, and there was no record of their whereabouts in the alumni rosters of the art school.

Although it is possible that these young men are actively painting in some remote corner of the world, it is more probable that they will never be known as artists, at least on a national scale. One can paint anywhere, but for a person's work to become part of the art world, he has to be known to fellow artists, to critics, buyers, and dealers. Otherwise his chances of being recognized as an artist are slim.

It is also possible that those who stop painting will start again and gain recognition despite their present lapse. This possibility is, however, rather remote. The obstacles are easier to surmount with the momentum gained in art school. This is the time when an artist has a fresh collection of work to show, when he is immersed in the world of art, when he has the support of his peers and the knowledge of contacts. If he breaks the flow of his work at this point, it takes far more motivation and energy to start afresh after an interlude of years, and to build up the backlog of recent work needed to prove the seriousness of his commitment. It can be done, but as far as we know it seldom happens.

Seven of the former students, or 23 percent, qualified for a score of 1. They have achieved a minimum of artistic success. They have kept up connections with the world of art, but only peripheral ones: They work as department store decorators, teachers of art in elementary school, model builders for architects, and so on. Several are not painting seriously any longer, and those who are have failed to show their work professionally. It is still too early, five years into their careers, to write off this group entirely. Some of them might abandon their marginal status and plunge into art full time. At present, these former students are clearly intermediate between those who have left art and those who achieved success in it.

The remaining nine young artists, or 29 percent of the original group, have established a recognizable artistic identity. To be sure, they range from those who show sporadically to those represented by major galleries. But despite the tremendous selective pressures, some have already reached a standing in the world of art. Of course, their fame must be kept in the perspective of their youth. Yet all have continued to do art work, and it may be expected that their stature will grow.

One has achieved unconditional success by any standard. He paints continuously, his work is shown in the best galleries, he is the subject of critical articles in prestigious art journals. One of his paintings is in the permanent collection of a great museum of art. Even though he works as an art teacher to supplement the income from the sale of his work, he has achieved as much in five years as any artist can hope for. Thus the range of possible outcomes available for study was complete: it varied from total withdrawal from art to convincing artistic accomplishment.

Success and Family Background. As a first step in determining the antecedents of artistic achievement, the 16 former students who five to six years after graduation from art school are still engaged in artistic work were compared with the 15 who have left the field. The point was to establish whether there were any differences in family background between the two groups. The data were available in the questionnaires filled out seven years earlier when the respondents were second- or third-year students in art school. The results are based on what they said at that time. The more interesting differences are reported in Table A1.16.

There were substantial but not significant differences in the occupational status of the fathers of the two groups. Fifty percent of the fathers in the successful group were junior executives, owners of businesses, or professionals, and 50 percent had white collar jobs or occupations of lesser status (for example, bank tellers, skilled or unskilled workers, farmers). The respective proportions for the unsuccessful group were 27 percent and 73 percent. This pattern is repeated throughout: The successful artists come from families of higher socioeconomic status, with higher overall income, and with fathers who have higher education. All four sons of professional fathers were successful, while three of the four sons of business owners were unsuccessful. Moreover, given the same education, the fathers of the successful group tended to attain higher occupational status.

The most notable socioeconomic difference, however, is in the occupational status of mothers. Sixty-two percent in the successful group, as against 20 percent in the unsuccessful group, had mothers employed outside the home ($p < .01$). It is not clear whether this means that working mothers contribute more income, and it is the total family income that is related to success; or that working mothers are more independent, and it is their personality that affects the sons' success. In any case, both the mother's education and occupation are more related to the son's artistic success than are the father's education and occupation. Finally, despite common belief to the contrary, family disruption through divorce, separation, or death of parents was three times more prevalent in the unsuccessful than in the successful group (40 percent versus 13 percent).

The largest difference concerns sibling position; the magnitude of the difference is remarkable and, we hasten to say, inexplicable. Thirteen, or 81 percent, of the successful artists as against only five, or 33 percent, of the unsuccessful ones were eldest sons ($p < .008$). A further analysis shows that the balance is accounted for by middle sons; none of the successful but more than half of the unsuccessful young artists were middle children ($p < .0008$). The proportion of only and youngest children was the same in both groups (19 and 14 percent).

Religious background also shows large differences. Sixty percent of the unsuccessful students marked Protestant as their faith; only 19 percent of the successful students did ($p < .02$). Disclaiming allegiance with a Protestant denomination may be more an indication of cultural marginality than of lack of religious belief per se. There is no difference between the two groups in religious practice; only about a third in each group claimed to attend worship at least once a month.

The data make clear that, to achieve success as an artist, it helps to come from a well-to-do, educated, higher status family. (This is a disillusioning thought. One would like to believe that, at least in art, money and status play no part in determining success.) What is not clear is how a high socioeconomic family environment sets the foundation for future success. Two explanations seem likely. The first is that talented young people with such backgrounds weather the hardships of artistic life more easily. Their parents will be more understanding and extend financial support. Sons of poorer and less educated parents will feel more pressure to abandon the economically unrewarding artistic career for a more lucrative occupation. The other possibility is that a higher socioeconomic family environment includes more sensory and intellectual stimulation. Children born into such a family may be exposed early in life to more varied artistic experiences. Perhaps interaction between parents and children is more complex. Hence the sons develop cognitive and affective skills that will enable them to be better artists.

The two explanations lead to almost opposite implications. If the first were true, then artists who succeed would differ from those who fail only in that they have access to more material and psychological support. There would be no need to postulate differences in talent or other personal qualities. The second explanation implies that a privileged socioeconomic background confers psychological and cognitive advantages that qualify for artistic success. In other words, money, education, and the life style that goes with them affect the ways of thinking and feeling in a manner advantageous to artistic success.

Although the question cannot be settled with the information at hand, independent evidence seems to favor the second possibility. We went back to the experiment on problem finding and compared the family backgrounds of those who scored high and those who scored low. There was a striking difference between the two groups, the former being more often the sons of wealthier families ($p < .006$). In effect, it appears that a higher socioeconomic environment favors a problem-finding orientation, which in turn might contribute to artistic success. While the first hypothesis cannot be dismissed completely, it seems clear that the second, which postulated cognitive differences between the two groups, is supported by complementary observations.

The other notable pattern that emerged unmistakably from the data is that students who are eldest sons are far more likely than those who are middle sons to succeed as artists. Why this is so is unclear. But again the same pattern holds true for problem finding. We went back to the experiment and divided the group into the 11 students with the highest problem-solving scores and the 14 with the lowest scores, omitting the six students with the middle scores. Of the 11 students with high scores, 9, or 82 percent, were eldest sons; of the 14 students with low scores, 7, or 50 percent, were eldest sons ($p < .06$). Apparently there is a peculiar constellation of experiences that firstborn sons undergo, alien especially to middle sons, which favors both problem finding or discovery orientation, and the achievement of artistic success.

What specifically these experiences are we do not know. Alfred Adler and his followers have written extensively about the effects of birth order on the psychological character of children and have postulated many unique effects for the firstborn. A considerable amount of empirical work has also been devoted to this question, but without clear-cut results. Lacking a viable theory to account for the birth-order differences, one can only point to the evidence, which is substantial, and suggest that important work remains to be done in this domain.

In any case, the data on the background of the artists show strong family and sibling position concomitants of success. Whether they directly affect talent, or whether they merely facilitate its expression is a moot point, although evidence from the problem-finding experiment favors the former possibility.

Success and School Background. To see if performances in school had any connection with later achievement, all the descriptive variables were correlated with the success scores. Only 7 of about 50 variables show significant positive or negative relationships to success; but the pattern and meaning of the relationships are notably consistent with previous results.

We turn first to the relationship between performance in school and success after leaving school. Three of the significant measures are judgments by teachers: ratings in originality and artistic potential (OAP 1) given nine years prior to the follow up, grade point average in studio courses, and grade point average in academic courses. Five to six years after graduation, students who had the best grades in studio courses tend to be the most successful artists ($p < .01$). The ratings in originality and artistic potential given during the first year of art school are also related to success five years after graduation ($p < .05$). So are academic grades, but in an unexpected way: good academic grades in art school are related to failure as an artist rather than to success ($p < .05$).

The fit between the teachers' judgment in school and the students' accomplishment after school is surprising; in general, one finds less of a relationship between college grades and later success in other occupations (see, for instance, Willingham, 1974). But the negative relationship between academic grades and success must also be kept in mind. Art students are required to take a complement of academic courses in addition to the studio courses, presumably in line with the ideals of a liberal education. It seems, however, that a good record in academic courses has no bearing on future success as an artist, and in fact may be counterproductive.

The other relationships can be summarized as follows. Of the cognitive tests, two are good predictors of success. One is the Object Question Test ($p < .025$), and the other is the "novelty" score of the Thematic Apperception Test ($p < .0005$).* Both these open-ended tests supposedly measure originality in cognitive style. None of the more standardized tests of intelligence, cognition, or divergent thinking was significantly related to success. In fact, the Welsh Art Judgment Test, which measures aesthetic taste (and on which the art students scored very much higher than other students) shows a low negative correlation with success. This might mean that while students in art school give what they know to be the expected judgment of good design, the successful among them may reject the commonly held standards. These findings again stress the importance of cognitive activity directed at problem finding rather than problem solving.

As we saw, male fine art students had lower economic and social values and higher aesthetic values than other students. The art students who were more successful five years after graduation also had consistently lower economic and social values and higher aesthetic values than those who were less successful, although the differences were not large enough to be statistically significant. Of course, the values of all fine art students—successful and unsuccessful alike—were already at the extreme, making it almost impossible for any further differences to emerge on the measure. Consistency of this pattern was all that could be expected; it confirms what has been shown to be characteristic of the artists' values time and again.

The same situation appears to hold also for the measures of personality. Only 1 of the 16 PF factors is significantly related to success: Students who became successful artists had lower self-sentiment scores than the unsuccessful ones ($p < .05$). The meaning attributed to a high score on this factor is "conformity to socially accepted behavior," "self-control," and "concern with social approval." Clearly it is lack of these characteristics that is related to success in art. The same factor was similarly related to performance in art school, the better students having lower scores. A · number of the other factors that distinguished art students from other students also distinguished the more successful from the less successful

---

*This correlation coefficient is somewhat inflated by outstanding matches at the high end of the scale. The distribution of scores on this variable was quite skewed; 50 percent of the scores were at the two lowest values of an 18-point range. Although success is clearly related to this variable, the relationship is not as strong as the correlation implies.

artists, but in view of the already extreme scores the differences were not large enough to attain statistical significance.

In summary, three sets of data were related to artistic success. One set derives from personal questionnaires. Several family background characteristics were implicated in whether a young artist will persist and prosper in his vocation. Of these the most striking is sibling position. Whatever the cause, art students who are middle sons are very likely to abandon art as a career, while the eldest are likely to persevere. The other strong link is between affluence and success. Young artists reared in wealthier families with better educated parents are more likely to survive in the competitive world of art. The role of the mother is particularly important in this respect. These are clearly important issues for understanding achievement in art and creative endeavor in general.

The second set of data derives from the cognitive, value, and personality tests completed by the artists while they were still in school. These measures were proportionately least productive; none of the conventional cognitive tests, none of the value scales, and only one of the personality factors—low concern with social approval—was significantly related to success. The lack of more significant correlations is in all probability due to the already extreme value and personality scores of all the art students, including those who later succeeded and those who did not.

It would have been interesting to determine whether the value and personality traits of former students who abandoned art have changed to resemble more closely the traits of the general population. Is their aesthetic value still as high as it had been in art school now that they have given up art as a lifework? Perhaps the value and personality system is congruent with one's goals only as long as the goals are perceived as attainable. The entire relationship between personality and commitment to creative work begs further longitudinal inquiry.

Although the predictive power of conventional paper-pencil cognitive tests was generally low, the two least structured measures of thinking- —the TAT novelty score and the Object Question Test—did show significant correlations with success. This finding points out once more that the sources of creativity are to be looked for in the questioning, metaphorical, playful, and problem-finding components of thought.

The third set of data derives from indices of performance in the art school itself. Two of the four indices are positively related, and one is negatively related to success. The teachers' evaluations of originality and artistic potential (OAP 1) and the grades in studio courses predict success five to six years after the students had left school. The correlations are not very high, but they are greater than similar correlations for other professions. In contrast to teacher ratings and grades in studio courses, those in academic courses had an inverse relation with artistic success. If one were to look only at the *total* grade point average, the significant relations would be missed, since the positive correlation with studio course grades and the negative correlation with academic course grades would cancel each other out. Just as the attitudinal commitment to art is shown by extreme value and personality scores, so dedication to studio work at the expense of academic performance points to the same single-mindedness of purpose.

CHAPTER 11

■

Success and Problem Finding

The relationships between artistic success and family background, sibling position, personality, values, and even art grades are only indirect indicators of whatever processes underly creative achievement. They reflect correlates of artistic activity, not the processes that constitute it.

In the experimental situation, where we observed the quality of artistic creation more directly, we saw that problem-finding was positively related to the quality of artistic performance. Students whose behaviors and attitudes before, during, or after the drawing process gave evidence of problem finding produced more original works than did those whose behaviors and attitudes were characterized by a problem-solving approach. The drawings of students who scored high in *problem finding* and *discovery orientation* throughout the three stages were rated more original and of greater aesthetic value by critics.

This raises a highly important question: Are problem finding and discovery orientation also related to long-term success? If they are, then problem finding and discovery orientation are central to the creative process not only in the short-run and in quasi-experimental settings but in the long run and in real-life situations.

Success and Problem Finding at the Predrawing Stage. The first set of relationships to be examined is that between problem finding at the predrawing stage in the experiment, and later success of the former students. Theoretically, it is at this stage of formulating the task that the main

171

difference between original and routine thinking should appear. And empirically this is the first step in the process—if one excludes the process of incubation and preparation which precedes conscious attempts at producing a work of art.

Table 11.1 reports correlations between scores on the first three behavioral observations in the experiment and later success. To allow for a more informed analysis, the evaluations of the drawings produced in the experimental setting are also reported. It will be recalled that the drawings had been judged seven years before the follow-up study by four panels of five members each: artist-critics, art teachers, graduate students in mathematics, and graduate students in business.

According to our model, the three behaviors observed at this stage —the number of objects manipulated (A1), the unusualness of the objects chosen (A2), and the amount of exploration of the objects (A3)—reflect whether a person approaches an indeterminate situation as a *presented* or as a *discovered* problem. People who score low on the variables A1, A2, and A3 act as if there was no question about what to do; they simply adopt an existing definition of the problem to impose on the situation. They are unwilling or unable to discover new possibilities in the task. In contrast, those who score high on these variables see a problem emerging from the situation itself. They do not identify the task in terms of an already existing definition; they are willing to experiment, to learn about the reality they confront in its own terms rather than in terms of previous assumptions. These are the people engaged in *problem finding*.

The data in Table 11.1 are clear-cut: two of the three measures of problem finding at this stage—variables A1 and A3—correlate significantly with later success. Variable A1 seems to measure the *breadth* and variable A3 the *depth* of discovery orientation when confronted with a potential problem. That behavior in the experimental situation should correlate so highly with artistic success seven years later can be explained only if we assume that it represents an orientation essential to artistic creativity.

It could perhaps be argued that A1 and A3 are measuring the same thing, making the two correlations redundant. But the correlation between the two variables is .48, which leaves room for independence. More conclusively, there is evidence that the two variables affect the artist's work in different ways. If we look across the "Originality" columns in the table, breadth of discovery appears to elicit high ratings only from artist-critics. Depth of discovery, however, affects final drawings in ways that result in high ratings of originality by all four groups of judges.

Table 11.1. Correlations Between Problem Formulation Behavior, Judges' Ratings of the Experimental Product, and the Artists' Success Seven Years Later

Problem Finding at the Stage of Problem Formulation	Success 7 Years Later	Evaluation of the Experimental Product											
		Overall Value				Originality				Craftsmanship			
		A.C.	A.T.	M.S.	B.S.	A.C.	A.T.	M.S.	B.S.	A.C.	A.T.	M.S.	B.S.
A1. Number of objects manipulated	.45[c]	.48[d]	.25	.05	.14	.52[d]	.26	.18	.29	.17	.15	−.05	.02
A2. Unusual quality of objects chosen	.21	.35[a]	.32[a]	.18	.14	.42[c]	.45[c]	.48[d]	.40[c]	.21	.20	.12	.07
A3. Discovery behavior while selecting and arranging	.43[c]	.44[c]	.57[d]	.30	.18	.58[e]	.59[e]	.44[c]	.46[c]	.34[a]	.43[c]	.38[b]	.26
AA. Total	.30[a]	.40[c]	.48[d]	.25	.26	.54[d]	.56[d]	.51[d]	.54[d]	.28	.30[a]	.22	.14

Key: A.C. = artist-critics; A.T. = art teachers; M.S. = mathematics students; B.S. = business students.
[a] $p < .05$.
[b] $p < .025$.
[c] $p < .01$.
[d] $p < .005$.
[e] $p < .0005$.

We should also note that the unusualness of the objects chosen (A2), while resulting in products that elicited high originality ratings by all four groups of judges, does not relate significantly to later artistic success. This finding suggests that the selection of uncommon elements with which to structure a problem may lead viewers to think of the finished work as original, but that an artist cannot rely on such strategy in the long run. Originality based on selecting what is unusual in the environment is ephemeral and exhausts itself with time. The creative person must learn to recognize the extraordinary potential of ordinary objects (or thoughts, or emotions). To do so, the processes represented by variables A1 and A3 are more effective than those represented by A2.

The results are clear: The behavioral observations made in the first stage of the experiment, the ratings of specific drawings, and the evaluation of the artist's general success years later are related in systematic ways.

Yet obscure processes are involved. How is problem-finding behavior at the predrawing stage translated into a visible quality in the finished drawing? How did the judges who looked at the drawings, and who had not been privy to our observation records, sense which artists had explored the objects in greater depth? In rating the drawings, they must have reacted to some concrete evidence of problem finding to which the drawing itself attested. Furthermore, the process that produced such evidence must be carried over into the future work of the same artists, influencing their relative success. But what this concrete manifestation of problem finding might be, we do not know.

We do know it is neither stronger motivation nor greater care that is reflected in the work. Time spent drawing is not correlated with judgments of quality. Nor is the craftsmanship rating usually correlated with problem finding. All this confirms our conclusion that the activity involved in formulating the problem is crucial to creative endeavor.

Success and Problem Finding at the Drawing Stage. When we examine measures that show how the former students acted while they were drawing in the experimental setting, we again find that two of the three variables are significantly correlated with later success, although one just barely. The data are presented in Table 11.2.

The highest correlation between any of the problem finding variables and success is the one attained by B1 ($r = .48; p < .005$). This score was the proportion of total drawing time elapsed before the final structure of the

Table 11.2. Correlations Between Problem Solution Behavior, Judges' Ratings of the Experimental Product, and the Artists' Success Seven Years Later

Problem Finding at the Stage of Problem Solution	Success 7 Years Later	Evaluation of the Experimental Product											
		Overall Value				Originality				Craftsmanship			
		A.C.	A.T.	M.S.	B.S.	A.C.	A.T.	M.S.	B.S.	A.C.	A.T.	M.S.	B.S.
B1. Problem-structure (lateness of closure)	.48[d]	.09	−.01	−.51[d]	−.39[b]	.08	.07	−.25	−.22	−.18	−.04	−.57[d]	−.46[c]
B2. Discovery-oriented behavior while drawing (changing media, arrangement)	.31[a]	.22	.27	.16	−.05	.37[b]	.39[b]	.28	.17	.01	.05	.16	−.12
B3. Changes in problem structure (difference between arrangement and product)	.20	.44[c]	.61[e]	.46[c]	.36[b]	.61[e]	.68[e]	.65[e]	.64[e]	.37[b]	.48[d]	.36[b]	.31[a]
BB. Total	.33[a]	.26	.46[c]	.03	−.16	.38[a]	.60[e]	.24	.18	.12	.34[a]	−.09	−.24

Key: A.C. = artist-critics; A.T. = art teachers; M.S. = mathematics students; B.S. = business students.

[a] $p < .05$.
[b] $p < .025$.
[c] $p < .01$.
[d] $p < .005$.
[e] $p < .0005$.

drawing was recognizable on paper. Two raters unconnected with the study examined the film strips of the evolving drawing taken by the observer, and judged when the final drawing could be recognized. The later this happened relative to the total drawing time, the higher the B1 score. In effect, it is a "delay in closure of the problem" score. The high correlation shows that students characterized by high delay in closure, that is, those who kept the problem open longer, achieved greater success as artists years later.

What this relationship suggests about the mental processes underlying overt behavior is not as simple as it might appear at first glance. Lateness in structuring the problem could merely be a by-product of an abstract style of drawing, since abstract artists might be expected to organize their drawings later than do artists with a realistic style. But this turned out *not* to be the case. B1 was not related to the abstract-realistic continuum.

The next explanation that occurred to us was that delay in closure was associated with the amount of time a person spent on the drawing. It might be that the longer an artist draws, the longer it takes for the final structure of the drawing to appear. Again, this was not supported by the data. B1 was not correlated with total drawing time.

We then thought that perhaps lateness of structure was a function of the amount of changes introduced in the drawing; thus delay of closure might be explained in terms of experimentation with various ways of stating the problem. But the data failed to support our interpretation: B1 was not correlated with B2 (changes in media and arrangement of the objects), nor with B3 (changes in problem structure). The respective correlations were $-.11$ and $.02$.

Only one explanation seemed to be left. A person who structures his problem late must do so because he has such a strong feeling for what the drawing should be that he does not have to put down on paper the outline of the finished drawing at the very beginning. He *knows* what the problem is; the final structure is so clear in his mind that he can work at unconnected details first, leaving the final synthesis to the end.

Yet this explanation did not seem to fit the problem-finding model at all. If the artists knew from the outset what their drawings would look like, then they approached the task as a presented problem. Rather than formulating the problem in the situation, they brought an already formulated problem to the situation. But then we remembered that most of those who delayed closure said in the interview that they *did not know* what the finished drawing would look like until quite late. In effect, their behavior suggests that they knew what the structure of the work would be like, while their subjective reports indicate that they could not visualize what they were going to do. We can reasonably conclude from the data that what we are measuring here is an unconscious process. *The artists' actions reveal that they are working in a goal-directed way, but without full conscious awareness of what the goal is.*

We may now summarize the most probable meaning of the B1 score. Artists who delay closure are guided by an unconscious feeling of what they are to do. Presumably they formulate the problem below the threshold of awareness before beginning to draw. They cannot tell what the drawing will be but their behavior shows that at some level the goal is quite clear. Once started they do not change their drawings any more than other artists. They may begin working at one corner of the paper, then turn to another, then focus on the center. To an observer it seems they are not getting anywhere. No pattern is recognizable, and the early photographic frames show no structure. Yet toward the end they pull the various parts of the work together into an organized whole.

It seems that delay in closure literally allows the artist *to discover at a manifest level what he already knows at a latent level.* But of course it is one thing to have a subconscious "feeling" for what one wants to do, and another to produce a drawing of that feeling. As he works on the paper, the late structurer finds out what he wants to express by sketching a line here, adding a mass of color there. Each detail helps to define the whole. Yet the goal was apparently clear to the artist from the beginning, even though he was not aware of it. Presumably this process occurs only when the artist has a deep personal concern with his work. To formulate a problem unconsciously one needs to be very involved with, and therefore very sensitive to, the problematic issues. Only then can an artist unerringly choose, say, a Japanese doll and a carburetor as objects that suggest new formulations of a problem, long before he realizes consciously why those objects are symbolically appropriate.

Those who had a low B1 score were consciously aware of their goal from the beginning. They outlined the structure of the final drawing in the first few minutes—a startling vanishing point, for instance, or a formal composition of light and dark textures. From then on, they might change large elements of the drawing, but the structure was not altered. In the interview these artists reported that they knew from the start how their work would look when finished.

Table 11.2 reveals other provocative relationships. Variable B1, which correlated so highly with later success, did not elicit higher ratings from the judges. In fact, both lay groups rated the work of late structurers significantly lower in overall aesthetic value and craftsmanship than the work of early structurers. If B1 is indeed an index of unconscious process, it seems that the visual expression of this process affects nonartists adversely. The untrained viewer finds the work inspired by the unconscious disturbing, or at least technically inferior. Yet in the long run the use of unconscious processes in problem formulation and solution is highly useful; art students who were open to them were more successful later than those who were not.

The data also indicate that problem finding might relate one way to success in the short run and another way in the long run. In the near term, B3 is the discovery variable that elicits the highest ratings from all the judges. B1 contributes nothing to the evaluation. In the long term, however, the effects are reversed. The tendency to change one's drawing a great deal results in work that is judged better at the time. But this way of working does not lead to lasting success. To achieve more permanent recognition, it seems better to build the painting around a deeply experienced—albeit unconscious—personal problem, and then discover through the emerging elements of the drawing the final structure of the work. Neither the use of preformulated problems, nor ones that emerge ad hoc in the drawing, lead to long-range success. What works best is the ability to relate conscious tasks to deeply felt subconscious issues in novel ways; the work is then infused with overriding personal concern, yet the artist is not self-consciously aware of it. It is the inner problem that shapes the structure of the whole. The artist "finds" the problem only in the end, but unbeknown to him, it had found him from the very beginning.

Success and Concern with Discovery at the Postdrawing Stage. The third set of measures that define problem finding was based on interview questions rather than on behavioral observation. Table 11.3 presents the relationships between these measures and later success.

Two of the five variables, C2 and C4, are predictive. C2 measures concern with discovery at the stage of problem formulation, before the drawing was begun. Although what artists said about their general attitude (C1) was related neither to the quality of the drawing made for our study nor to later success, and what they said about concern with discovery after they began drawing (C3) was related to the quality of the drawing but not to later success, expressed concern for discovery prior to

Table 11.3. Correlations Between Concern for Discovery as Related in the Interview, Total Problem Finding Score (ABC), Judges' Ratings of the Experimental Product, and the Artists' Success Seven Years Later

Concern for Discovery	Success 7 Years Later	Evaluation of the Experimental Product											
		Overall Value				Originality				Craftsmanship			
		A.C.	A.T.	M.S.	B.S.	A.C.	A.T.	M.S.	B.S.	A.C.	A.T.	M.S.	B.S.
C1. In general	.00	.22	.12	.23	.01	.27	.23	.13	.21	.15	.25	.08	.11
C2. Concern with discovery at the stage of problem formulation	.38 [b]	.40 [b]	.48 [d]	−.02	−.11	.60 [e]	.58 [a]	.33 [a]	.30 [a]	.26	.29	.06	−.05
C3. Concern with discovery at the stage of problem solution	.02	.31 [a]	.36 [b]	.29	.23	.31 [a]	.45 [c]	.45 [c]	.46 [c]	.24	.23	.12	.13
C4. After solution*	.45 [c]	.36 [b]	.59 [e]	.19	.05	.45 [c]	.64 [e]	.39 [b]	.31 [a]	.33 [b]	.63 [e]	.10	.07
CC. Total	.28	.42 [c]	.52 [d]	.19	.09	.56 [d]	.62 [e]	.36 [a]	.42 [c]	.31 [a]	.52 [d]	.07	.11
ABC. Grand total	.41 [c]	.47 [d]	.64 [e]	.22	.09	.65 [d]	.78 [e]	.50 [d]	.50 [d]	.31 [a]	.51 [d]	.11	.02

Key: A.C. = artist-critics; A.T. = art teachers; M.S. = mathematics students; B.S. = business students.

*This is a dichotomous variable, hence Pearsonian correlation is a questionable statistic for the measure of concordance. A nonparametric Fisher exacta test shows approximately the same probability values for the concordance between C4 and the other variables as the correlation does (e.g., teachers' originality rating and C4: p. = .0007; success and C4: p. = .04). In this table the correlation metric was retained to facilitate comparisons.

[a] p < .05.
[b] p < .025.
[c] p < .01.
[d] p < .005.
[e] p < .0005.

the start of drawing related both to higher evaluations of the drawing itself by both groups of expert judges, and to later success.

One of our interview questions was: "Why did you arrange the objects as you did?" Students who answered that "it was the only way to arrange them so they would look good," or who indicated that they wanted to produce "a pleasing harmony" or provide "a startling vanishing point"—that is, those who used objects to set up canned problems —tended to fail as artists when measured by the study's criteria for success. Students who claimed that the drawing emerged out of the situation itself, and that the arrangement did not conform to any set principle, tended to be successful.

Once again, the importance of problem finding in creative work, especially during the early stages, becomes apparent. It is in the period before the problem is fully visualized that creative thought most differs from routine thinking. Furthermore, problem finding seems to persist over time: Students who reported it in the experiment were the ones who met with success later.

Variable C4 also shows a strong relationship both to the ratings of the drawings and to later success. The C4 score was based on a yes or no answer to the question: "Could any of the elements in your drawing be eliminated or altered without destroying its character?" Of the 15 students who dropped out of art after leaving school, 4 had answered yes and 11 no. Of the 16 students who remained in art and were to some extent successful, 10 had answered yes and 6 no.

This simple observation helps to understand why the problem-finding approach is conducive to creative achievement. The person who sees his problem as solved, completed, finished, is less likely to continue to ask questions. The only reason he can claim the problem is solved is that he applies a *presented* criterion both to its formulation and to its solution. He believes there is a single right solution. When the problem is *discovered*, there is no single right way of solving it, because there is no exact precedent that can certify the solution. There are only closer approximations to be made, new problematic levels to be discovered.

Presumably this is why so many great artists have found the same subject inexhaustible, why they have experimented with the same theme over and over in their work, as if attempting to achieve a "right" solution, all the while knowing that it would remain elusive, that each apparent solution was the harbinger of a new problem. Cézanne's versions of Mont-Sainte-Victorie, Monet's variations of the lily pond and the Rheims

Cathedral, and Picasso's series on the Damoiselles d'Avignon are recent examples that illustrate the point.

Correlation coefficients alone fail to do justice to the connection between the measures taken in the experimental situation, and real-life accomplishment seven years later. For instance, a closer examination of the delay of closure variable (B1) shows that of the 10 students with the highest delay scores, none had dropped out of art six years later; 3 had success scores of 1, 7 of 2 or higher. Of the 11 students with the lowest delay of closure scores, 8 dropped out of art by the time of the follow up, 2 had scores of 1, and only 1 had a higher score ($p < .002$ by median test).

The pattern was so strong that we were drawn to examine the deviant cases to see if they were "explainable." This is ordinarily risky since it may lead to ad hoc arguments to "save the theory." In this case there was no danger; the relationship was already strong enough to support the theory. The closer examination was illuminating. All high delayers (the 10 students with the highest B1 scores) achieved success but 3 had the minimum success score. The low score of two of these three did not, however, adequately represent their creative achievement, since they were creative in fields other than graphic art.

One of these young artists had almost completely abandoned painting and sculpture. He was working in New York as a lyricist, songwriter, and independent producer of his own recordings, and thus was not known to our critics as a graphic artist. The other was a young black artist, who by performance in art school should have been among the most successful artists in our sample. But he was abandoning art in part to dedicate himself to bettering the conditions of his people. Both are creative, and both were identified as such by the delay of closure score. Neither achieved a high level of success by our criterion, for reasons having nothing to do with their creativity.

Altogether, 6 of the 10 measures of problem finding taken in the experimental setting show positive correlations with success seven years later. The total problem-finding score was also related to success at the .01 level of probability.

Despite these promising results, the measures of problem finding have not delineated completely the cognitive processes underlying creative performance. Nor do we believe that we have devised the most fruitful way of studying problem finding in all its manifestations. We are aware of the great complexity and beauty of the process and know that it is not to be encompassed by experimental approach. Although the discovery of problems has been described many times and with deep insight, it has perhaps never before been examined empirically at such close quarters, nor been related to longitudinal criteria of creative success. We need hardly add that much remains to be done.

Perhaps the assumptions that artists are unpredictable, that the creative process is impervious to controlled experimentation, and that success in art is beyond the reach of systematic analysis have discouraged longitudinal studies of artists and of creativity. But these and similar assumptions are now open to question. Although value and personality traits measured while future artists are still in school are not predictive of later success, they do determine who will attempt to become an artist. Successful artists develop from an extremely select group in terms of values and personality. Several family background variables have also emerged as antecedents of success. Crucial among these are the economic and educational attainments of parents, and especially the sibling position of the young artist. Performance in·art school also predicts later achievement. Grades in studio courses and teacher ratings are positively related to professional success; grades in academic courses tend to be negatively related.

Most important, our study shows that artistic creation, when conceived as a continuous process of problem finding and solution, is amenable to systematic inquiry. Problem finding can be observed and is positively related to success in the world of art.

Artists who approach their work with personal commitment yet without stereotyped problems in mind not only produce drawings that are rated more original and of greater aesthetic value, but persist in art longer and achieve greater success in their creative profession. It would seem that problem finding is an integral part of a person's cognitive style; it is a reliable characteristic, not just a temporary trait accidentally elicited by the experiment.

The longitudinal validation of the effects of problem finding on creative work raises again the issue of the generality of the present results. Are there similar effects on creative work outside the realm of art? The steps by which problems are formulated were observed by methods devised specifically to study artistic problems. The next question is how they may be adapted to other fields that involve creativity. Only then will we know if the same process of discovery is characteristic of all forms of original thinking, regardless of subject matter. If the results with artists are confirmed for other fields, the present overwhelming emphasis in education and research on problem solving will have to be moderated. We shall have to discover how to facilitate the process of problem finding.

Of course, our findings may not apply to really successful artists. Those we studied were no Rembrandts, Picassos, or de Koonings. Nor was our task to explain the great masters, whose achievement will probably remain unfathomable, determined as it is by multiple forces within the artist and surrounding him. We wanted instead to explore the characteristics that distinguish talented young people who enter art school, who perservere in the world of art, who five years after leaving school have gotten a foothold in the art world, and who may have gained temporary recognition as artists. From among these one or two may attain more than local fame; but without obscure but committed young artists such as those we studied the world of art would have no aspirants for future admission to the pantheon of masters.

Despite personal and social forces that prevent more than a few students from attaining recognition, the longitudinal results show that those who endure in art are suited to their calling. They are not merely luckier or more persistent; they also possess the problem-finding orientation that seems necessary for creative work. Whether this also helps one to reach the ultimate accomplishment of genius is a moot question; but problem finding seems to help make an artist successful at his chosen task.

These conclusions made us wonder what an artist needs these days in addition to talent and training. What do young artists encounter as they attempt to establish themselves after leaving school? Success in art, as in other fields, does not depend only on personal qualifications; the social environment is also a critical factor. Skill and perseverance are necessary, but not sufficient. They must be adaptive in a milieu that allows their productive expression. The field of forces into which young artists step at the beginning of their career is the topic of the next chapter.

CHAPTER 12

■

The Social Context of Art

On leaving school, young artists face the same task as other graduates—they have to find a place in an occupation that will satisfy material needs and provide them with a positive identity.

To become established in an occupation means far more than working to make a living. A young person's standing in the eyes of others, and to a great extent in his or her own eyes, depends on the job that a person holds. One's occupation is not only a source of income; it is a definition of who one is.

Most occupations provide a gradual transition from apprenticeship to full career status. The steps that lead to becoming a physician, lawyer, accountant, or engineer are well marked; those through which one becomes a bricklayer, plumber, carpenter, or electrician are also fairly plain. There are institutions that facilitate entry into almost every skilled vocation, and others that protect the interests of persons already in it: professional schools, professional associations, trade schools, trade unions, licensing boards, employment agencies, political lobbies, and so on.

But what institutions can the young artist count on to establish and maintain occupational status? The obvious answer seems to be: none. There is something absurd about an American Artistic Association modeled after the American Medical Association, or an Artists Union to parallel the Teamsters Union, or an employment office for fine artists out of work. Indeed, can one think of a fine artist being out of work? Artists do not need institutional supports; they are supposed to be above such things; they are free spirits, autonomous, independent, and self-sufficient. As long as they paint and like what they are painting they are artists, and that is all that counts.

In reality, things are not that simple for young persons just out of art school. It is not enough to paint and enjoy their work if there is no one else to appreciate it. Even artists are not completely self-sufficient in this respect. Perhaps a very few can work in isolation and maintain their artistic identity with the support of only a small group of intimates. But almost all of those in our sample wanted to "show" their work and hoped that eventually society would recognize their talent.

One does not become an artist just by painting. To paint might be the only thing that matters subjectively. But to be able to earn a livelihood and to develop a self-concept as a bona fide artist distinct from a "sometime painter," artistic behavior is not sufficient. One must be legitimized by the appropriate social institutions.

In art as in other occupations the two issues are separate: The behavior necessary to perform the role is to a certain degree independent of the status that gives legitimacy to the role. A person who behaves like a physician, doing successful surgery and maintaining a satisfied practice, would immediately lose his status as a physician if it were discovered that he did not have a valid medical diploma. The best expert at plumbing or electricity would run into serious trouble if he used his skill without an appropriate license or union card. Whether a person is an effective teacher has little to do with whether he will get a teaching job; what counts is whether he has the seal of legitimacy bestowed by certification.

Perhaps business is a partial exception to this rule. In business, a person's actions are directly related to his status: success has its own legitimacy, and there is no need for other legitimation. But this is true only of the self-made businessman who starts without any capital. A person who works for a large firm, or one who is backed by strong creditors, is ipso facto recognized and legitimized by the institutions with which he is connected.

To attain legitimate status in a social role one must gain symbolic approval of his behavior in that role. It is not enough for a person to operate as a good surgeon or as a good artist. To be taken seriously, he must submit himself to the legitimation procedures of that role. Artistic legitimation may take widely different forms. Among the Mundugomor of New Guinea, for example, a boy born with his umbilical cord twisted around his neck is expected to become an artist when he grows up.

Whether he has talent or not, his paintings and carvings will be accepted as art while the work of someone more talented but born in a normal way will be ignored (Mead, 1935).

What institutions, then, bestow legitimacy on artists in our culture? During the Middle Ages and far into the Renaissance, artistic status was tied to rules of entry and of promotion closely enforced by guilds. At present, however, no formal institution is directly concerned with the young artist's career.

But the absence of formal institutions does not mean that the work of artists is free of societal evaluation and legitimation. A number of informal systems have emerged to regularize the relationships between artists and public. These systems played a decisive role during the five years after the former students left art school, and while they sought to establish themselves as independent artists. In the following pages, we shall try to reconstruct the early stages of the artist's progress as these emerged from the interviews.

Conflicting Requirements.   The first legitimating institution is of course the art school itself, even though it fulfills a different function for the artist than a school does for other professions. A Bachelor of Arts degree in Fine Arts has little effect on the holder's future as a painter or sculptor. At best, it allows entry into graduate school and hence might lead to a teaching job in high school or college. Art school might be indispensable as a socializing institution where young people learn what is involved in becoming an artist, but the certification it gives does not bestow artistic status in the sense that a school of law or medicine grants legal or medical status.

A number of informal institutions are much more significant in this respect. The first of these spontaneously developed mechanisms for the making of artists is the loft, a large room often in a vacated factory. The stated purpose for renting a loft is to have plenty of space in which to work. But the loft has outgrown its initial utilitarian purpose, and has become an important symbolic institution for launching young artists on their career.

When a person rents a loft, he is communicating the message that he is in earnest about becoming an artist. Since the art world is so unstructured, formal channels of information are not available for spreading the news of one's intention. The young artist cannot put an advertisement into a trade or professional paper, nor can he hang out a shingle. For his message to be effective, he must spread the word himself as widely as possible; to do so he invites to his loft everyone who is willing to come.

The essential decor of a loft includes finished canvasses stacked against the walls, and the work in progress prominently displayed. There are parties at least once a week; the more memorable they are, the more likely it is that the young artist's name will be widely known. At this stage the main need is for exposure, to be recognized as one who has committed himself to being an artist and is seriously at work. Among the people coming in and out of the loft, there might be a few potential customers. This is very important since developing a "following"—a group of people interested in purchasing his work—is a prerequisite for an artist's next professional step.

The loft is not just physical space. It is an informal institution that allows artists to get in touch with the public. A loft without parties and without visitors, a loft that is not known in artistic circles, is not a *loft* in this institutional sense.

Most of the young artists we studied who met with success after graduation started their careers in a loft. The six with the highest success scores had all rented lofts even before they left school. Most of them rented jointly with colleagues, but each had taken this step toward establishing a public identity as an artist while still a student. So far as we know, none of the unsuccessful former students did this. They also painted and sculpted. But they did it in private; their name and work were known only to a few close friends.

Nowadays the loft, or its equivalent, seems almost necessary to certify a person's entry into the role of fine artist. Yet this requirement entails a deep contradiction for the young artist. It demands behavior that is at odds with some of his most basic personality traits and values. Time and again, observations have shown that artists are withdrawn, self-sufficient, and introverted. They hold conventional economic and social values in low esteem. These traits and values are functional because they make possible a tolerance of the solitary and subjective conditions under which works of art are created. But a loft requires artists to be entrepreneurial and sociable. It requires them to be their own caterer, master of ceremonies, and public relations man. These demands made most of the successful artists in our sample uneasy; they were aware of the contradiction between the intrinsic need for solitude to practice art, and the extrinsic need for sociability to gain artistic status. After an initial success, some artists abandon their well-known lofts and continue their work in smaller, more private studios. But they are aware that they do so at great risk; unless they have already established followings and gallery contacts, the solution of the contradiction may mean the end of their careers. Some gifted students who realize that they have to pay this price for success cannot bear to do it, and therefore fail even the first step toward their intended career.

The second informal institution that helps bring an artist to the public eye and to establish his status is the art show. The extent to which an art show is able to legitimize an artist depends, of course, on the prestige of the show itself. At the lowest level are the sidewalk exhibitions, or "chicken-wire" shows, organized by neighborhood clubs, shopping centers, and so forth. Our successful artists felt that they were not likely to gain any reputation by participating in these. At best, they might attract some customers who could later develop into permanent buyers. But even this is unlikely; serious buyers rarely patronize "sidewalks." Exhibitors at these shows are likely to be amateurs, part-time artists, or those who have resigned themselves to local reputations. Those who harbor the hope of making it in the "legitimate" art world tend to shun chicken-wire shows as undignified and useless affairs.

A different kind of show is the one organized by a number of independent artists who decide to exhibit their work together. Several friends might decide on a common theme or a common style, select an appropriately intriguing title, and rent exhibition space in an art club or minor gallery. If they are lucky, they will attract enough attention to be written up by art critics in local papers. Many solid reputations have been established this way, from the Salon of the Independents in Paris that launched the Impressionists, to one of the artists we studied.

This young artist (S.06) made his reputation through a show that he arranged with four other artists. Even though it was a great success, still remembered in artistic circles and included in a recent written account of Chicago art, our artist was ambivalent about the show. Like the loft, the independent show requires organization, publicity, and salesmanship, all characteristics that go against the artist's grain. Moreover, if the group is successful, a paradoxical danger arises. The young artist becomes identified with the group and people expect him to perform according to the group image. His style might become restricted to a single set of successful problems, preventing the discovery of new ones; he runs the risk of being typed. Instead of being encouraged to keep working on his own "discovered problems," the young artist may be constrained to continue working on the "presented problems" defined for him by the group. In fact, S.06 left the newly developing "school" of which he had been one of the founders; he did not want "to be trapped by its success."

Finally, there are the institutional juried shows organized by major art associations and museums. If such a show is sponsored by a nationally known institution, it can bestow a great deal of legitimacy on an artist who is selected to exhibit in it. But juried shows are not easy to enter. The artist must know about deadlines and conditions of acceptance. The more he knows about the theme of the show and the ideology of the jury members, the better his chances for acceptance. Then he must submit slides of his work to the jury. If the slides pass muster, he will be invited to send along his paintings or sculptures. The artist must crate his work, and ship it to the jury. If they like his work, he will appear in the show; otherwise his materials will be recrated and shipped back at the artist's expense. Time and money are involved in this process, and for most of those who submit their work it will all be wasted.

The institution of the art show also clearly poses contradictions for a young artist. He must use social contacts, organizational skills, and economic judgment to exploit effectively the exhibition channels. These are all qualities he lacks, because they are the antithesis of the qualities that enabled him to become an artist in the first place. Yet if he wants to succeed, he must find ways of compromising between his personal preferences and the demands of the social milieu.

Perhaps the most crucial legitimating institution in the art world is the private art gallery. A person who gets a contract with a reputable gallery is sure to have achieved artistic status, at least for the time being. When his work is shown in a gallery it will automatically attract customers and critical attention. But very few artists reach this stage. A gallery dealer's business is to monitor the art scene. He or she listens to the gossip about artists, visits the most promising lofts, and keeps an eye on local shows. If he finds a young artist who seems to be committed and who has already developed a following of customers, he might ask him to send in slides of his work. Artists who have not begun to sell their work on their own will rarely be approached by a dealer. The average art gallery might consider closely the work of 150 to 200 new artists each year. Perhaps one or two artists of the crop of "promising" ones will be pursued further and eventually offered a contract.

If the young artist is lucky enough to be accepted by a gallery, a new set of contradictions comes into effect. The dealer, who knows what will sell, begins to make demands on his "property." He will drop by the artist's loft, look at his work, and shake his head. He will give advice on style and content, on the media to use, on the size that the work should be. He will set deadlines and production quotas. The young artist who has learned to treasure independence and self-sufficiency as conditions for producing art is now confronted by the need to follow the dealer's directions, and to compromise his standards. If he is not careful, the dealer will soon turn him from a problem finder into a problem solver.

In addition, the young artists report that a certain amount of business sense is required for dealing with the dealers. Some marginal firms will ask for up to 80 percent of the artists' sales as their share, and many items in the gallery's bill are open to bargaining. Even some of the best galleries have idiosyncratic accounting procedures. It might take many months, sometimes years, before the artist finds out that one of his works has been sold. He will have to ask over and over to be paid his share of the sale, because the gallery itself might have trouble collecting from customers, or simply because the galleries that deal with young artists are operating on thin budgets. Sometimes the gallery will pay a promising artist an advance on his future work. But even this arrangement creates tensions —the feeling of having mortgaged one's future work is not easy to live with. In any case, working with a gallery requires a managerial attitude and financial sophistication, requirements that run counter to the artist's previous training and expectations, and to some of his most salient personality traits and values.

Indeed, the dealer may undertake to "improve" the artist's personal image. He will encourage public appearances and suggest potentially profitable acquaintances. He might try to influence the artist's life style and behavior. This expected malleability, to adopt an artificial public role, is the very antithesis of what we know of the artist's personality and preferred life style.

It is no wonder that the young artists feel extremely ambivalent toward galleries. They recognize their importance in the scheme of things, and the successful artists learn to get along with them. But there is always some resentment about the compromises required. Several people in our sample claimed that they either never sought contacts with galleries, or that they rejected offers from them, or that they decided never again to work through a gallery after a first experience. But others admitted ruefully that although they recognized how much a gallery contract might threaten everything they believed in, it would be hypocritical for them to deny that they wanted it and hoped for one.

Out of this dissatisfaction with the existing channels of exhibition, some new forms have developed in recent years. Groups of artists have banded together and opened galleries to show their own work and that of their friends. Again, the task of promoting and merchandising one's work in a cooperative gallery requires talents that are usually missing from the artist's background.

Another step in the acquisition of an artistic role is to move to New York. Most members of the art world believe that unless a person is recognized in New York City, his artistic status remains at best marginal. For reasons that are too complex to explore here, the power to confer legitimacy is more centralized in art than in almost any other field. Florence in the early Renaissance, Rome later on, and Paris for several centuries afterward held virtual monopolies on the assignment of artistic status. In the nineteenth century a young painter or sculptor from Russia, England, the Americas, or anywhere else for that matter, had to go to Paris to find out how good he was. His artistic stature could be established only by Parisian dealers, critics, and patrons. At present it is New York that fulfills this function.

In our sample, four out of the six most successful artists eventually moved to New York. The remaining two were planning to make the move; they felt that their success depended on it. The reasons given for having to be in New York were varied, but they agreed on some central points. For one thing, artistic changes take shape in New York at least six months before they spread to the rest of the country. One artist (S.31), who had spent two years teaching art at the University of Minnesota before moving to New York, explained that one can find out what is happening in art from journals, but one cannot find out what is going to happen unless one lives in New York, where party gossip foreshadows new trends. As he said, "The new is what people are only just talking about; it's ideas that count, not products. One can see where it's at from magazines, but it's not the same thing as living it." As long as it is widely believed that only ideas developing in New York will determine the future, young artists will inevitably want to participate in the "New York Scene."

The young artists recognize the rationale for the monopolistic position that New York holds in conferring status. The superiority of the city as an art market is obvious. Yet they find it ironic that to attract the attention of Chicago buyers and dealers they have to leave Chicago. But moving to the center of action is just one more sign of a person's commitment to art. The dealer who knew an artist's work back home will take a second and more thoughtful look at it after the artist has moved to New York. "The kid must be serious after all," he thinks to himself, and the artist's status moves up a notch.

This institutional recognition, like all the previous ones, contains its own set of conflicts. When promising young artists feel that they have to move to New York, they contribute to at least three sociocultural processes that are at odds with their own beliefs. They exacerbate the competitiveness in the already crowded art world of New York. If they want to survive in it, they have to use a certain amount of aggressiveness, shrewdness, entrepreneurship, and one-upmanship—all qualities that, as we know, are foreign to their personality. Second, by paying attention to the trends, they risk becoming "trendy" themselves. And finally, by their presence in New York they confirm the city's preeminence in art, a circumstance they personally deplore.

Again it is paradoxical how success exacts a price from the young artist. To gain recognition, he must recognize the existing social system of art, which he finds disagreeable. Yet only those are legitimized, as a rule, who with their adherence to the legitimizing system help to maintain its legitimacy. What makes this situation so intractable is the difficulty to imagine any realistic alternatives. It is easy to visualize the confusion that would follow were New York to lose its standard-setting function. Who would know what is good or bad art? Everyone would have to decide for himself or herself what was worth admiring and what was not—clearly an untenable critical position. Sooner or later a new centralized set of values would have to emerge. What is wrong with New York's position in the art scene is not that it creates a monopoly on values, but that by so doing it forces artists into situations that are disruptive and self-defeating. Perhaps this cannot be helped under existing conditions, but it is felt as a severe problem by the beginning artist.

Instead of moving to New York, a young artist might decide to move to a provincial center. There are not many of these, but some of the older art colonies in New England, San Francisco, or the Southwest, confer a certain amount of status on the aspiring artist. So do those regional universities that have well-known art departments. In our sample, five of the six most successful artists spent time "in the provinces"; three of these later moved to New York, and the others are planning to follow. The alternative of settling down in Chicago was not considered viable by them. They felt that there were already too many good artists in the city, and not enough recognition to go around. Chicago lacked for them the high stakes of New York, or the immediate visibility they could achieve in a smaller place.

The problem with working on the faculty of a university, or in a rural art colony, is that life tends to be slow, the art tends to be inbred, and its practitioners tend to be either defensive or self-satisfied. As long as New York is out there, young artists in the provinces keep feeling that they are missing out on something. To a certain extent they are right. That one can sell paintings anywhere, and might more easily gain a following in Dubuque than in New York, is not the point. The young artist feels that national recognition, the permanent legitimation of his status as an artist, can only originate from New York. While there is still hope of becoming one of the masters of his generation, he will seek to find a place in the capital of art. Only after he has accepted a more restricted estimate of his status will he be able to feel relaxed outside New York, and in fact one of our more successful artists did return to Chicago after his "go at New York." Opting out of the race for immortality might lead to greater self-respect and deeper peace of mind, but in the here and now it also reduces the young artist's standing in the art world.

Moving away from one's home base presents other challenges as well. The new environment often has disorienting effects on the style and content of an artist's work. One young artist (S.22) had developed in Chicago a body of paintings that were inspired by problems of urban life. His canvasses were filled with technological symbols: gears, machines, neon signs, skyscrapers, and so on. When, after graduation, he left the city for a farm near the University of Georgia where he took a teaching position, his previous concerns appeared irrelevant. It took him two years to find a new set of ideas to work with, and at the time of our follow-up he was still unsure whether the alternatives he found were meaningful to him.

A similar experience was recounted by another artist (S.27), who went to teach in the South West. His work was affected by the strong lights and colors of the desert. As a reaction to the overwhelming impression that the environment was making on him, he toned down the range of his palette and developed a colorless, rigid style, a style he did not like but could not help under the circumstances. It also took him more than two years, and another change of location, to regain control over his style.

Another case (S.10) is also to the point. In Chicago this student had done paintings and sculptures of average size, and was developing a personal style of his own. After leaving art school, he went to the University of Ohio as a graduate student and teaching assistant. There he had access to far more space to work in. His creations expanded in size to fill the available space. He kept experimenting with larger and larger sculptures and paintings. Two years later he moved back to Chicago and rented a large loft on the West Side, which he soon filled with gargantuan-scaled work. But his 50-foot canvasses and large pieces of sculpture could not be taken out through the doors of the studio, and neither galleries nor customers were willing to have them hauled out by a crane through the skylight. Finally he moved again, this time to New York City, taking with him pieces that could be dismantled for shipping, and leaving the rest in the abandoned loft.

Critics who review the work of artists for newspapers and magazines perform an intermediate legitimating function. They do not bestow status directly, since to qualify for a review an artist must already have enough of a following to have his work shown in an exhibit or a gallery, but a few good notices from reputable critics strengthen the artist's standing considerably. The danger inherent in critical legitimation is again the loss of autonomy. The young artists in our sample complained that the critics' expectations were based on different principles than the ones that motivated their work; they felt that the price of recognition was often compromise with their own artistic goals.

There are other institutions that legitimize a person's artistic status, but they only touch a small minority of artists in any given generation. The final stamp of recognition is purchase of a work by a major museum. Museums are the shrines that record a culture's choice of values, and the works they contain represent the artistic benchmarks of an age. One of the young artists in the group has qualified for this recognition. When the work of an artist rates an article in a national art magazine, he can also feel that his professional identity is assured. Art books devoted to one person, or a position as artist in residence on a major campus, are also unmistakable signs of having achieved the higher rungs of success.

All the institutions that have evolved to help the artist in his quest for recognition also produce strong conflicts. Of course role conflict is not unique to the artistic profession. Young doctors imbued with humanitarian values have a difficult time adjusting to the grim demands of a profession that requires many actions at variance with an ideal of service to mankind. Young teachers with notions of a Socratic education or pure research have to adapt to the realities of crowded classrooms or publication requirements. Police officers trained to uphold the law and help the community often find themselves caught in pressures that force on them favoritism and collusion.

The artist has his own personal idea of what is a meaningful product. Society, through its various institutions, develops its own notion of what it needs from the artist. Unless the artist compromises by adapting his vision to society's demands, society will withhold recognition of his status. The conflict has existed at all times and in all places, but may be uniquely acute in the United States at the close of the twentieth century. The contradictions are less obvious but they cut deeper. In China or Stalinist Russia, as in the Middle Ages, a young artist would not expect to be rewarded for being original, self-sufficient, or asocial. From the first days of his training he knows that he must work within a system of beliefs sanctioned by the culture. It is the culture that presents the problem for the artist to solve. There is no need for him to find out what the problem should be; in fact it is safer for him not even to try. The artistic problem is defined by societal needs. In New Guinea this may involve representing ancestral spirits in the correct relationships to one another; in Soviet Russia it may mean motivating young people to become tractor drivers in Siberia. The tasks of the artists is translating these "problems" into visual form. This situation of course also creates conflicts, but they are perhaps easier to grapple with, because the issues are relatively clear and out in the open. Our artists are encouraged to be subjective and independent, yet at each step of their career subtle forces pull them back toward conformity. To compound the paradox, the conformity that is asked of them is undefined, shifting, and seemingly devoid of justification.

Conflicts in the Cultural Context.   When historians of civilization, scholars like Spengler, Toynbee, or Sorokin, come to writing the sections in their work that deal with modern art, their scorn is difficult to contain. They decry the artist's loss of values, his loss of faith, his sensuality, his lack of principle. They believe, like the majority of Middle Americans do, that art is being destroyed by incompetent artists.

From our young artists' point of view, the situation looks exactly reversed. They say they would be happy to spend their lives painting Pre-Raphaelite Madonnas or Byzantine icons if doing so made sense. But they know that Madonnas and icons are no longer part of the symbolic reality on which culture is based. They would gladly embrace a faith and serve a set of principles if there was one available. They cannot be blamed for not being able to create a faith ex nihilo. The few principles that are generally accepted in our society, such as electoral democracy, private ownership, or civil liberties, are poor subjects for inspired pictorial representation.

Historical periods that produce great art tend to have a rich store of universally shared symbols for artists to draw on. The head of Anubis suggested to the Egyptian viewer many mysterious yet fathomable meanings that are beyond the expressive range of a giant can of Campbell soup. European artists were able to work for centuries with the elements of a symbolic universe that had meaning for people from every walk of life. The same has been true for the great Oriental civilizations. But contemporary artists are painfully aware that what they try to communicate will be understood only by a few people, and perhaps only for a few years. They know that they cannot use a symbolic language of any permanence, because there is no agreed-upon system of meanings in our culture.

Or perhaps, to state the matter differently, there *is* after all a system of meanings in our culture, but its unprecedented character places a heavy burden on the practicing artist. It might be said that the main element of our symbolic universe is a profound belief in progress, or perhaps more exactly, change. Just as the Egyptians based their ultimate hope on permanence, we base ours on change. That would explain why we prize originality so much, why we force artists to produce always new symbols, to use ever novel styles. Modern art would then be the visual representation of the one reality that our elite believes in, the reality of progression, if not progress. Ironically, most artists and critics believe that modern art is a reaction against society and its values. It might well be that instead it actually buttresses the deepest value of our culture. The more "revolutionary" art tries to be, the more in the mainstream of society it is. After all, it shows that things are changing, and we believe that change is necessary. We need only to label the change "good," and then we have progress. So the artist produces his revolutionary statement, the critic puts his seal of approval on it, and then we rest content because we have taken another great stride for mankind.

The young artists we interviewed were all asking a question familiar to contemporary art critics: Is art possible in our time? (Schulze, 1972; Rosenberg, 1973) Whether it is really true that their work supports the symbolic universe or not, most artists feel alienated from the work they produce. Either because his own faith in progress is wavering, or because he feels that his work does not reflect progress adequately, none of the artists interviewed felt satisfied with what his art could do.

It is important to note that this dissatisfaction is not related to the role conflicts described earlier. This particular malaise is not due to the con-tradictions forced on the artist by the social institutions responsible for his legitimation. It is due instead to a deeper cause, reflecting a more general problem—a problem that is not social in nature, but rather cultural. It is not something that could be solved through institutional change. To solve this problem we would have to agree on a set of priorities, values, and beliefs, and create a symbolic reality that was meaningful to all. Then the artist would have access to a set of common meanings that he could refer to in his art. As it is, the artist's efforts to communicate his vision are frustrated by the lack of an expressive vocabulary of any universality or permanence. And it is not possible to have a generally accepted vocabul-ary for meanings as long as there is no agreement on what is meaningful, and why.

One of our most successful artists (S.31) talked for a long time about this problem. He feels that his work—paintings of magnified fabric patterns—and that of his friends is "hideously ritualistic." He finds most of contemporary art "distressing." Abstract art is a cheap solution —everybody can do it, and it is too easy to use an abstract style without having anything to say. He thinks that postexpressionistic art relies too heavily on symbols, yet the symbols are forced; they lack the direct simplicity of those used in former times. Modern art reflects itself or the art of the years just past, rather than "where people are at." Artists are not inspired by reality any longer but only by one another. This artist envies the cultural atmosphere in which David painted almost two centuries ago. He feels that the smooth realism of David is more complex than anything being done now. It is "fantastically interesting, neither fresh nor old—as if it just got there."

He told us further that "the business of the artist is to sit down and ask, What am I going to do next?" He, however, feels that there are not many options. One can either stop painting, or react to what other artists are doing; there is no other source of inspiration left. Neither external nor internal reality can provide shared symbols or experiences: The only reality with any common currency is the limited reality of the art world itself. Art is not only for the sake of art, but it originates in art, it is about art, and it only results in more art. It is a closed system with few references outside itself.

The latest attempt to evade this impasse is for artists to deemphasize the importance of their work. Since the painting cannot communicate, it should be ignored; instead of the art object itself, the important thing becomes the artist's experience, feelings, and vision. As in action painting, it is the process that counts, not the product. But since the process must be objectified to prove its existence, the artist unfortunately has to produce something. Hence he is constantly searching for objects he can make that have self-evident meaning, a direct impact untainted by the breakdown in symbolic communication. For instance, one of the dreams of this artist is to cast a 30-room Victorian mansion. He figures that to do this in urethane foam would cost only about $20,000—but then it would not have the permanence of cement, which is what he would really like to use.

In some ways it would be a brilliant solution: There are few things as self-evident as a 30-room house. A Victorian house, and one cast in cement, can produce nice symbolic associations. But of course there is one fault in this solution: It is impossible to carry out.

The problem is compounded by strong doubts about the efficacy of the media the artist uses to express himself. Not only is the reality to be communicated unclear, but the means of communication are suspect. As one of the more successful artists (S.06) says, and he speaks for others of his group, "The possibilities of painting are exhausted. The world of painting is closed and artificial. After you have seen your millionth painting, you are sick of it. People are becoming increasingly restless with the useless, reserved, artificial world created by a canvas hanging on the wall."

Another relatively successful painter (S.17) feels that "in the fifteenth and sixteenth centuries there was more validity to painting, because it was the only thing to do." That he is still using materials developed three centuries ago instead of mastering the new materials made available by technology bothers him. "Art is wedded to science," he says, but he "has no feeling for modern materials." As a result, he seriously questions whether he deserves recognition as an artist.

To cope with this crisis of confidence in the arsenal of materials, many of the former students are contemplating drastic steps. Three of the six most successful artists, and others as well, hope to work with film. Movies seem to offer a solution both to the message problem and to the medium problem. They reach larger audiences that are socialized to the expressive vocabulary of movies. As a medium, film is modern, flexible, and allows the artist to work with the time dimension, which is not available in painting or sculpture. But filmmaking is expensive, and the artists are ambivalent about the constraints involved in financing and producing a movie. Moreover, they are not interested in low-budget, underground "flicks," which they all think are "awful"; they would like to be involved in legitimate motion pictures with mass appeal.

Then there is the rest of the modern arsenal of visual media: laser beams, fluorescent lights, video, electronic devices, computerized mobiles, epoxy, sprays, sound-light combinations, fiberglass, masonite, aluminum, glazes, and any other technological discovery that can be used to project a visual stimulus. Some of the artists swear by these new products, and feel it is their duty to master their use. But when they do, they often realize that "everybody else is trying to use the latest gimmick," and that their ability to communicate is not necessarily improved by the new materials. Ironically, those who rely on old-fashioned techniques feel guilty for not using the available new resources.

Despite these conflicts and contradictions, at least one-third of the former students in our sample are still producing art, and continue to consider themselves artists. A few are even returning to conventional painting or sculpture after a fling with movies, photography, or electronic media. And although only one person we interviewed said that in five years he expected to be doing the same kind of art work he was doing now, all of the young artists were planning to remain in art. They hoped "to have more resources and freedom," or "to have the chance to do my own thing, but on a bigger scale," or "to use any medium that's appropriate."

So while the artist worries about what to say and how to say it, he may in fact be saying exactly what people need to hear. The very indecisions that tear at the artist are responsible for the constant changes in his work, and hence produce the message that is demanded and rewarded by contemporary society. Like the oyster that builds a pearl around its pain, the artist paints his canvas to cope with his conflicts.

But on second thought, the young artists say, it might be better for the artist not to see the situation in this light. It only increases his feelings of being misunderstood, of being exploited by impersonal forces. It is not very pleasant to realize that your confusion is a product appreciated by others, that your function in society is to be bewildered, and that your tentative responses to the bewilderment are going to be relabeled as forward steps in the process of culture.

This is not to say, of course, that all a person needs to succeed as an artist is to produce works that have never been seen before. There are other prerequisites—working within the social system of art, for example, and applying what we have called in preceding chapters a problem-finding approach.

As for the first of these requirements, an already legitimized artist can do anything and call it art with relative impunity. He can wrap a few miles of Australian shoreline in plastic and call it art, or exhibit a sandbox full of ants and be taken seriously by art critics and museum curators. Once he has been granted status by the legitimizing institutions, he can in turn bestow the status of art on any object or action. The process is not unlike the sacramental powers that the Church vests in its clergy.

On the other hand, any work produced by a nonartist, however accomplished, will remain a curio until it is recognized and blessed by a representative of the artistic hierarchy. The situation is well summarized by the art critic Franz Schulze (1972):

> Nothing is more likely to send the ordinarily broadminded official art world into a towering snit of unbroadmindedness than an artist who achieves success without its benediction. The toniest galleries and museums may stage the most egregious follies without raising so much as half a critical hackle in the art journals, but let some outcast bourgeois hero like Andrew Wyeth or Norman Rockwell get a two-page spread in Life Magazine, and the establishment esthetes will sound off like Savonarola haranguing the Florentines.

As this excerpt suggests, there are alternative channels of legitimation to success. Painters might become "bourgeois heroes" if they are recognized by the mass media or if they strike a chord in the sensibilities of the affluent. It is likely that permanent fame will depend on the official imprimatur of the art world; but temporary success can be reached by alternative routes.

As for the requirement that works of art depend on talent, or original thought, or creativity, or some other outstanding human quality, the evidence is admittedly less overwhelming. There is really no way to prove that the most highly praised and priced works of the past 50 years are in any way more original or creative than those passed over by critics and buyers. The criteria of assessment used in art are all open to the charge of being based on "after the fact" rationalization. As a number of the young artists charged, it is not that we appreciate good art, but call good art that which we appreciate. And what we appreciate is dictated by the convergence of many needs, most of them unconscious, or at least not well understood. If this is true, then the art that passes muster at any given time is the one that happens to fit the needs of the public not because of any exceptional quality of the artist, but because of a fortuitous coincidence between his product and the public need.

There is no way to tell whether this view of artistic gifts is true. All we know is that to become an artist in our time, a certain constellation of personality traits and values appears to help. And we know further that to become successful, it helps an artist to be open to novelty, it helps to look at problems as if they had never been formulated before. It helps if the artist is curious about his environment, if he approaches objects from a multisensory perspective. It helps if he can work with a subliminal goal in mind, painting or sculpting with a deep purpose that is below the threshold of his awareness.

There are, then, some objectively recognizable qualities that artists who survive in the art world share. There is no way to know whether these qualities are necessary to produce "good" art anywhere and anytime. It is possible that each culture selects and nurtures a different type of artist, as it evolves a different style of art.

Patterns of Development in the Artistic Role. Given the nature of the institutional channels for artistic legitimation, young people who intend to be recognized as artists will have essentially similar career lines. At the same time, because of the highly informal and loosely integrated structure of artistic institutions, the timing and the sequencing of steps in career development will be flexible.

This section will deal in more detail with the occupational choices confronting the nine persons who by our criterion had achieved a moderate-to-good success in art five or six years after graduation from art school.* The other 22 former students who had met with little or no

*Those young artists who had been juniors in art school at the beginning of our study had been graduated six years before the follow-up phase; those who had been sophomores had been out of school for only five years.

success will be left out at this stage. That 29 percent of the initial sample has been able to achieve any status as an artist is important in itself. Now, however, we want to focus on the ways that they have found to develop for themselves an artistic identity.

The first thing to keep in mind is that none of the young artists could support himself exclusively on the income he gets from his vocation. Even the most successful one, who has had gallery contracts for years, whose work has been bought by a museum and favorably reviewed by critics, hopes to earn only half of his moderate income from the sale of his work. The highest sum anyone earned from art sales, in his best year, was just over 3000 dollars. But this source of revenue cannot be counted on, as it can vary sharply from one year to the next.

Young artists must find some permanent work to supplement their income, no matter how much they would prefer to devote their time solely to art. In the first years after graduation, the work they do is often unrelated to art (three of the nine artists had such jobs), but most often it involves working at the fringes of the art world. Four out of the nine at one time or another worked for art galleries, most of the time helping to crate or hang paintings, but in one case as assistant manager.

Five went on to graduate school in art, partly as a respite from survival pressures, partly to get a degree for teaching art later in a relatively comfortable position. By the time five years had elapsed after graduation, eight of the nine artists were teaching art to supplement their incomes, and the ninth was a consultant to a trade journal.

But art teaching is also an impermanent role for people whose main interest lies elsewhere. The young fine artist is not going to devote his energies to making a cozy berth for himself on an art faculty. He keeps moving from job to job either because he cannot get along with his more entrenched colleagues whose vocation is to teach art, or because they cannot get along with him.

The artist who teaches still has to have other sources of income, both to round out the meager part-time teaching salary and to tide him over between academic jobs. He might even be working at three or four jobs simultaneously, and seeing each as a drain on energies that should be used for creating art. He might be teaching at two different schools, working at a gallery, printing etchings for a fee, and in extremis taking on a freelance commercial job.

All of these activities are in a sense irrelevant to the artist's role, in that they do not advance his status in the eyes of the legitimizing institutions.

Moreover, they take away precious time from the essential task of producing a body of personally meaningful work. Yet these activities are also necessary, since in their absence the artist would be unable to retain a foothold in the art world and practice his vocation in his free time.

A closer look at the career line of one of the artists (S.31) shows how it is possible to manage artistic progress and earn money at the same time, although the two activities often demand contradictory performance. When this artist was graduated from art school, he was already relatively well known for his work. Nevertheless, he decided to stay in school two more years to obtain a Master of Fine Arts degree, rather than trying to start his career at once. The school provided him with studio space and the opportunity to build up a collection of his own work. His father paid for his expensive art supplies (the young man painted very large canvasses). To make a living while he attended graduate school, he operated a punch press, a drill, did die-casting, and worked as a shipping clerk. These jobs took up most of his evenings, as well as the summer months for two years. During this period he exhibited in several group shows in the Midwest, and had his first one-man show. Despite these promising beginnings, his budding status brought practically no material advantages; he sold very few of his paintings.

Two years later, with the graduate degree in his pocket, the artist wanted to move to New York City, even though he lacked the money to start out in style. But to avoid the draft, he accepted a teaching job instead. To get a decent position teaching art, connections and recommendations are perhaps more important than in any other field. The director of a museum where he had exhibited recommended him to the dean of an art school. As is usual in such cases, the young man sent color slides of his paintings to the dean; the latter liked his work and he was hired.

He spent the next two years in Minnesota, in a pleasant outdoor atmosphere with other congenial young artists. Life was easy, the income adequate; he was able to marry and settle down. In these two years, he earned $4500 from sales of his work. But there were disadvantages: He felt that teaching responsibilities and concerns with academic routine were turning him into a mechanic. Moreover he felt too comfortable, with little motivation to do better. The lack of motivation was due to a sense of futility; he felt that his provincial teaching post made it almost impossible for him to show on a national level. There was no way for him to attract the attention that would legitimize his full artistic status.

He then did what he wanted to do all along—move to New York in quest of recognition. As in the other cases we studied, adjustment to the highly competitive world of New York art was traumatic. It took the artist almost two years "to get out from under financially" after the initial investment in his new loft was made. During this prolonged period spent searching for an adequate place in which to work, his output dropped dramatically. For months he had little energy left to paint.

In the meantime, he supported himself mainly with a part-time job teaching Environmental Studies (six hours twice a week) and with his wife's income as a social worker. Their savings had gone into the down payment for the loft. Making it habitable and paying for the necessary materials and supplies required every penny of their joint income.

Two years after moving to New York, he was getting close to the moment of truth. He would either start painting in earnest again, find himself a gallery, and resume the dual process of working for money and for art; or he would get caught more and more by survival demands, and postpone forever the resumption of his artistic production. If he stops painting consistently, he will probably continue to live on the margins of the art world. Teaching art, once a means toward affording his true vocation, might become a substitute vocation. He would still paint, his friends will still consider him an artist, once in a while he might still show his works and sell some of them. But without the steady, unremitting dedication to painting—with all the incidental interpersonal maneuverings involved in attracting attention—the young artist slips out very easily from the arena where artistic reputations are established. All the young artists agreed, one cannot let anything interfere with the steady output of art. Once the spell is broken, it is very difficult to recoup one's courage, and to recover the attention of the world.

This brief sketch could serve as a blueprint for the "professional" development of almost all the young artists who have pursued their vocation. Perhaps the only atypical part of this particular artist's story is that he has never worked for a gallery. Like all the others, six years after graduation he is at a crucial stage, poised between striving for success as an independent artist, and accepting a more secure occupation which, fulfilling as it might become personally, would bar him from the achievement to which he aspired when he entered art school.

It is at this stage that the young artists must confront the Tocquevillean paradox in our culture, a paradox that is felt especially by persons dedicated to art. The personalistic, equalitarian ideology that imbues our value system proclaims that fame and social recognition are irrelevant, corrupting, and invidious. In painting, what counts is the inner experience; every artist is as good as all others, so long as he is honest with himself and tries to do his best. Yet, at the same time, the history of art with its few semidivine geniuses; the social organization of art with its few successes and many failures; the competition for the attention of critics, curators, galleries, buyers, and so on—all of these concrete pressures contradict the ideology that places emphasis on equality and inner satisfaction.

Of course, the young artists are aware that it is always possible to stop heeding the call of fame. One can step out of the competition, and paint only for one's own pleasure. There is a price to pay for this solution, too. None of the young artists who tried it found the peace they were hoping for. Perhaps they had been socialized too deeply into depending on external rewards, or perhaps this problem cannot be resolved by choosing either horn of the dilemma. The fact is, those who had opted for what the Greeks would call the "idiotic" life felt hemmed in by it. Dissatisfied by the futility of their self-imposed seclusion, they soon returned to the fray.

A person who plans to devote his life to art is likely to encounter three main sets of obstacles which will threaten the integrity of his art and of his mind. The most concrete of these are the contradictions built into the social institutions that lead to artistic status. The loft, the exhibition channels, the galleries, the New York art scene are all necessary steps a serious artist must learn to negotiate. Yet each one of these institutions requires a kind of behavior that runs counter to the artist's deep-seated values and personality traits. He is aloof and withdrawn, and must be sociable; he is shy and sensitive, and must promote himself; he is disinterested in money, and must learn to fend for himself in what seems a financial jungle; he is independent, and must take on images that others have prepared for him. Perhaps more important, subtle pressures threaten to change him from a free discoverer into a routine problem solver. If he is not alert, the necessary interaction with the agencies that make his work possible will end by destroying the very core of the work, its originality.

The second set of obstacles is less tangible, but no less real. These are the rents in the "seamless web" of culture: the segregation of values, beliefs, and experiences which makes for a breakdown of communication between different segments of society. Rightly or wrongly, young artists feel isolated from the rest of mankind, unable to share their concerns. They would like to communicate, but cannot find appropriate means to do so. Visual symbols lack common currency, no one style is accepted by a stable majority, no medium of visual expression is inevitably right. The cumulative impact of these conditions saps the artist's self-confidence, and tends to induce a feeling of cynical helplessness. Like a man in a nightmare who keeps shouting while none around him notices, the artist feels impotent to reach his audience.

Finally there is the set of obstacles which is not so much the fault of malfunctioning social institutions or of a specific cultural crisis, but is built into the very center of the artistic role. This is the tension between the intrinsic and the extrinsic aspects of the process. On the one hand, making a painting or a sculpture should be its own reward. A person should be happy just because of the pleasure inherent in the action. He ought not to be concerned whether his work will be liked by others, or even whether it will be preserved. On the other hand, as our young artists confessed, each person also hopes to achieve fame in the bargain. And perhaps wealth; after all, why not? So he will do what he can to get the attention and the approval of others for his work. This leads to competition with other artists, and possibly to other compromises. Subtly the emphasis shifts from concern for painting to concern for the external rewards that painting might get. In this process the artist risks losing his unique identity. It becomes easy for him to change from a creative artist bent on defining the problems of existence, into a talented draftsman who *knows* what the real meaning of life is—namely wealth, power, and fame.

Are these unavoidable conflicts that confront a man who wants to become an artist any more stressful than those awaiting anyone else? Are they just particular cases of the universal problem of social existence which every maturing individual must solve in the course of his life? In some ways, of course, it would seem that the young artist is exposed to unusually harsh tensions in his social environment. Doctors, army officers, factory workers, people in business would seem to have far fewer contradictions inherent in their roles. *What* they have to do, *how* they should do it, and *why* their work is needed is usually clear. The artist cannot take for granted anything. But since this struggle to preserve one's character and vision may reward the artist with the achievement of creative resolutions, on balance, his lot has its compensations. The conflicts he must face are more severe, but the very conditions in his social environment that are responsible for this also allow him to painfully carve out for himself an independence that can compensate for much ordinary hardship.

CHAPTER 13

■

Becoming an Artist

One of the most intriguing enigmas about creative people is the origin of their motivation. Biographers delve into the early experiences of the artist for the source of his inspiration; depth psychologists seek out fascinating events in infancy for the key to his creativity. Legends describing the exceptional childhood of artists abound. The tales are almost always based on recollections gathered after the artist had achieved success—in most cases after his death. Inevitably, the accounts are prejudiced by the propensity to establish logical continuity between present and past.

Since our first interviews with young artists took place while they were art students, the retrospective accounts of early childhood we recorded are much closer in time to the actual events and thus less liable to distortion than are most biographical accounts. We also have subsequent interviews with some of the same students who attained a measure of success after leaving school. These accounts are not retrospective; they are contemporaneous with the events that are being reported. From these interviews we hoped to construct the pattern of socialization into art. The central questions are: How does one become a fine artist? How does one become a creative problem finder?

Early Childhood. It is often thought that artists are marked by signs of an exceptional destiny at an early age. Either the infant experiences some traumatic event that bends his temperament in the direction of art, or as a

208

child he shows unusual talent, which is then carefully nurtured until it blooms into full accomplishment. There are many archetypal—and perhaps apocryphal—stories to this effect: The kite that thrust its tail between Leonardo's lips, the discovery of young Giotto drawing beautiful pictures on boulders in the pasture where he was tending sheep.

We were unable to find in the early lives of our young artists any incident that served by itself as an unmistakable sign of an impending artistic vocation. Emotional crises that seemed to stimulate the beginnings of artistic expression could be traced, but these appear more as temporary coping mechanisms than as the outburst of a clear and permanent talent. Under stress, the future artists turned to drawing; yet neither they nor their parents saw this as the beginning of a vocation. In several cases, enrollment in art school and the decision to become an artist seemed more a matter of accident than of rational planning.

The backgrounds described in the interviews show only a chance design at first. There is no clear message in the record saying: This child will be an artist. Instead of finding an inevitable destiny springing from a single source, we began to make out a highly complex formative process—innumerable events slowly building up to a final commitment. Instead of the superficially satisfying picture of a calling that attracts the artist with the finality of a divine order, we find an intricate web of actions and reactions, which sometimes seem not so much engineered as fortuitous.

The artist as child, like other children, draws cartoon characters, copies comic-book heroes, and makes caricatures of his friends and foes. Most of the young artists insisted that although their first attempts were not substantially better than those of other children, their drawings were noticed more and praised more. He may be an eldest son and therefore received more attention, or someone in the family may be interested in art. Perhaps he has simply found no other way of attracting attention. In this sense, the ability to draw becomes an adaptive skill for some children, just as for others physical toughness, intelligence, or good looks become a preferred way of controlling the environment.

The first memories of artistic expression take many forms. Most of the young artists recall beginning to draw more or less self-consciously when they were six to eight years old; often the recollection is tied to a specific event involving feelings of loneliness.

One young artist, Robert, remembers that when he was about seven his mother had to take up employment and was away from home most of the day. At the same time, he developed measles and had to remain in bed for several days—alone. To make his isolation more tolerable, his mother gave him a giant set of watercolors and paper to paint on. By the second day Robert ran out of paper, and in his boredom began to decorate the bed sheets with his colors. His mother did not mind this too much, and since she forgot to buy more paper, Robert went on to paint the walls. By the time the measles were over, no wall was unpainted in the room.

This early memory exemplifies one of the adaptive possibilities of visual expression: For a person who is lonely and helpless, the ability to create visual images is a sign that he exists, that he can change and control his environment. All children must at one time or another feel the sense of reassurance that Robert got from personalizing his room. But while most of them find other, more congenial and reliable ways of controlling the environment, Robert and the other young artists learn to rely more and more on art. As one of our artists said, he paints in order to "make a world of his own."

Another example of the first stirrings of artistic expression is the early drawing by Jan. Until he was seven years old, he lived on an island farm in Northern Europe. Jan remembers the place as a bucolic paradise. He spent most of his time scrambling for mushrooms and strawberries, surrounded by "water, sun, grass, animals," and "sacred trees." The end of paradise came when Jan was five. His mother gave birth to another son and abruptly shifted her attention to the baby. Jan's first memory of the act of drawing is a scene of his mother doing a sketch of the sleeping baby. After this time Jan himself began to draw on "every available scrap of paper," and he recalls that people commented favorably on his work. Between the ages of 8 and 12 he became fascinated with the theater and built innumerable stage settings with paper and glue. He also made plates and cups out of baked clay, which attracted attention. Jan still remembers with pleasure how when he was eight a visiting uncle borrowed one of Jan's plates so that he could show it to his friends back home.

Jan's memories suggest how a child who feels threatened may turn to art as a way of reestablishing a feeling of competence. In this case the threat was due to the birth of a sibling. Nor was this an isolated instance; most of the successful artists in this sample are first-born sons and a number of them recalled that the beginning of intensive drawing activity coincided with the birth of a sibling.

While mothers are remembered as warm and close—at least during the first half dozen years—the artists with few exceptions have harsh memories of their fathers. Jan describes his father as "stern," "ambivalent," "fluctuating," and "ready to beat" him without provocation. Another successful artist in the group reports his father as an "odd, moody, quick-tempered bastard," who beat his son fairly often. A third remembers his father as formal, "far away like India," and semi-alcoholic.

It is difficult to know how much these memories of a cruel father have been colored by the Oedipal scenario, which is perhaps de rigeur nowadays. It seems clear, however, that when the young artists were adapting to the balance of forces in the family, they used art as a way of identifying with the mother and at the same time establishing their own competence and independence from the father.

School Years.   Elementary school is remembered as a bleak experience by almost all the artists. Ron, who turned out to be the most successful one in the group, stuttered badly when he entered school, and felt that the other children made a scapegoat of him because of his impairment. Characteristically, he remembers "drawing pictures all the time" in school, and slowly gaining some measure of recognition for them. He drew caricatures of the boys who tormented him, which sometimes silenced them. Drawing became both a demonstration of competence and a defense against aggression. Moreover, teachers began to rely on his emerging skills and encouraged him by asking for posters, teaching aids, layouts, and mock-ups.

The effect of the admiration of the other children and the requests of the teachers on the development of artistic skills can hardly be overstated. Practically all the artists recall how they were able to amuse or impress their schoolmates with their sketches. They all remember being asked to design and build things for their teachers.

Again, however, one has the impression these youngsters had discovered a skill, not a full-blown "gift" that established their artistic identity once and for all. While other children were experimenting with baseball, arithmetic, popularity, and perhaps also drawing as ways to establish their reputation in the small world of the school, the future artists were devoting most of their energy to drawing as a way of establishing their identity. Although this is impossible to prove, it seems, at least by their own account, that what made them special was not so much a greater skill but a greater dedication and hence a more consistent and predictable output of visual products. With time, of course, this led to greater skill also. By then these children were differentiated from their fellows by competence as well as persistence.

High school is remembered as only slightly more pleasant than elementary school. Sports, which are the main way of establishing competence for most boys, were usually alien and threatening for the artists. Tom recalls his first (and last) venture to the football field; he had put on his shoulder pads backwards, and retreated to the dressing room pursued by the laughter of the coach and the teammates.

Besides continuing to produce drawings, stage settings, and posters, most of the young artists became involved in crafts that required the careful use of hands and a taste for design. They built models of airplanes, furniture, and antique cars.

High school was also the time when some of the parents began worrying that their sons were not turning out as they had hoped. Ed's parents, who thought his paintings "pretty" when he was in elementary school, became "uptight" when they realized that he was in earnest about art. Ed reports, "Because they were Catholics they thought painters only did naked ladies, so they sent me to a convent school." In Ed's opinion, "The school was terrible." He resented the rote learning, the discipline, the ubiquitous statues of Jesus. His only relief was provided by the sensuous stimuli: he remembers "tripping" over the colors of the stained glass windows, the smell of the incense, the aesthetically pleasing rituals that he enacted as an altar boy.

The high school years are a time to establish a sense of one's self, to take a stance toward life. Like other adolescents, the young artists were uncertain about their ultimate vocation and identity. Despite their manifest aptitude in art, most of them did not think of themselves as potential artists until they had been graduated from high school. Under family pressure, they thought of becoming architects, engineers, mechanics, businessmen—everything, in fact, except full-time artists. Yet they continued to develop their skills in the one area where they felt competent; several attended courses at the Junior School of the Art Institute.

During this period the function of art as a means of formulating and solving problems appears explicitly. Even before the high school years, drawing had served a rudimentary problem-solving purpose—to reduce loneliness, to attract attention, to prove one's competence. But by adolescence, the problems that are formulated and solved through art become more complex and less obvious. The work becomes more expressive and less defensive.

Jan, for instance, tells at some length how he had been hoping while in high school that art would help him "to understand the universal order." He was looking to art for a set of rules that would give direction and meaning to his life, which after the shock of immigration to the United States he felt to be "fractured and confused." Uprooted from his culture and its values, he expected art to provide him with a set of principles that would transcend particular cultural values. At this point in his life, the main dilemma was the confusion produced by a new environment. Art, with which he was already familiar, seemed to provide a way of formulating this vaguely felt problem and to suggest a solution.

A different problem confronted Tom as an adolescent. All the male members of his family were highly skilled and independent craftsmen, including his father, who went his own way, stubborn and strong, leaving Tom free to do as he wanted. Yet Tom felt that his father was silently critical, and the more he was left alone to do as he wanted, the more Tom wanted to impress his father and be accepted by him. Tom's ambivalent feelings were still evident in the interview. He often mentioned his father in connection with his work, which he described as having "hints of violence, a peculiar energy in them." Many of his sculptures consist of thickets of sharp blades, some stationary, others moving, that are threatening and menacing, "ambiguous and efficient."

The main function of art for Tom was to help him formulate and perhaps resolve in visual terms a problamatic relationship with his father. The ambiguity, the violence, the efficiency, and the threat of his work were the concrete representations of his feelings toward the father, which also involved issues of independence and identity. By controlling, manipulating, and experimenting with these highly charged visual elements, Tom was expressing and trying to cope with the salient problematic force in his life. These symbolic transformations were not conscious; if they had been, Tom's problem would have become a presented problem.

It is precisely because Tom was unaware of the connection between his intangible feelings for his father and the tangible characteristics of his work that he was able to explore creatively both his complex feelings and the various ways that these could be represented visually. If he had consciously decided to represent visually the problem he was having with his father, he would probably have resorted to conventional, readily understandable symbolic communication—something on the order of an advertising poster. It is unlikely that such standardized statement of the problem and resolution would have helped Tom cope with his furies, nor would the viewer obtain any fresh insight from the representation of the problem in such a "presented" form.

For Jan the main problem during high school was that he did not know which values, which style of life, which cultural identity to embrace. For Tom the main problem was how to resolve his relation to his father. In each case, the deeper issue underlying the artistic work was: What kind of person would the artist become? The formulation and solution of central existential problems determine the attitudes one will take toward life, and these in turn determine the formulation of one's artistic problems. For each young artist visual representation becomes the means by which he tries to define and cope with the experiences that affect him most deeply. The experiences dealt with during the high school years are predictably universal: loneliness, lack of direction, alienation from a world that does not seem to make any sense, ambivalence toward parents, the need to find a person who will understand.

These problems affect every adolescent, and standard ways of defining and coping with them have been institutionalized. Most adolescents accept these presented formulations and solutions of the problems. Some turn to accumulating money, power, material comforts; others to intellectual eminence, professional status, good works. These are standard solutions to standard problems. Few experiment with changing the formulation of the problems themselves. What makes the young artists different is that their developing skill at visual representation leads them into attempts at reformulating the standard definitions of the problems and solutions. As they develop the means for exploring the most ambiguous and intimate experiences, they uncover new contradictions, new questions, new problems.

In this sense, the predicament of the young artist as an adolescent is similar to that of a scientist who, while studying a hitherto undetected virus, becomes infected with an unknown disease, and must find a cure that will save his life. The artist projects on the canvas a visual expression of the experiences that trouble him. In working with these elements, he discovers the shape of his problem, a problem with no known solution. Now he must find a way out of this bind.

Developing a Vocation. The decision to become an artist does not come easily. Most of the young men who majored in fine art and almost all of those who would later be among the more successful artists first tried other careers. It is almost as if even in the choice of a career, the successful artist has to discover his decision instead of taking it for granted from the beginning.

The first and in many ways the major step toward full commitment is entry to art school. The investment for the artist-to-be is great: he often leaves "regular" college, he must pay tuition, more often than not his family is opposed, he risks testing the extent of his talent, he puts his pride on the line by announcing he will be that unique being, an artist. How, then, does one decide to enter art school?

The interviews suggest three forces contributing in various degrees to the final decision. First, practically all the artists who had tried academic studies in college had performed poorly. The three who had tried architecture "just couldn't hack the mathematics." Ed, who was graduated next to last from his high school class of 168 (the last being a mentally retarded student) did no better in college. Yet our records show that all of Ed's scores on cognitive tests were above average. On the divergent thinking tests he scored about two standard deviations above the means, and on several instruments his performance was three full standard deviations above the norms. Clearly Ed's academic record was not an accurate reflection of his intellectual potential. The same seems to hold for most of the artists whose academic ventures ended in failure. Concerned with the visual formulation of subjective problems, they seemed hard put to deal seriously with objective problems at a conceptual level. They just did not have the motivation to do academic work; it did not "make sense" to them. They gave it a try but soon decided to follow their own bent, even if doing so meant sharp disagreement with their parents.

A second reason for entering art school is alienation from the "nine-to-five routine." Many saw their fathers as trapped, defeated, and unfulfilled by jobs with few challenges or opportunities for personal expression. After a stint in the army, one of the artists worked for a while with his brothers in his father's brokerage firm. But he found the selfishness and competition, even within the family, intolerable. Although inducements were offered him to remain, he left the family firm, saying he would rather starve than spend the rest of his life that way. This may of course be merely "sour grapes"; unsuccessful in academic and business ventures, the young artists disparage that which they cannot reach. But it seems at least equally likely that their lack of success is caused by a prior disinterest in money, status, security, and the other goals of traditional occupations.

Finally, there are of course various positive reasons for entering art school. In addition to the opportunity for acquiring greater technical skill, one of the most frequently mentioned ones is the attractiveness of the life style, and especially of the camaraderie, of artists. Although artists are by temperament withdrawn and asocial, they feel comfortable in the company of other people who are working in art. Many had experienced this sense of belonging when they were taking supplementary courses at the Art Institute while they were in high school; for them entering the school after graduation was like a homecoming. Some look forward to a relationship with teachers as the way to acquire an identity as well as skill; Jan mentioned that he "always wanted to become involved in a master-disciple relationship with an art teacher."

The existence of the artist with its glamorous and bohemian overtones is a powerful attraction. Yet contrary to conventional notions, the life style does not necessarily entail dissipation or romantic excess. Nietzsche made a correct, and as usual with him, unpopular diagnosis: "Artists," he said, "are not men of great passion, despite all their assertion to the contrary . . . that vampire, their talent, generally forbids them such an expenditure of energy as passion demands. A man who has a talent is sacrificed to that talent; he lives under the vampirism of his talent" (Nietzsche, 1960, 258–259).

There is much insight in this observation as well as a misinterpretation, due perhaps to semantics. The artist is not vampirized by talent but by the need to set and resolve, with the help of his expressive talent, the problematic experiences of his life. Talent is only a handy tool, not the source of the compulsion; advertising artists and copyists also have talent. But otherwise Nietzsche is right. The demands on the young artist leave little room for extravagant behavior. The sexual mores of the artists we studied seemed a great deal more subdued than those, let us say, of the swinging junior executive.

What appeals most to the young artist is not so much freedom from moral restriction, although the art school is free of restrictive social controls, but the freedom to work in a situation where he can define what to do and how to do it. It is impossible to overemphasize the intrinsic rewards that art work provides. The complete control over each action, the immediate results of each movement, the concreteness of the products are powerful rewards. Squeezing a tube of paint becomes a pleasurable sensation, the smell of the pigments is exhilarating, and so is the yielding feel of the clay in one's hands. These sensory rewards, as well as the highly subtle psychological benefits derived from coping visibly with the emotional stresses of existence, all contribute to the decision to become an artist.

By the third year in school, most fine art students have become deeply immersed in the artistic subculture. They spend long hours in the studios of the school working on their projects. Renting a loft becomes an important step in affirming their identity. Whether they work at the school or the loft they are surrounded by people with the same goals and the same skills. The interactions reaffirm and consolidate their choice. The free time they allow themselves to drink coffee at the school or to have a party at the loft is spent in shop talk with other artists or with people who are part of the art world in other ways. (Hard drugs were rarely used, marihuana not more often than one would expect; all respondents claimed that drugs were no help in their work.) If "conversation is the most important vehicle of reality-maintenance," as some claim (Berger and Luckmann, 1967, 152), it is easy to see how after a few years of such interaction the young man conceives of himself as having really become an artist.

Whenever possible, the part-time job art students take is related to this developing view of themselves. Private art galleries offer the most coveted positions; while crating and uncrating paintings, one learns the ropes, the behind-the-scene transactions in marketing art. One meets dealers, critics, future customers. Yet the experience of working in the gallery is often disillusioning; the young artist learns that the art market entails practices that are often in opposition to his own principles. But then this too is part of the ambiguity and conflict that is an integral component of the artist's experience in our time. The ability to accept the commercial side of fine art is a selective factor in its own right, determining which student will continue in art. Several highly gifted students, whose work was held in high esteem by teachers, left the field because they were averse to the self-promotion, "gallery-fawning," and occasional duplicities involved in developing a clientele.

Other part-time occupations students take are constructing models for architects, dressing department store windows, casting toy statues, selling art supplies, teaching art in summer camps, conducting museum tours, and so on. The young man who casts Smokey Bear or helps dress mannequins at Marshall Field's is still called an artist; others who are now renowned artists once held the same job.

These jobs which bring in some money are, however, marginal to the young artist's future. The school helps him develop skills more central to his intended career. It organizes fellowship competitions, exhibits, juried shows; the student learns the mechanics of submitting his work, the criteria by which the work is appraised, how aesthetic judgments are formed and altered. This information does not necessarily make him happy, but the practical knowledge it provides is needed for later survival. And like all schools, it gives direct assistance on a selective basis to the students who are considered most talented. Teachers recommend them for independent fellowships, scholarships to advanced degree programs, instructorships, and other positions in the art world.

Besides giving instruction in technical skills, therefore, the art school confirms the student's artistic identity and provides him with experiences needed in his future career. A young man who has enrolled still undecided regarding his future, but with a history of using visual expression to cope with the environment, will find in the school a congenial atmosphere. It gives immediate legitimacy to his skills and temperament, which are often held in contempt elsewhere. His talent and aspiration are taken seriously by the faculty and fellow students. If he has felt embarrassed in other settings, he need no longer be ashamed to want to be an artist. Courses in art history demonstrate the centrality of art to human life and history. Everything reinforces the importance of art and the artist: the location of the school in the museum, the activity in the studios around him, and the conversations with senior students and teachers, who are themselves artists.

Other career plans, which had been kept alive because art appeared to be such an unlikely occupation, fade away. The school becomes a crucial link in the long sequence of experiences from preschool experiments with crayons to final success as an independent artist. At any point along this sequence, however, a person may "go wrong" by finding a more satisfying fit between his skills, motives, and external pressures. Despite superior talent, he may abandon art.

Two black students in our sample, for instance, were highly promising young artists. One had an extremely high score in our problem-finding experiment, and his work received almost the highest all-around rating by the expert judges. Neither student lacked the talent to become an artist. Yet after graduation both decided independently that in this particular historical moment their efforts ought to be directed to more immediate social problems. Instead of continuing to formulate personal problems through the symbolic medium of art, they felt that the concrete problems affecting their race were too pressing to be ignored. They ceased to do creative work in art and turned to social work and education in the inner city. Their view of art has changed, too: They see it now as a tool for social reform.

To illustrate in greater detail the development of an artist, we present three case histories from our group. The emphasis will be not only on key events in their career, but also on the kinds of problems expressed by their work. The three examples are not intended to stand for any larger groups: When the analysis becomes refined enough, no two artists are alike. The brief histories illustrate only a few of the ways artists become what they are.

Roy. In some respects Roy is the least typical of the group we studied. He was much older than the other students we interviewed, and independently wealthy (unique in our sample). We give his history because his work gives clear evidence of the existential problems in tension below the artist's level of consciousness.

Roy was born into an affluent Midwestern family. The family moved around a lot, and despite the Depression Roy remembers all his homes as "nice and warm." He "never wanted for material comfort," and says his childhood was "pleasant," "without any traumas." The memories of his early childhood are strangely vague, almost surrealistically empty. Roy mentioned in a different context that he had been very close to his mother. But when questioned more directly about this, he is very reticent. He does remember copying cartoon characters when he was six or seven years old. Otherwise he cannot recall anything worth relating. Although we felt that Roy's present work is more clearly influenced by his family background than is the work of any other of our artists, he truly believes that his childhood "held nothing germane to later artistic interest."

Roy began drawing in elementary school. But he was not outstanding, and nothing was done to develop his talent. Nobody in the family had any artistic bent; his ability was neither encouraged nor discouraged. It was something of a surprise when, at the end of high school, Roy announced that he had decided to become an artist. He himself cannot explain why; it just seemed to him that was what he wanted to do. His parents were strongly opposed to his quixotic notion; they felt he should prepare himself for a business profession befitting his background. Roy compromised and took courses in commercial art, which he detested. This was the first occasion he remembers of "serving two masters"—a phrase he was to use to describe his relation to art throughout our talks.

Roy soon became "disgusted" with commercial art and changed to journalism, again a cross between creative and commercial work. After getting his undergraduate degree, he went back to art school, but again in advertising rather than fine art. He explains that he wanted to go back to painting but he felt guilty about assuming the "useless" role of the artist. The war came, and Roy enlisted. When he returned, he took a series of editorial jobs and seemingly forgot about painting. From 1942 to 1959, for 17 years, he did not touch a brush.

In 1959, riding an airport bus to downtown Cleveland where he had flown to attend a business meeting, Roy saw a poster advertising summer classes at the Cleveland Art Institute. "That rang a bell"—it occurred to him that the Chicago Art Institute must also offer summer courses. On his return to Chicago, he went straight to the Art Institute and found that in fact they did offer summer courses. He took three weeks off the job and spent them in intensive work in a basic painting course. For the next two years he took evening, Saturday, and summer courses. He then enrolled full time, and was graduated four years later.

During all this time Roy continued to work as a part-time editorial consultant. In addition, he had a substantial income from inherited securities. He often thought of devoting all his time to art, but always pulled back at the last moment and continued his editorial work, even though his art is excellent and he "enjoys painting more than anything else."

In part Roy feels that it would be arrogant of him to "chuck everything" and claim to be a full-time artist. He says it would be "presumptuous" to do so. He has "always waited for a sign that would say, 'now I am a hundred percent artist.' " But he now knows that the sign will never come. In part he feels that holding back may be a way of preserving his dream of greatness, which could be shattered if he devoted all his time to art. Suppose he failed. Some people, and Roy includes himself among them, live absorbed by dreams of future accomplishment. They dare not attempt to reach their dream for fear of destroying the illusion. By painting on the side, Roy believes he is "facing at least some of the reality —which can be grim sometimes."

He has given serious consideration to abandoning painting altogether, but feels the need to "do something lasting." He thinks it sinful not to develop fully one's potential. In this respect, Roy has been influenced by the theosophy of Teilhard de Chardin: What will become of a man after his death depends on the level of complexity his consciousness has achieved during his life. To develop one's creative potential is a moral imperative. Roy says he is not sorry for those who lead a hard life, do the best they can, and die without recognition. It is much sadder to live a successful life and be thought of as a charlatan by posterity.

In his senior year at the school, Roy and two other students rented a loft where they painted and entertained. The other two artists had adapted themselves to the need for sociability, and a constant stream of friends, potential customers, and even art dealers were in and out of the place. Roy, who thinks of himself as a "loner," was at first fascinated by the atmosphere of vitality and success. But he soon became annoyed by people watching him work and having his work displayed "like a cucumber." He was "afraid that people would laugh, or, even worse, not say anything." Moreover, he felt he was not "maturing" in the glamorous milieu. So after a few months he left his friends and rented a studio for himself.

Just after he was graduated from art school, Roy's mother, with whom he had been living, died. Within a year, Roy, by now in his midforties, was married to a young woman, and after a visit to a quaint suburb of Detroit, they decided to move there. They bought a Victorian house surrounded by an overgrown garden, and furnished it with antiques from the best New York shops. Two upstairs bedrooms were joined to create a studio where Roy can paint. The mornings he usually spends doing editorial work in a separate study—he has kept his job, although he commutes to Detroit only once or twice a month. He is still "serving two masters." In the late afternoon he paints, sometimes continuing to the early morning hours. Roy produces a maximum of eight finished canvasses a year—large, museum-quality works.

The style and content of Roy's paintings have undergone a remarkable change since he left art school. In school he painted small, very carefully drawn abstractions that resembled organic shapes. Now his paintings are large and figurative, in the current hard-edge manner. They usually include female figures dressed in nineteenth-century clothes, standing in empty Chirico-like landscapes. Roy characterizes his theme as the representation of enigmatic relationships between a few people. He stresses that the relationship between the people on the canvas must be ambiguous and stylized, to save the painting from becoming obviously "moralistic or propagandistic."

One of the canvasses that Roy pointed to as an example, one that he considers his favorite work, depicts three people. An enlarged figure of an old woman dressed in clothes from the past century, her face almost covered with a shroud, is hovering like a shadow over two other persons who are in the sunlight. One is a young boy, about eight, dressed like Little Lord Fauntleroi. The other is a young woman in modern dress, reading a book. Roy said that he had used an early snapshot of himself as a model for the little boy; his wife posed for the young modern woman. He explained that the old woman in nineteenth century dress who recurs through many of his paintings is inspired by pictures of his mother he finds in old family albums. He claims to have a "nostalgia for former times."

Roy believes that the paintings have no relationship to his own experiences. So far as he is concerned, the personal references are incidental. It was only because the family snapshots were handy that he used them; others would have done just as well. The dramatic group in his favorite picture, with the shrouded old mother hovering over the young wife and the child-artist, is simply an ambiguous and stylized composition having no other meaning. It does not reflect anything about the artist's own problematic feelings about the charade. It was our impression that he was unaware of any relationship between his life and his paintings. He would have been skeptical if the relationship had been pointed out to him. And perhaps he would have been right. Yet there seems to be a deep personal unity in his work.

Perhaps an incident might make the point more clearly. On our arrival, we saw from the doorway a large, vigorous, colorful painting of human figures that covered almost an entire wall in the hallway—the painting he was later to describe as his favorite work, and one that was characteristic of a number of other paintings. It was so at odds with the small, etching-like, line abstractions we had known as his typical output in Chicago that one of us exclaimed, "What a splendid thing! Who did it?"

He said he had done it, and went on to describe how he had used the snapshot of himself to model the little boy, his wife as the model for the young woman, and the photograph of his mother for the hooded crone. At the same time he told us that his mother had died since we saw him last, and added that his style had changed since his move from Chicago.

No deep analysis is needed to infer that the composition is closely related to Roy's life, to the ambivalence about his vocation, and more generally to his feelings of self-worth and guilt. It seems clear that painting to Roy is a means—however unconscious—of finding out what has happened to him. It is an attempt at expressing the forces that have influenced his life. No one can know all the forces involved in this case. But surely aspects of his relationship to his mother have produced unresolved conflicts between a need to accomplish something important through art, and a fear of being incompetent. Roy himself seems unaware of this relationship. If he were aware of it, his paintings would turn into single-level "presented" problems, or as he would put it "moralistic propaganda," instead of the multiple-level "discovered" problems in which the hooded old woman hovers.

To a certain extent, Roy is aware of the personal function of his work, if not of its content. In another context, he answered a question about what he thought of when he worked by saying that painting was a personal expression, a release, an act he feels compelled to carry out. He also added that the finished painting brought no final relief and that he "didn't know what had happened" when the work was completed other than he had had to do it. The problems in Roy's life seek their own solution by compelling him to paint to gain release, but it is difficult even to recognize the statement of the problem, let alone be satisfied once and for all with the solution that he sees on the canvas.

Over and over we found that the parallels between the artists' work and the problems they confronted in daily life were dimly perceived. Whether the theme was rebellion, loneliness, or jealousy, none of the successful artists could give a clear account of what their painting represented about their experience; it was not only as if the vision could not be expressed in words, but that its true meaning was not available to their consciousness.

This unawareness of the relation between personal motives and occupational activity is of course not confined to artists. How many surgeons, lawyers, army officers, or psychologists are aware of the connections between their professional acts and their deep-seated needs? What differentiates artists, perhaps, is that despite their relative lack of awareness the medium in which they work allows them to give expression to their problems more directly.

Where worldly success in art is concerned, Roy is pessimistic. Although his work has been shown in juried exhibitions now and then, he dislikes the process of trying to have it become known and accepted through the usual channels of gallery marketing. Caught in the ambivalence between wanting to be a painter and the fear of being presumptuous, between wanting recognition and the fear of rejection if he seeks it, Roy keeps fighting the problem of his own maturity in private, with an arsenal of majestic and nostalgic canvasses, which he hopes will one day find their way to popular acceptance.

Ed.   While the tensions expressed in Roy's art are almost entirely private (though possibly universal in their occurrence), Ed's career and work are riven by tensions between the goals of the artist and the demands of the art market. This is not to say that Ed lacked personal problems. But the vicissitudes of his life coincided with a paradigmatic conflict betwen the artist's need to find his own artistic problems and the art market's requirement that he work on problems that are presented to him.

Ed was the last of several children born to a wealthy New York family. His father had been married before, and the other children were from his earlier marriage. He was 50 when Ed was born. Ed remembers him as a formal and distant figure. His brothers amused themselves by telling Ed he was an orphan; they teased him relentlessly. When one older sister whom Ed remembers as-"sweet and beautiful" died, he was left at the mercy of his brothers. His mother was never mentioned directly in the interview, but it appears that she was unable to take Ed's side in the family drama.

There was one advantage to Ed's position in the birth order; he "missed out on the conditioning" the other children received from their father because he was so old by the time Ed was born. Although he felt lonely and rejected, he was relatively free. Before he was of school age, the family moved to a ranch in the country. Ed feels that this was the point when it was all over between him and his family; he grew to be "closer to the house than to [his] parents."

By the time he was six or seven, Ed was drawing and painting. His parents thought his painting "pretty," and for the first time Ed enjoyed the experience of his family paying attention to what he was doing. On the walls of his room he painted landscapes and wooden machines rescuing people from all sorts of horrors. His parents, "always uptight about cleanliness," let him go ahead. When they realized, however, that Ed was in earnest about drawing (and he might have been earnest only because of their attention), they became upset.

To get him away from drawing and into discipline, Ed's parents sent him to a traditional Catholic elementary and secondary school. He describes his experiences in the school as "miserable." By this time his overall strategic posture toward life seems to have already developed. Basically unsocialized, lacking an adult with whom to identify, resentful of siblings and peers, stifled by authority, art became for Ed a symbol of rebellion, as well as a medium for working out his feelings and for establishing control over a hostile environment.

After being graduated from high school in the next-to-last position, he was nevertheless accepted by the architectural department of a state university. He lasted less than six months, at the end of which he was glad to be drafted into the Army. The two-year enlistment was uneventful, the only memory that Ed mentioned from this period being a wistful reference to how he used to "make everybody laugh" with his caricatures.

Back from the Army, he went to work for his father. Everybody wanted him to be in the family business. His half-brothers were already in it. According to Ed, they and their wives were in ruthless competition for the shares. Ed lasted four months in the firm. He left to work on a construction site, sold records, ski-bummed for six months, became involved with a "wealthy chick" whom he followed from the ski slopes to the city and under whose thrall he lived for a year, and then worked for a while as an illustrator.

After these stages of a contemporary *Entwiklungsroman*, Ed was ready to enter an art school. He felt that art was "partly a rebellion" against everything his family stood for. In addition, the only rewards he had experienced had come from his drawing—the attention of his family, the amusement of his Army comrades.

Ed did well in Art School: B+ average in studio courses, C average in academic courses, and the highest rating of all students in originality and artistic potential. All his scores on the cognitive tests were above average: those on Unusual Uses, Brick Fluency and Flexibility, and Word Association Fluency were more than twice the mean for Fine Art students. On some of these tests he was over three standard deviations above norms. Superior performance was turned in also on the Object Question Test and the Perceptual Tests. On the intelligence measure he was slightly above average for college norms. Clearly his abysmal high school record did not reflect his intellectual ability. Finally, Ed placed in the upper quartile of artistic success in our sample.

When he was graduated from art school, Ed was already well known in Chicago art circles as an up-and-coming young artist. He was in the middle of the most exciting artistic experiments, went to the right parties, had good contacts. The same year he married a fellow-graduate, a young Jewish woman; the marriage severely upset Ed's parents.

At the time of graduation Ed was offered a fellowship for a Masters in Fine Arts degree at a Southwestern university. He says it "sounded like a good deal"—he would get $2200 a year to teach a few courses, and the degree after one year. He also had "romantic reasons" for going: He "dug that part of the country" and wanted to explore it in his art.

Graduate school was a "mistake." In the first place, the Masters program stretched out to three years instead of the one year that had been promised. Ed felt his teachers were not interested in what he was doing; they just wanted him to become another "tenure-grubbing" instructor. They used "lots of shenanigans, playing with stipends to keep the students on the line." After three years, Ed had to write a 65-page thesis for his very "uptight dean." Here again his rebelliousness against outside requirements asserted itself; he "couldn't bear" to do it, and so he left without the degree.

Living in the romantic desert environment also turned out to be a disappointment. Things were too slow, and Ed was bored. For a while he turned to poetry "to save myself from looking at Albuquerque." But that did not help either in the long run. Worst of all, the change did not suit Ed's work. The vast open spaces overwhelmed him, and as a reaction his paintings became rigid and defensive. The strong lights and colors of the desert, and even the symbols of Southwestern paintings—the vibrating discs, the mesas, the canyonlike shapes—filtered into his work against his will. He tried to oppose the change for a long time by forcing himself to avoid the obvious environmental influences, but finally realized that he might as well adapt to his new surroundings and "do more of what was around me." By then, however, it was time to leave the region—without his MFA.

The Southwestern interlude illustrates a principle we saw at work in a number of instances: whenever one of our young artists moved to a new environment he had to change the elements of his art. The new environment provided new experiences, the problematic forces rearranged themselves in different configurations. The artists needed a new set of forms and colors to cope with these changes. To paint inhuman machines and congested streets in neon colors makes sense when one lives in the city, but after living a while in the open country these themes lose their point. Some were able to make the transition from place to place by formulating a new set of problems or by reformulating the old problems though a different set of visual symbols. Others could not adapt; this seems in part to have been Ed's trouble with the Southwest.

The frustrating experience chastened Ed. He "didn't want to be a superman any more," just being a person who "dug himself" was enough. Returning East, he took a job as a crafts director at an Army missile base. It was a way "to pay the rent" and "keep the kids alive"—he had two children by now. At the post he was able to paint on his own. But the soldiers "were so abstracted they didn't need any hobbies"; all they wanted to make were beer mugs and ash trays. "To top it all off," he said, "they blew a cannon every day at 5 P.M." Its ominous boom reminded Ed of the voice of authority he was trying to escape. He left after six weeks.

When he arrived in New York he had 40 finished canvasses with him. Four months after his arrival he had a one-man show in a minor gallery. He had to haggle with the owner, who asked for 80 percent of the sales; they finally agreed on a 40/60 split. But the show did not gross much money anyhow, and Ed contemplated going on welfare. For a while Ed's wife took a job, leaving their children with a sitter. When they noticed that the older boy was beginning to use "TV lingo" and talk in commercial clichés, Ed's wife left her job to stay home with the children. These were bleak and even hungry times.

Slowly, however, Ed was able to work out a viable situation. From 7 P.M. to 10 P.M. one day a week he teaches printmaking in a university. All day Saturday he prints etchings on the school press for five dollars an hour. From 10 A.M. to 5 P.M. on Mondays and from 1 P.M. to 5 P.M. the rest of the week he works for a downtown gallery where he "moves paintings around." The rest of the time he does his own work at home.

The gallery fills an important role in Ed's life; it keeps him "alive" psychologically as well as economically. The owner provides encouragement, therapy, direction—and commissions. Ed does his art work in two phases. The first involves filling pad after pad with sketches, some just a few lines, others meticulously executed. They are mostly in India ink, although some have splashes of color. None is a "picture"; they are rather visual concepts, germs of ideas, statements of problems. These sketches are usually done at home, often at odd moments. Phase two begins with Ed's bringing a sheaf of drawings to the gallery. If the owner likes one of the ideas, he asks, "But how will it work in 3-D?" Ed answers, "It will look fine." The owner says, "Do it in wood." So Ed goes home and translates the idea into a sculpture. If it turns out well, the gallery buys it.

Despite this apparently successful symbiotic relationship with the gallery, Ed is troubled. The form of adaptation he has developed has plunged him directly into the center of a conflict between the demands of originality and those of conformity.

During our visit to his loft on the Bowery in New York, it became clear that the sketch pads are the medium in which the problem-finding crucial to Ed's thinking and development as an artist is taking place. The commitment and action are all in these drawings; they are the source of his pleasure and his pride as an artist. It was his sketchbooks that he showed us when we asked him what he was up to.

Ed admits that as the gallery is increasingly successful in selling his work, more and more of his time and energy are being "sapped" into fulfilling the commissions of the gallery—into, as he says, "working to order." And he feels that despite the apparent success of his work as represented by sales, building sculptures to specifications is uncreative and a damper on his originality. They are, so to speak, solutions to presented problems; he cannot help feeling that the more successful he is with the gallery, the less successful he will be in his own terms.

He knows that sales depend on making the huge objects the gallery orders. But Ed is, in his own words, "ambivalent about making things large scale." It is not what he would be doing if the choice were his alone. He identifies his true creativity with the sudden inspirations represented by the small sketches in his pads. The drawings he makes for the gallery and the large structures that clinch the artistic image of the drawings are often only mechanical translations to satisfy the market. Their character depends on the money they bring in, the "gallery politics," and the demands of the interior decorators who buy his work from the gallery.

Doing what will bring him "sales success" is forcing Ed into the same business situation that his brothers are caught up in, and that Ed had sought to escape. It is not only a cruel paradox but a terrifying predicament for one who has dedicated his being and sacrificed his patrimony rebelling against a style of life imbued by the values of the marketplace.

Perhaps more than any of the young artists, Ed is caught at the intersect between his personal problems imposed by the conditions of the market in art. Success in sales is important to Ed, as it is to any artist; he wants to show and sell his work. In his own words, he wants to stop "running around saying, 'Daddy, Daddy, I want to be an artist,' "while he, his wife, and two children live in a cold-water loft on the Bowery. He wants to settle down and do what he has to do as an independent artist. To support himself and his family he has to devote more and more of his time and energy to working on the problems presented by the gallery. Yet the hope of becoming an artist, of achieving genuine originality and personal satisfaction, draws him toward experimenting with the problems he discovers but which find their way only into his private sketch pads. He can work successfully for the gallery, or perhaps successfully for himself. His dilemma is that he feels he cannot do both.

(When we were preparing our study for publication, we received new information that bears on the case of the painter we have been calling Ed. He has had a one-man show in one of the most prestigious New York galleries to very encouraging critical reviews. It seems that Ed has been able to resolve the dilemma that almost paralysed him a few years ago. Apparently he has found a successful compromise. His new paintings are very large, as expected by the public; yet he has retained the freshness and vitality of his small sketches, qualities that the art critics praise in his work.)

Ron. Of all the young artists, Ron comes closest to meeting the criteria for genuine artistic success, at least within the limited time span of the study. His name is known to art dealers, critics, and other artists. One of his paintings hangs in an important museum. He is written about in art journals. He has no trouble getting a gallery to mount a one-man show of his work. Whether he will remain the most successful artist in this group or not, he is so at present. In an article written before the follow-up phase of the study, (Getzels and Csikszentmihalyi, 1969) we had already singled him out as the "artist of the hour" on the basis of his performance and evaluation in the problem-finding experiment. (This is no self-fulfilling prophecy, for Ron was unaware of our assessment.)

There are three major clues to Ron's achievement. The first is his attitude toward what he is about; more than any of the other students, he talked repeatedly of the need for "originality" and "discovery" as the key to his work. The second is a peculiar sense for what both critics and public will find attractive; in the problem-finding experiment, his drawing was the one both expert and lay groups liked equally. The third clue is more difficult to delineate and perhaps more important. Ron has managed to merge the tensions of his personal life with the conflicts in art as practiced today to an extent that none of his colleagues approached. By dealing with the one set of problems, he is also able to deal with the other.

The other young artists are fighting their own troubles *and* the difficulties they face in art. Ron appears to be moved only by the forces that affect his art. This subliminal, symbolic translation of personal issues into artistic ones allows Ron to devote all his energies to his work. His field of attention is not split into "life" and "art," as they are for Roy and Ed; the two are one for him. Consequently he is more sensitive to what happens in the art world, he is more at home in it, he is surer of his judgments, his artistic reflexes are quicker, he is unambivalent about what he is doing.

This does not mean that he has found the philosopher's stone and is enjoying a conflict-free existence. For one thing, the practice of art involves contradictions of its own. To mention one example, which is an important one for Ron, the artistic ideology of our time places supreme value on the creative idea itself (as in conceptual art) and discounts the solution in the tangible product. Yet artistic fame is still achieved only through things that can be hung, seen, walked around. There is no way to gain recognition just by formulating the creative problem; one must also carry out the "menial" solution. To someone as closely identified with the world of art as Ron, the disparity between the ideal and actual evaluation of discovery in art can itself become a strong existential problem, which he would want to formulate and resolve in his work. However, since it is the current practice of art that creates the problem in the first place, attempts at solution can only exacerbate the problem by showing there is no solution—unless Ron were to break out of the prevailing dilemma and resolve the conflict by ceasing to worry about what is or is not "Art" and formulate the whole question in terms that make sense to him and perhaps to others. This is what he is attempting to do now.

Ron remembers his family as open and warm. He insists that he has "no hangups at all" from his early years. His present "restrained bohemian" existence is not a rebellion against the family; he "was raised this way." In his childhood as now, Ron claims, he was treated by his parents as a "person"—with acceptance, respect, and love, never with hostility.

Ron's father was a lawyer and his mother was a writer involved in social causes. As a child Ron was "pretty solitary"; his sister was seven years older and not often available as a companion. Despite the closeness to his parents, Ron felt lonely; he had few friends. Partly this was due to his stuttering, which made it difficult for him to feel control in interpersonal relations. Throughout the account of his early life, Ron cited contradictory evidence without showing much awareness that he was doing so. Loneliness and warmth, "no hangups" and stuttering were mentioned with equanimity and in the same breath.

"On the whole," he said, "I had a ball" in childhood. The first four years were spent in the country, then the family moved to Chicago. Ron remembers having a lot to do with animals, even in the city. He raised dogs, rabbits, and chickens. But this idyllic period must not have lasted long, because his memories of grammar school are quite contrary. The "kids were hostile" because of Ron's stuttering. Things reached such a point that his parents transferred him to a private school, where life appears to have been tolerable. During this time Ron "drew pictures all the time" and made posters and charts for his teachers. In high school he placed even more emphasis on drawing and totally excluded sports from his life. By the time he was ready for graduation, Ron had decided to become an art teacher. He was "very proud to have decided" himself. His family was understanding, and the transition to art school was smooth.

Ron seems to have put a distance between himself and his past. Although he talks about his early years at length, he does so coolly, with detachment and little insight. It is as if his present concerns have preempted his interest; or, to put it another way, as if the unresolved tensions of his childhood had become transmuted into the artistic problems he is currently dealing with.

When he entered art school, Ron was planning to become an art teacher or a commercial artist. But soon he began "wanting to do more," and by the second year he was in fine art. Ron has much to say about art school and art education in general. He remembers the four years as boring and frustrating. Basic drawing courses were "irrelevant to human experience," painting courses concentrated on developing the students' "style and statement" too soon, before they knew what art was all about. Ron believes that an artist's education should "begin loose and end tight" rather than the other way around. What is most important, the teaching "should emphasize discovery" instead of technique.

Ron's performance in art school was far from brilliant. Art grades averaged B−, academic grades D−. His teachers' ratings in originality and artistic potential were, however, a full standard deviation above the mean. Cognitive test scores were about average—higher in divergent thinking, lower in convergent thinking. His TAT production of novelty score was outstanding, by far the highest in the group. All of Ron's TAT stories were surrealistically imaginative, irreverent, funny. He tied for the highest problem-finding and discovery-process score in the drawing experiment.

As a senior in art school, Ron had his own loft where other artists, potential customers, and an occasional art dealer would come to have a good time and to become familiar with his work. Before graduating he had a painting in a prestigious show, and the work was later added to a museum's permanent collection. Two of his paintings traveled for two years across the country in a national art exhibit. He had a one-man show at one of the best Chicago galleries, and his paintings were included in a number of lesser group shows and galleries.

Despite these successes, Ron had to find a job to support himself after graduation. He began by working six months in a Chicago display firm casting large Smokey Bear figures in epoxy. If nothing else, the employment taught him three-dimensional casting techniques. Another half year he took charge of 43 children in a third-grade class. One summer he taught art in a camp, but he was fired because of his methods, which he called "discovery-oriented": Ron thought it more important for his pupils to learn about themselves (by rolling down slopes, playing volleyball without a ball, doing self-portraits blindfolded, and so on) than about the techniques of drawing.

About two years after graduation, Ron married a wealthy young woman from the suburbs of Chicago, who had also been at the art school. Immediately after the wedding, Ron and his wife moved to a loft in New York City. Since then Ron has continued producing and showing his work with regularity. In the year before we saw him, he made "60 pieces, 15 of them major." But during the same period, only slightly more than 10 percent of Ron's earnings came from his sales—the rest he earned teaching art at a private school. He estimates that usually he can bring his freelance income to about 30 percent of the total, and in the future he hopes to achieve a 50-50 balance.

What Ron says about art and what he does in art constitute a strange contradiction. He is adamant in his ideology that there are "too many paintings turned out in the country today." The art object must be deemphasized. Art should not be used by the artist as a "vehicle for recognition and status." The activity itself "is where it's at," not the product. "My cans of paint, my palette with cigarette butts can have more meaning than any painting," he says. "Any time an activity is isolated, it is art." Every concrete object can also be a work of art: "No artist could make an environment like 42nd Street"; "the greatest piece of environmental art would be to spray the Lower East Side". To "dig a hole in the desert" is art, not because of any quality of the hole, but because of the digger's attitude toward what he is doing.

To deemphasize the artifact, to make a strong "antistatement against style," to reduce the artist's visibility, Ron is planning the following activities. He hopes to convince a gallery to show 25 large paintings of his own name. If the gallery agrees, Ron will go home and start painting his name in six-foot letters. He has also thought of doing a series of works each in the style of one of the modern masters, again with his own name incorporated in the paintings. While these projects are still "up in the air," he has already started a series of 20 pictures, all exactly alike, that will hang together in the same show. They are intended to force the viewer into questioning, "Are these 20 different paintings, or only one? Do I see just an environment, and not *paintings* at all?"

These projects are conceived by Ron as concrete formulations and solutions of the problems besetting art, and therefore indirectly besetting his life. By confusing the viewer, by forcing him in a problematic situation, by making him realize that style, individuality, uniqueness do not matter, that the product is irrelevant, that it is the attitude and experience that counts, Ron hopes to clarify what art and life are all about. Irony and the "put-on" are his weapons, but his goals are serious.

However, there is a deeper irony in this effort that seems to have escaped Ron. He attempts to deemphasize the object my making more objects. He attempts to deemphasize style by using stylistic devices. He intends to efface the artist's status by producing huge paintings of his own name. One is reminded of other self-defeating activities like preparing for peace by stockpiling armaments, or using syllogisms to prove the imperfection of reason.

Ron cannot be blamed for not seeing the futility of all this, for it is difficult to be a successful artist and not be concerned with the current ideological problems of art. It is ironic, though, that one should spend so much time feeling apologetic about success. But here too there is a contradiction between Ron's ideological disparagement of his success and his well-directed drive toward success. While he is cultivating these put-ons—if that is what they are—he is at the same time producing paintings that are shown in galleries and written about in journals. Although at one point in the interview he decries that "too many paintings are turned out in the country today," at another point he talks of his own work and success as follows:

I always know where I'm at. There has never been any question about what I wanted to do. I've always got a big kick out of what I've done, without being heavy about it. I always come to quick conclusions about what is good. I have a strong ego which permits me to reach conclusions without worrying about them. Yes, I am going to do it; no, I won't do it. I can always make situations suit my needs by being in control of people and situations. I like to take chances. I am aware of how incredibly short life is, and I don't want to waste time. I want to accomplish something both in the eyes of society, and more than anything else, for my own sake.

I do a lot of things with joyful desperation, like work four days in a row stretching canvasses, 20 at a time, then fall exhausted like after making love. A lot of people approach their work as if it were a job. Work is what you must do by nature.

To work with such assurance and enthusiasm, despite the conflicts he sees in the symbolic system within which he works, is the key to Ron's success as an artist: His own existential problems have become identified with the problems of art. Therefore he can say "work is what you must do by nature"; what is artifactual for others has become natural for him.

In *The Act of Creation,* Koestler (1964) cites Dubos's description of the development of genius:

It is often by a trivial, even an accidental decision, that we direct our activities into a certain channel, and thus determine which of the potential expressions of our individuality become manifest. Usually we know nothing of the ultimate orientation or the outlet toward which we travel, and the stream sweeps us to a formula of life from which there is no returning. Every decision is like a murder, and our march forward is over the stillborn bodies of all our possible selves that we'll never be. (Dubos, 1950, 383)

After visiting with the young artists in their studios and listening to them recount the stages in their development, we were impressed by the same lack of a single "cause" that accounts for what they have become. The artists do not experience their talent as a quality that sets them apart, let alone makes them "superior" to others. They do not think of themselves as different, nor of the events in their lives as exceptional.

Nevertheless, they *are* different from other people. This difference does not stem from an irresistible force, like early artistic giftedness or a single, fateful family trauma, however; it grows from a convergence of ordinary events that result in choices that move the artist closer and closer to his career commitment.

All our artists began what Dubos calls the "march forward" by tracing outlines of Donald Duck or Superman. But other children were doing the same thing. It is impossible to tell the precise pattern of family interactions—a sickly child seeking his parents' approval, a youngest son rebelling against his elder brothers, a stutterer who finds reward in nonverbal competence—that explains why these children continued to draw while others abandoned drawing for other activities. A difference in "talent" might account for the circumstances. But it is likely that future artists kept on drawing because they took the activity more seriously: it was more important to them, they took more pains with it, and hence they *became* more talented.

The specific reasons why they took the activity more seriously differ from artist to artist. In some cases, like that of the stuttering child, the reason seems quite direct; in others it is less so. But in every case the future artist finds that he can control his environment more effectively through drawing than through any other means at his disposal. This competence gains him attention and praise. He learns to give order to space and time, to deal with daily concerns through visual representation. Dreams are played out on paper, emotions channeled into color. Threats he is afraid of are defeated in a drawing, people he loves can be remembered. Later in school, the child who has learned to achieve control and release through art will apply this talent in the new situation. While others are exploring *their* ways of attaining competence and mastery of the world—through physical exploits, intellectual superiority, social popularity—the young artist continues to explore *his* way.

The increasing skills also begin to provide motivations for their own use. The developing artist then acquires values that are compatible with the practice of his future profession and personality traits that are functional for creative work. He slowly learns that art can be more than a means to gaining attention and praise, that it has the power of stating and resolving the problems of life. By this time his contemporaries will have ordered their lives through other means—occupational security, academic training, or the use of some other skill. The young artist enrolls in art school, rents a loft, enters the world of art, and finds it hard to believe that he could be anything but an artist. Art has become his way of coping with the world, his way of formulating and solving the problem of existence.

CHAPTER 14

■

Problem Finding and Creativity

As has often been pointed out (Wertheimer, 1945; Getzels and Jackson, 1962), psychological explanations of creative thinking have traditionally followed two major approaches. One places emphasis on rationality. Thinking, it holds, involves approximation of logical truth. Being true or false is a quality of assertions and propositions. Inferences can be drawn from them, and formal operations applied to test their validity. Combinations make it possible to derive "new" propositions, and logic establishes the various forms of syllogism which guarantee correctness of the conclusion.

Deduction through logic and rationality is the substratum of creative production; the discovery of the planet Neptune, for example, was the result of this process. Induction, with its reliance on experience and experimentation also depends on logic and rationality. The focus here is not on deriving lawful relationships from general propositions but on gathering facts and establishing their relationships, until new lawful generalizations are found. But whether thinking proceeds by deduction or induction, the emphasis is on rationality and logic.

The second approach is classical associationism. From this viewpoint thinking is a chain of ideas, or more accurately a chain of stimulus-response connections. There is no difference between so-called lower and higher mental process, between trial-and-error, logical, or original thought. New ideas result from associations of old ideas by trials and errors. Habit and past experience—retrieval rather than reason—are the essential features of thinking. The distinction between higher and lower

236

forms of thought is more apparent than real; it lies not in fundamental qualitative but in quantitative differences. As Thorndike put it, "In their deeper nature the higher forms of intellectual operations are identical with mere association or connection forming, depending upon the same sort of physiological connections but requiring *many more of them*" (Thorndike, 1926, 415; italics in original).

Wertheimer, speaking for the Gestaltists, was sharply critical of both approaches. Thinking does not proceed piecemeal, either by logic or by association. It proceeds by the structuring of Gestalten. The organism first experiences a problem situation in the environment S_1, which acts as a trigger for the process, and then a solution situation, S_2, is reached, after which the process ends. The problem situation is structurally incomplete; it involves a gap or a "structural trouble." The solution situation is structurally complete; the gap is filled, the structural trouble has disappeared.

When the task is finding the area of a rectangle, the process of thinking from S_1 to S_2 is clear. The problem is presented: What is the area of a rectangle with side a and base b? The mode of solution of this problem, as of all problems entailing thought, is characterized by "grouping," "reorganization," and "structurization" of elements into subwholes and wholes with reference to the task at hand. The structural features and requirements of the situation set up certain strains, stresses, and tensions in the thinker. These strains and stresses yield vectors in the direction of improving the problematic situation (S_1) along a "structurally consistent" line into a solution situation (S_2) (Wertheimer, 1945, 41–42).

This model fits well conditions where the problem can be thought through to a recognizable solution. But there are conditions that do not fall readily in the S_1–S_2 classification; the thought process does not begin with an already formulated problem. Instead the issue involves realizing that the situation is not as good as it might be, that it needs to be improved. In this case, the first step is the realizing that there *is* a problem, in *finding* the problem. This is the case of the scientist or mathematician who must pose his own problem, or in Einstein's words "commit his own crime"; or of the artist who sets up a still-life, literally creating a problem that had not been there before. The problem is not presented; it must be discovered.

Wertheimer himself distinguishes between presented problem situations with a given S_1, and discovered problem situations without it. He writes of the latter, which he recognizes as characteristic of creative work:

The process starts, as in some creative processes in art and music, by envisaging some features in an S_2 that is to be created. The artist is driven toward its crystallization, concretization, or full realization. . . . Whereas what happens in instances of the type S_1 . . . S_2 is structurally determined by the nature of S_1, or of S_1 in relation to S_2, here [it is] determined by the structural features in the envisaged S_2, even though S_2 is still incomplete, still vague. This somewhat changes the dynamic nature of the outline given above [that is, in the S_1–S_2 situation] . . ." (Wertheimer, 1945, 197–198)

When the situation is of the S_1–S_2 type, Wertheimer's formulation is fruitful, and much empirical work on problem-solving and creative thinking has been done it its terms. But when the situation is one where the S_1 plays little or no role and the individual must find his own problem, the model is less satisfactory. It fails to deal with two issues touched upon but left unanswered: the source of the substantive problem that is found or created, and the source of the drive toward its realization in a creative product.

It is to issues of this sort that psychoanalytic explanations seem to be directed. Psychoanalytic accounts focus on the origins of creativity, and on the motivations for formulating and solving creative problems. Although Freud dealt with creativity in numerous contexts, he left no single conclusive statement on this issue, and varied views have been derived from his work. Nonetheless, there seems to be general agreement on the following basic points. Creativity has its source in conflict, arising from the repression of libidinal desires. The unconscious forces that motivate the "creative solution" parallel those that motivate the "neurotic solution"; the psychic function and effect of creative behavior is the discharge of pent-up emotion until a tolerable level of psychic balance is reached. Creative thought derives from the elaboration of "freely rising" fantasies and ideas related to daydreaming and childhood play; while the creative person accepts these freely, the uncreative suppresses them. When the unconscious processes become "ego-syntonic," it is possible to achieve "special perfection." The role of childhood experience in creative production is emphasized, creative behavior being seen as "a continuation and substitution for the play of childhood" (Getzels and Jackson, 1962, 91–92).

One aspect of the Freudian formulation, however, seems to have attracted less general attention. This is the emphasis on "questioning" and the "investigation impulse"—in our terms, problem finding as a characteristic of the creative process. Significantly, Freud stresses this aspect in his *Leonardo da Vinci*. He points to the "untiring pleasure in questioning" observed in little children—a curiosity that disappears in most adults. The first source of this curiosity is "infantile sexual investigation." If this period comes to an end through repression, the "investigation impulse" may take three different courses. It may share the fate of sexuality, in which case curiosity remains inhibited and narrowed for life. Or the repressed sexual investigation may reemerge from the unconscious as compulsive reasoning. The third possibility, which in Freud's words is "the most rare and most perfect type, escapes the inhibition of thought and the compulsive reasoning. . . . The libido withdraws from the fate of the repression by being sublimated from the outset into curiosity, and by reinforcing the powerful investigation impulse." Curiosity can freely express itself in the form of intellectual interest and creative production (Freud, 1947, 46–50).

Despite obvious differences, these various conceptions of creative thinking are founded in a similar paradigm of the human being: a combination of the homeostatic model of self-maintenance, and of the tension (or conflict) reduction theory of behavior. According to this paradigm, the organism's optimum natural state is a form of equilibrium, and the organism always acts in such a way as to return to this state of balance. Problems produce tensions driving the individual to logical or associative mental activity to reduce the tension, and the individual ceases the activity when the tension disappears at the solution of the problem. Lack of closure in a situation raises tension which prompts the person to seek closure, and the person ceases to act when the structural balance is restored. Conscious or unconscious conflict produces tensions that lead the individual to seek resolution, and he or she ceases to seek it when the tension is alleviated. Mental activity, thinking, imagination, creative behavior always involve reduction of a drive, a diminution of conflict, a decrease in tension and stimulation.

More recently a different basic paradigm has been advanced. Although it is recognized that thinking, problem solving, intellectual exploration, imaginative activity may be means of reducing certain drives, mental activity may be an end in itself. The organism may seek to increase stimulation as well as to decrease it. Piaget (1951, 1952), Schachtel (1959), Hunt (1961), and White (1959) among others have pointed out that children do not learn best when they are hungry or thirsty; only after their basic needs are satisfied do they manifest curiosity and exploratory activity. A child whose needs are taken care of does not, as the homeostatic model would suggest, remain at rest. On the contrary, it is just then that the child's play is most vigorous. As early as the first year, a child gives evidence of active exploration and even experimentation. The behavior is directed, selective, and persistent; it is continued not because it serves primary drives, but because it satisfies an intrinsic need to deal effectively with the environment.

Moreover, a conspicuous portion of adult life is devoted to activities which by no stretch of the imagination can be said to contribute to bodily maintenance through satisfying primary drives and attaining states of rest. As Schachtel says:

> The main *motivation* at the root of creative experience is man's need to relate to the world around him. . . . This is apparent in the young child's interest in all the objects around him, and his ever renewed exploration of and play with them. It is equally apparent in the artist's lifelong effort to grasp and render something which he has envisaged in his encounter with the world, in the scientists's wonder about the nature of the object with which he is concerned, and in the interest in the objects around him of every person who has not succumbed to stagnation in a closed autocentric or sociocentric world. (Shachtel, 1959, 243)

This need to explore and control is not limited to artists or scientists, but shows itself also in such common activities as working at riddles, reading mystery stories, traveling to strange places, or fantasizing, all of which provides pleasure not by reducing bodily drives or diminishing basic conflicts but are sought out because they raise the level of excitement. As Berlyne suggests, albeit in a somewhat different context, "Few human impulses are more inexorable than the urge to escape from boredom" (1950–1951, 68). Or to put the matter more positively, few human impulses are as inexorable as the need for novelty. As Hebb and others have shown, normal people need to deal with problematic issues just as they need food and shelter, and they will seek out the problematic when they have reached a homeostatic balance (see, for instance, Hebb and Thompson, 1954; Bexton, Heron, and Scott, 1954; Csikszentmihalyi, 1975).

The core of this alternate paradigm can be expressed most briefly as follows: In addition to familiar viscerogenic drives like hunger, thirst, and sex which can be satiated, there seem to be also as yet ill-defined neurogenic needs that are gratified by stimulation—needs for excitement, sensory variation, and perhaps above all the challenge of the problematic.

From this point of view, the mental processes of the human being are not like thermostatic or information processing devices that lie idle until sparked by some stimulus, drive, tension, or presented problem; rather, mental processes in humans are autonomous entities that must remain active to function at an optimal level. Human beings need not be driven by outside pressures to explore, to think, to dream, to imagine, to seek out problems for solution; their mental functions are constituted to do just that. They are not only *stimulus-reducing* and *problem-solving*, but also *stimulus-seeking* and *problem-finding* organisms (Getzels, 1964).

The two explanatory paradigms—the tension-reducing and the tension-seeking accounts of behavior—are different ways of explaining motivation for creativity. Historically, the homeostatic model arose as the basic "thesis" of modern psychology; the stimulus-seeking model developed in reaction to it as the "antithesis." It has been difficult to reconcile the two; more often than not, one view prevails over the other, as when exploratory behavior is explained as reduction of an "exploratory drive," which amounts to a reinterpretation of stimulus seeking in homeostatic or drive reduction terms. Since evidence can be adduced to support either model, neither can be discarded on empirical grounds. Until a synthesis of the two views emerges, one must choose one or the other to account for the psychological roots of creativity.

The question that confronts us then is: Which of the two explanations is more compatible with what we have observed in our study of artists? Is their work motivated by the need to reduce some instinctual drive—be it libidinal, viscerogenic, or exploratory—or is it spurred on by a positive goal of increasing challenges to reach more intense levels of interaction with the environment? When confronted with this categorical choice, one immediately realizes that neither view alone does justice to the observations. Neither explains completely the source of problems artists find, or the motivation for grappling with them. The creative activity of artists cannot be explained adequately by either model. One needs an integration of the two principles, a synthesis of the apparently antithetical positions.

At first glance it may seem that the tension reduction model is adequate to explain the creative behavior of the artists we have studied. In their case, problem finding tends to originate in some conflict or tension. The tension is not usually consciously perceived by the artist himself, although it can be inferred with considerable confidence from the consistency of his behavior. For example, some subjects seemed clearly motivated to creative effort as a means of recapturing a blissful childhood experience; others wanted to resolve dilemmas of love, or time, or death, or the frustration of urban living. It is not difficult to interpret their work as a response to tensions, as an attempt to reduce conflict, or as a drive to return to an undisturbed "homeostatic" condition.

But as soon as this much is admitted, the inadequacy of the apparent explanation also becomes obvious. The source of the tensions that inform the artistic effort is not as clear as it seems to be. The conflict is not due to an "inner" state such as physiological changes in blood sugar level, or high hormonal output, or the nervous system's need for stimulation; nor can it be explained by reference to the transformation of libidinal energy alone, or even by regression in the service of the ego (Kris, 1952). The tensions that direct the artist's work arise out of symbolically mediated relationships with the environment, with other people, with abstract ideas like "love," "jealousy," or "universal order." If there is a homeostatic level to be restored, it is not only an "inner drive" state but a state of affective, social, and cognitive equilibrium with one's surroundings.

The homeostatic model assumes that the sources of tension (hunger, sexual drive, the need for novelty, and so on) have concrete locations within the individual; they are *there,* already preformed as problems within the individual. But our observations suggest that this is not so. The conflict artists address exists initially only as diffuse, free-floating tension without structure or aim. The creative process consists exactly in trying to formulate the parameters of the vaguely perceived conflict into a problem that can be dealt with and in trying to resolve the problem through symbolic means.

The work of several of the artists illustrates this process clearly. One artist, for instance, was trying to resolve his ambiguous relationship with women at the time of the study. In particular he was puzzled by one young woman who behind a serene facade seemed to be hiding a tragic, almost schizophrenic temperament. In formulating the problem for the experiment, this artist was attracted to the sexually suggestive elements of the objects and structured with them a dynamic representation of the conflict he was experiencing. By formulating the problem in this concrete way, he made its sources accessible to consciousness and therefore amenable to expressive solution.

In another case, one of the artists was building a series of sharp blades that, powered by batteries, could move around a room. The interview suggested that the threatening, mechanical forest of blades was related, in the artist's subconscious, to his relationship with his father, whose influence he saw as a threat to his individual development. The moving sculptures served as a concrete expression of a vexing existential conflict; an expression which by symbolic means brought out in the open the feelings associated with the conflict.

If the tension-reduction paradigm alone seems inadequate to explain artistic creation except in the most general and amorphous terms (what behavior cannot be attributed to tension reduction?), so is the stimulus-seeking model by itself also inadequate. Artists are not motivated only by a generic need to increase stimulation, nor by a search for novelty per se. They do engage in exploratory activity, and the end result of their work is novel, but the exploratory behavior is directed by conflict. On the one hand, the source of creative exploration is a conflict that needs resolution; this seems in accordance with the stimulus-reducing model, in which the goal of behavior is seen as the achievement of the stasis condition prior to the conflict. On the other hand, it is *not a return* to a former condition which governs the creative person's action, but the search for a new condition that is yet to be discovered—a search that involves finding and formulating problems; in this sense the artists' behavior fits the stimulus-seeking model, in which the goal of behavior is to achieve an emergent condition.

If we read the evidence correctly, the creative behavior of artists suggest a modification and synthesis of these models. To be sure, art (or science, literature, religion, and other forms of symbolic activity) has its source in tensions. But the tensions that underlie the creative work are not already structured problems. To obtain meaning and substance, the initially ambiguous tensions must be embodied and formulated as problems. The crucial task of the creative person is precisely that of transforming potential into actual problems. Creative work is the concrete statement of existential problems which previously were experienced only as diffuse tensions.

The tensions that motivate creative activity are neither viscerogenic, nor strictly speaking psychogenic; the work is not directly aimed at reducing physiologic imbalance or alleviating libidinal conflicts in the organization of the psyche. One might perhaps as well call them sociogenic in that they have their source in the symbolic ambiguities of the artist's time and place. In any case, the specific forces underlying artistic creativity are not already structured problems but issue out of and are integral to the problem-finding activity itself. The aim of the creative activity is not to restore a previous equilibrium, but to achieve an emergent one.

Consider in this respect the case of the artist whose favorite paintings dealt with a triangular relationship between himself, his mother, and his wife. Surely he was trying to resolve an emotional tension. One might infer that he was attempting to recapture the feeling of security he had experienced in childhood. Yet the figure of the wife represents an element that had not been there in childhood; its presence in the painting shows that the artist did not simply return to the past by denying the reality of the present. He had to discover a way of relating the three conflicting elements—or persons—to achieve an equilibrium that had never existed before. The paintings are expressions of this existential conflict.

For another artist the main source of tension seemed to lie in the abrupt changes brought about by war. Here again an idyllic childhood and a loving mother are lost, and their loss mourned. But in this case the artist is also exposed to a shift in cultural values; after immigrating to the United States he is confronted by an alien life-style. The issues he must resolve center around the achievement of a new state of security and harmony, one which denies neither the past nor the present reality. The artist does not know exactly what "bothers" him, nor what memories salvaged from the past may be useful to him in the present context. Hence he constructs "stage setting" problems, visual combinations in which past and present concerns, reality and fantasy, interact in symbolic disguises.

Through "trial and error," "logical" analysis, and preconscious "inspiration," the artist moves closer and closer to a statement of the specific problem that his unique experience has produced. He may or may not recognize the underlying forces engaged in the problem he creates; indeed, several of the artists said they understood their work *only after* they saw the "solution" on the canvas. It is probable that the artist who understands at a rational level the problem he has stated will not use his artistic talent as a way of dealing with the issue. As the conflict or perplexity rises to conscious analytic awareness, it ceases to provide the stimulus for preconscious imaginative problem finding. In this sense, the activity of our artists conforms simultaneously to both the stimulus-reducing and the stimulus-seeking models; *they were reducing the ambiguous tensions through finding structured problems amenable to symbolic solutions.*

The integration of the two models of creative activity is based on several assumptions that can now be stated more directly. Creative behavior is motivated by tensions generated within or among affective or cognitive symbols. Intrapsychic drive states are not sufficient to explain creative products; the symbols we use to code experience are sources of imaginative production in their own right. This alone is of course not a radical insight: The psychological theories of cognitive dissonance, cognitive development, and ego development have suggested as much. What our observations have brought into the open and emphasized, however, is the diversity and complexity of the intangible social, emotional, and intellectual experiences that produce existential tensions which artists translate into tangible creative problems.

One artist's feeling of social isolation may therefore become preconsciously linked to the reflecting properties of a chunk of glass found in the experimental setting. As the colors of surrounding objects are filtered through the glass, they come to express facets of the artist's relationship to people he knows. At the visual level, the problem relates to how light, color, and shape are affected when viewed through an irregular piece of glass. But at a deeper level, the problem echoes the existential question that disturbs this person: Is the world really as he sees it, or does his perception distort everything just as the glass distorts what is around it? When the strange colors and forms of the desert find their way into another artist's paintings, they no longer permit him to transform his tensions into problems he can deal with artistically, and he must seek more congenial surroundings. These glimpses suggest the complexity of the relation between underlying conflicts and their translation into works of art. This relationship cannot be explained by the viscerogenic or neurogenic models alone; the autonomous power of human imagination to create symbolic problems from formless emotions must also be taken into account.

The stimulus-reducing and stimulus-seeking models assume that the need which is the source for an act can only be one of a finite number of needs. Motivational theories take it for granted that at the root of all activity there must be a cause reducible to one "need" or a single urconflict. These conceptions take insufficient note of the possibility that new exigencies of existence, irreducible to previous "causes," may arise in the lifetime of a person or in the course of history. The proposed integration does not deny the significance of universal viscerogenic drives or psychological needs. Much of our behavior is concerned with the maintenance and restoration of physiological and emotional equilibria. Similarly, certain widespread institutions have evolved, such as the nuclear family, which produce basic tensions like the oedipal conflict. But these "causes" can give only extremely generalized, approximate explanations. One needs to take into account also affective tensions and cognitive experiences that may arise for the first time in the life of the particular individual existing in a concrete historical moment—tensions and experiences introduced by city life, unprecedented political situations, new family arrangements, scientific discoveries, and changes in aesthetic styles.

In the homeostatic model and the drive discharge theory of behavior, the creative act simply restores the psychological state that existed prior to the act. From this point of view the achievement of Picasso is not qualitatively different from that of Praxiteles; the work of Einstein is psychologically equivalent to that of Democritus. Creativity becomes a misnomer since the supposedly creative act does not alter anything; it simply restores a natural state that is unaffected by the passage of time, cultural change, or new developments. All historical depth is lost; every human accomplishment shrinks into the same matrix of basic needs. Again, this is not to gainsay that there are basic equilibrium needs that drove people to action in ancient Greece and still drive us today. But it also seems obvious that in addition there are emergent needs for new accomplishments that build on, incorporate, and move beyond the old equilibrium.

Creativity entails sensitivity to previously unformulated tensions and the ability to express them as problems that can be solved. To explain this process in terms of a closed model of needs distorts the reality to be explained. Nor can one make sense of the process just in terms of a generalized tendency to explore, to produce novelty, to seek stimuli. Both conceptions are necessary, integrated into a dialectical model. One might then describe artistic creativity as follows. It is a process by which an individual (1) experiences a conflict in perception, emotion, or thought, (2) formulates a problem articulating the previously inarticulated conflict, (3) expresses the problem in visual form, (4) succeeds in resolving the conflict through symbolic means, (5) thereby achieving a new emotional and cognitive balance. The aim of the creative act is not to reduce a drive in order to restore a previous equilibrium, but to reach out for a new equilibrium. The key to creative achievement is the transformation of an intangible conflict into a tangible symbolic problem to which the creative solution will be the response.

These are the issues brought to light by our study. To deal with them conclusively one will need to know a great deal more about the kinds of tensions that disturb the homeostatic processes—the emergent ones as well as those which are constant. We need to know much more about how vague tensions are transformed into articulated problems, how they are expressed symbolically. In the meantime, the observation of artists at work has provided some ideas about what is involved in the process of problem finding. Taken together, these observations suggest a process that has not hitherto been studied systematically.

The creative process is stimulated by tensions that cannot be expressed in existing conceptual or symbolic terms. If they can be expressed in already known terms, the resulting problem will not be original. Even in the limited experimental situation, artists who began to conceive their drawing with a personal formulation (for example, the use of a piece of glass to represent the filter of one's relationship to others) produced more original work than those who began with a known formulation (such as representation of a "startling vanishing point"). Consciously or unconsciously the creative artist transforms his deeply felt emotional tensions into an expressive tangible counterpart; when he has arranged these symbolic elements in an appropriate dynamic relationship, he has found the creative problem.

It seems to be essential for the artist to consider a variety of potential expressive elements, even if later he will make use only of a few. If he restricts himself to a few elements from the beginning, the problem he structures is likely to be less original. The artist must be sensitive to many visual forms; if he responds only to objects conventionally felt to be "beautiful," or only to their obvious aesthetic qualities, he is likely to formulate a "presented" problem—that is, one that is defined by known rules—rather than a "discovered" problem—one that includes a new relationship between conflicting elements.

Artists who defined their problem soon after starting to work produced drawings that were less original than those who kept the problem open longer. It seems that a creative problem cannot be fully visualized in the "mind's eye"; it must be discovered in the interaction with the elements that constitute it. Delay in closure helps to insure that the artist will not settle for a superficial or hackneyed problem. Yet this delay is not due to lack of direction; our observations suggest that those who wait to structure their drawing work toward a definite goal, albeit one that is not accessible to conscious awareness. Artistic success in our sample was most strongly related to this phase of the problem-finding process; therefore it is likely to be one of the central issues of creativity in general.

In addition to keeping the structure of the problem from crystallizing too soon, the more creative artists experimented with various problem-solving strategies in the course of their work. The "solution" of the artistic "problem" can be said to consist in the harmonious or consistent combination of various symbolic, expressive, and formal elements on the canvas. At the same time, as Wertheimer has pointed out, in a creative work the formulation of the problem only becomes manifest in the solution itself. Formulation and solution proceed apace. In our experiment, the artist who tried different means of solution—experimented with different arrangements, pigments, surfaces, tools—was more likely to discover a new way of representing his problem, and to produce a more original solution.

Finally, another concomitant of the creative process in art is the artist's attitude toward the "solution". Creative artists were not only unaware of the exact parameters of the problem until the drawing was almost finished, but they were also unsure whether and when it was finished. This is again consistent with the nature of creative problems. The tensions involved in basic existential conflicts can never be expressed once and for all. Each statement can only be partial; it can deal with only a few dimensions of the experience, and then only from a selection of the possible points of view. A person who claims his painting is finished—the problem ultimately solved so that it cannot be altered any more—must believe that he has found *the* correct solution; but correct solutions exist only for problems that have already been solved before.

In principle the same problem-finding paradigm seems to apply to forms of creativity other than the artistic. Time and again outstanding scientists have stated that the formulation of a problem is more essential than its solution, and that it is a more imaginative act. The specific content of the problem-finding process will vary depending on what form the tensions, conflicts, and dilemmas take—whether they are primarily perceptual, theoretical, social, political, mechanical, or whatever. But regardless in what field the problem lies, whether a person approaches his or her task in a creative way or not depends on the following criteria: Does he or she approach the task as a presented problem situation in which the problematic elements (the ones that produce the tension) are already known, or as a discovered problem situation in which the crucial elements are not yet known or foreclosed? Does he define the problem, that is, what must be done, in a routine way, or does he feel that there may be things to be done that are not yet clear? Does he use only a few familiar symbolic elements to build the definition of the problem, or does he consider a variety of alternatives? In working toward a solution does he seem already to know what the outcome must be, or does he keep refining and if necessary redefining the problem as a result of the interaction with the symbolic elements? Does he rely on a single, familiar problem-solving strategy, or does he attempt a variety of strategies—in effect does he accept closure on method at once, or is he able to delay methodological closure? When the problem is apparently resolved, is he content with the solution, or does he think of the solution he has attained as only a step toward other, perhaps more fruitful statements of a problem still to be resolved?

If one substitutes concrete terms for the abstract variables like "what must be done," "problematic elements," and "alternatives," which are obviously different for different fields, then questions of this order provide a guide for observing how creatively a person approaches a given task. The list is not exhaustive, of course; it includes only the variables which, within the limits of our experimental design, appear to be related to the creative success of artists.

Suppose, however, that one wished to apply this model to scientists, or more specifically to mathematicians. What are the problematic elements for them—numbers, formulae, derivations, some abstract relations among forces and quantities? And how would an observer know whether one mathematician explored a greater number of relevant elements than another? In general, it would seem difficult to develop an abstract test of problem finding as one can of intelligence or problem solving. Problem finding appears to depend on sensitivity to and intimate knowledge of a specific realm of experience; hence it is doubtful that a general test of problem-finding ability is feasible. But this does not mean that problem finding and its relation to the originality of solutions may not be investigated in other fields along the lines of our study of young artists.

The same model and method have in fact begun to be extended to problem finding in other domains. For example, in a recent study, college students were confronted with a Duncker-type array of objects (quite like in the study with artists) and were asked to generate questions and formulate problems with these materials. The quantity and quality of problems posed were related to the personal and intellectual characteristics of the problem finders. In the sample of 60 subjects, the number of problems generated by each person ranged from 2 to 31. When the quality of problems was classified on a 6-point scale from "simple" to "complex," the range varied from an individual mean of 1.4 to 4.7. Significant relations were found between the quality of problems and the quality of cognitive functioning as reflected in measures of thinking and concept formation. Thus there are differences among individuals in problem-finding ability (as there are in problem-solving ability), and the quality of the problem finding is related to the personal characteristics of the problem finder (Arlin, 1974).

Similar studies have been started in the domain of social interaction. In one study, subjects were asked to formulate interpersonal problems, and the quantity and quality of the problems were found to correlate with measures of cognition and personality. In a second study, the way interpersonal problems are posed is being related to the way in which the problems are solved. To comment on the results of these studies is premature, since they are still under way. But whether the problematic situation deals with objects or persons, it seems that there are individual differences in the style by which problems are found and formulated and in the quantity and quality of the problems posed. There are also systematic relationships in the style, quantity, and quality of problems a person finds and his cognitive and personality traits.

These tentative illustrations, taken together with the study of artists, show that problem finding and its crucial role in thinking and creativity can be studied empirically. Problem finding may turn out to be no less important than problem solving for understanding creativity; the gift of genius is not only the possession of technical skills or the facility for solving problems, but also the sensitivity and imagination for finding them.

One may well ask: Need problems be *found?* Are there not enough conflicts and dilemmas within and among people, at home and in business, in the arts and in the sciences? There is, of course, a surfeit of unease; much anxiety is caused by conflicts peculiar to our times. But many of these do not *present* themselves as problems capable of resolution or even of profitable contemplation. The unease must be articulated in productive ways if it is to be moved toward resolution.

The supreme problem solvers of the day are information processing machines (Mackworth, 1965; Getzels and Dillon, 1973). But the rate and quality of discoveries depend on people who can articulate out of vague tensions the significant problems. Some individuals, like the copyist in art, the technician in science, the pedant in scholarship, the bureaucrat in government, deal with problems that have already been identified. The fine artist, the inventive scientist, the creative scholar, the innovative statesman, the self-actualizing person are in addition aware of unformulated problems potentially present in the conflicts of their own experience; unlike machines they devise their own programs and work on *discovered problems.*

This ability is not based on a quantitative superiority in memory, reasoning, or conventional cognitive capacities. The ability to formulate problems seems to be a faculty of a different order. It entails a process far more in touch with the deeper layers of being than reason alone usually is; it is far more holistic in that it encompasses the person's total experiential state. The process is goal-directed, but it often pursues goals beneath the threshold of awareness. It seeks out similarities between external objects and internal states; it uses symbolic means to express formless feelings, thereby disclosing that which otherwise would go unperceived, articulating what otherwise would remain unarticulated. Problem finding may well be at the origin of the creative vision. Despite its elusiveness, this process deserves the attention bestowed on the more familiar and accessible components of thought.

APPENDIX 1

■

Additional Tables and Figures

Table A1.1 Cognitive Tests—Comparison of Art Students with College Norms

Groups		N	Mean	SD	Significance level of t
Wonderlic Intelligence Test					
Males	Art students	86	21.9	5.3	<.001
	College norms *a*	3232	24.6	7.4	
Females	Art students	93	22.1	5.0	n.s.
	College norms *a*	1282	22.6	7.3	
16 PF Intelligence Test (Factor B)					
Males	Art students	86	8.1	2.0	n.s.
	College norms *b*	535	7.9	1.7	
Females	Art students	93	8.1	2.1	<.05
	College norms *b*	559	7.6	1.8	

a Wonderlic Personnel Test Manual (Wonderlic, 1961), Table II(a).
b IPAT, 16 PF Test, Preliminary Norms for the 1962 Edition.

Table A1.2. Perceptual Tests—Comparison of Art Students with College Norms

Groups		N	Mean	SD	Significance Level of t
Spatial Visualization					
Males	Art students	130	18.6	7.5	<.01
	College norms *a*	446	16.6	7.2	
Females	Art students	133	13.0	6.0	<.001
	College norms *a*	356	9.0	6.2	
Welsh Art Judgment Scale					
Males	Art students	97	34.5	11.9	<.001
	College norms *b*	75	17.3	11.5	
Females	Art students	113	35.2	9.5	<.001
	College norms *b*	75	19.3	12.2	

a Guilford-Zimmerman Aptitude Survey, Manual, 2d ed. (Guilford and Zimmerman, 1956), Table 8.
b Welsh Figure Preference Test, Preliminary Manual (Welsh, 1959), Table 2.

Table A1.3. Values—Comparison of Art Students with College Norms a

Values	Male Art Students (N = 129)	Male College Students (N = 2489)	Significance Level of t	Female Art Students (N = 134)	Female College Students (N = 1289)	Significance Level of t
Theoretical	44.16	43.75	n.s.	42.68	35.75	.001
Economic	36.16	42.73	.001	33.07	37.87	.001
Aesthetic	52.02	35.00	.001	55.04	42.67	.001
Social	31.94	37.00	.001	33.46	42.03	.001
Political	38.82	42.94	.001	37.34	37.84	n.s.
Religious	37.03	38.20	n.s.	38.32	43.81	.001

a From Allport-Vernon-Lindzey *Manual, Study of Values,* 3d ed. (Allport, Vernon, Lindzey, 1960), p. 12.

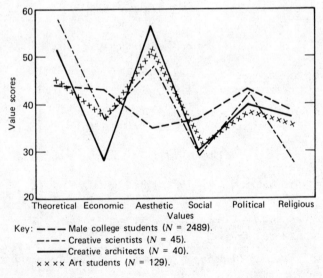

Key: — — — Male college students (N = 2489).
----- Creative scientists (N = 45).
——— Creative architects (N = 40).
x x x x Art students (N = 129).

Figure A1.1. Value profile of art students compared with those of college students, creative scientists, and creative architects.

254

Table A1.4. *Personality Traits of Art Students—Analysis of Variance by Sex and Major*

	N	A	C	E	F	G	H	I	L	M	N	O	Q1	Q2	Q3	Q4
							16 PF Factors									
Male																
F.A.	35	6.28	13.28	13.54	11.83	10.60	10.23	11.14	10.48	15.26	9.66	11.28	10.74	13.54	9.34	14.46
A.E.	12	8.50	14.58	13.00	11.17	11.92	11.83	10.50	8.92	14.75	11.00	10.83	11.17	14.67	10.58	12.75
A.D.	16	9.19	13.44	14.50	15.25	12.62	12.19	8.62	10.87	13.87	10.87	13.00	10.12	12.62	9.31	14.31
I.A.	23	7.78	15.30	15.00	12.78	11.35	11.48	10.61	9.65	13.74	11.13	10.69	10.00	13.13	10.61	14.39
Female																
F.A.	44	8.13	14.48	13.48	13.34	8.73	12.23	12.52	10.16	16.66	8.43	11.34	11.16	14.34	8.61	14.41
A.E.	15	9.67	13.27	11.67	11.40	10.00	11.07	11.80	8.80	15.13	10.00	11.87	10.60	13.27	8.67	13.80
A.D.	7	10.43	16.28	12.43	12.57	12.00	13.00	10.43	6.14	13.57	12.43	8.28	10.43	11.86	10.86	10.43
I.A.	27	9.48	13.37	12.55	13.52	10.74	12.44	11.48	9.30	14.52	10.41	11.81	9.67	12.44	10.74	13.85
F Values Effects																
Sex		13.57[c]	.03	4.57	1.01	9.17[b]	2.21	14.75[c]	3.52	3.50	3.88	.00	.01	.09	.97	.40
Major		5.48[c]	.12	1.16	2.61	6.41[c]	.38	6.14[c]	2.23	5.37[b]	8.67[c]	.03	1.85	2.75	4.14[b]	.67
Interaction		.12	2.78	1.24	1.39	.62	.51	.48	3.63[a]	.48	1.69	3.13	.29	1.18	1.73	1.14

Key: F.A. = fine arts; A.E. = art education; A.D. = advertising; I.A. = industrial arts.

[a] p < .05.
[b] p < .01.
[c] p < .001.

255

Table A1.5. Correlations Between Wonderlic Intelligence Test and Perceptual Variables

Perceptual Tests	Fine Arts Males (N = 35)	Applied Arts Males (N = 39)
Spatial visualization	.39*	.60***
Hidden shapes	.36*	.42**
Match problems	.01 a	.43** a'
Perceptual memory (errors)	−.02 b	−.47** b'
Welsh Art Judgment Scale	.01	−.22

Note: The differences between correlation coefficients marked a and a' and b and b' are significant at least at the .05 level of probability.
*p < .05.
**p < .01.
***p < .001.

Table A1.6. Correlations Between 16 PF Factor C (Ego Strength) and Nine Cognitive Variables

	Fine Arts		Applied Arts	
Cognitive Variables	Males (N = 35)	Females (N = 44)	Males (N = 39)	Females (N = 34)
Unusual Uses	.24 a	−.05	.15	−.25 a'
Brick Fluency	.00	−.16 b	.31 b'	−.15
Brick Flexibility	.33 c	.10	.04	−.30 c'
Ideational Fluency	.01	−.12	−.02	.06
Object Question	.03	−.11	−.04	−.28
Word Association Fluency	.31 d	.11	−.08	−.17 d'
Word Association Flexibility	.61*** e	.17 e'	−.15 e'	−.08 e'
Wonderlic IQ	.47** f	.02 f'	−.20 f'	.12
16 PF IQ	.20	.17	−.07	−.22

Note: The differences between correlation coefficients marked a and a', b and b', etc., are significant at least at the .05 level of probability.
**p < .01.
***p < .001.

Table A1.7. *Average Standard Scores of Ten High and Ten Low Achieving Male Fine Arts Students on Ten Cognitive Tests*

Tests	10 High Achieving Students	10 Low Achieving Students	Difference in Favor of High Group
Unusual Uses	48.1[a]	53.0[a]	−4.9
Brick Fluency	52.3	51.1	1.2
Brick Flexibility	50.5	55.1	−4.6
Ideational Fluency	50.7	50.3	.4
Object Question	55.3	46.1	9.2
Word Association—Flexibility	46.3	48.3	−2.0
Wonderlic IQ	48.4	48.3	.1
16 PF IQ	49.5	51.0	−1.5
Spatial Visualization	46.4	49.7	−3.3
Hidden Shapes	48.8	51.2	−2.4

[a] Standardized scores for all male art students; mean = 50, SD = 10.

Table A1.8. *Average Standard Scores of Ten High and Ten Low Achieving Male Fine Arts Students on Six Values*

Values	10 High Achieving Students	10 Low Achieving Students	Difference in Favor of High Group
Theoretical	52.1[a]	46.4[a]	5.7
Economic	41.8	54.2	−12.4
Aesthetic	55.5	46.1	9.4
Social	43.0	57.5	−14.5
Political	51.6	46.5	5.1
Religious	53.1	48.6	4.5

[a] Standardized scores for all male art students; mean = 50, SD = 10.

Table A1.9. Scoring Reliability of Problem Finding Experimental Variables (Two Raters)

Process Variables	Placement Above or Below Median				Correlation Between Two Raters (product-moment)	
	Number of Agreements	Number of Disagreements	chi²	p Value	r	p Value
A. *Problem formulation*						
1. Number of objects manipulated	31	0	....a	.....	...	.....a
2. Unusualness of objects chosen	31	0	....a	.....	...	.....a
3. Exploratory behavior	27	4	12.5	.0005	.82	.0005
AA. Total	29	2	19.9	.0005	.95	.0005
B. *Problem solution*						
1. Openness of problem structure	...	...	...	...	.86b	.0005
2. Exploratory approach to drawing	27	4	12.5	.0005	.98	.0005
3. Change in problem structure content	28	3	17.1	.0005	.87	.0005
BB. Total	29	2	19.9	.0005	.86	.0005
C. *Concern with problem finding*						
1. In general	24	7	8.8	.005	.79	.0005
2. In problem formulation	28	3	17.5	.0005	.85	.0005
3. In problem solution	25	6	11.7	.001	.74	.0005
4. Changes	31	0	...c	.....	...	.0005
CC. Total	24	7	8.8	.005	.70	.0005
Total discovery process	26	5	11.4	.001	.89	.0005

[a] These scores are actual counts of behavioral observations recorded during the experiment. Therefore, any lack of reliability could have occurred only while recording; however, the objective nature of the behavior recorded argues for high reliability.

[b] Median of six coefficients between three raters.

[c] This category is scored on the basis of a yes or no answer to a specific interview question.

Table A1.10. Correlations Among Subtotals and the Total Problem-Finding Score (N = 31) [a]

Process Variables		1	2	3	4
1. Problem formulation total	(AA)	—	.34*	.38**	.74***
2. Problem solution total	(BB)		—	.42**	.73***
3. Concern with problem-finding total	(CC)			—	.81***
4. Total problem-finding process	(ABC)				—

[a] The correlations between the three subtotals and the grand total (column 4) are inflated due to the effect known as "spurious overlap." In the present case, this means that each subtotal contributes approximately 30 percent of the grand total's variance so that even in the absence of any correlation between one subtotal and the other two, the *rho* between one subtotal and the grand total would still be .55. For our purposes, the important fact is that the "total problem-finding score" should be representative of all three stages of the process, and that it is.

*p = .05.

**p = .025.

***p = .001.

Table A1.11. *Correlation Matrix of Ten Problem-Finding Variables, Three Subtotals, and One Total Problem-Finding Score* [a]

Process variables		Problem Formulation				Problem Solution				Concern for Problem Finding				
		A1	A2	A3	AA	B1	B2	B3	BB	C1	C2	C3	C4	CC
Problem formulation	A1	—												
	A2	.43												
	A3	.48	.22											
	AA	.64	.58	.77										
Problem solution	B1	.51	.23	.15	.25									
	B2	.05	.17	.18	.13	-.11								
	B3	.30	.33	.56	.49	.03	.44							
	BB	.26	.13	.35	.34	.34	.58	.44						
Concern for problem finding	C1	.31	.32	.29	.24	.17	-.10	.16	.13					
	C2	.17	.10	.68	.39	.14	.38	.55	.34	.17				
	C3	.16	.08	.16	.14	.02	.13	.37	.34	.38	.28			
	C4	.29	.23	.31	.22	.19	.29	.66	.41	.02	.30	.26		
	CC	.44	.16	.55	.38	.18	.20	.66	.42	.53	.60	.66	.59	
Total problem-finding score	ABC	.57	.38	.74	.74	.32	.39	.71	.73	.41	.60	.52	.56	.81

[a] With $N = 31$, r of .30 is significant at the .05 level, .36 is significant at the .025 level, .48 is significant at the .005 level, .57 is significant at the .0005 level.

Table A1.12.   Degree of Agreement Within Groups of Judges[a]

	Intraclass Correlations		
Judges	Overall Aesthetic Value	Originality	Craftsmanship
Artists	.29 (.13-.44)	.31 (.15-.45)	.22 (.03-.36)
Art teachers	.59 (.47-.69)	.47 (.33-.59)	.36 (.21-.49)
Mathematics students	.36 (.21-.49)	.45 (.30-.57)	.44 (.30-.57)
Business students	.34 (.18-.46)	.35 (.20-.48)	.51 (.37-.62)

[a] For all intraclass correlation coefficients in this table $p < .05$. The 95 percent confidence interval is given in parentheses.

Table A1.13. *Correlations Between Ratings Given by Five Artists to Thirty-One Drawings* [a]

	Dimensions of Rating																	
	Overall Aesthetic Value						Originality						Craftsmanship					
Judges	A	B	C	D	E	Total 5 Raters	A	B	C	D	E	Total 5 Raters	A	B	C	D	E	Total 5 Raters
A	—	.08	.31	.43	.29	.80	—	.19	.40	.33	.24	.55	—	.21	.09	.33	.34	.62
B		—	.03	.45	.09	.54		—	.11	.29	.13	.50		—	.20	.38	.09	.55
C			—	.34	.59	.71			—	.45	.79	.74			—	.03	.36	.55
D				—	.40	.93				—	.41	.74				—	.27	.77
E					—	.79					—	.68					—	.60

[a] Significance level of correlation coefficients: .31 to .35 $p = .05$; .36 to .41 $p = .025$; .42 to .45 $p = .01$; over .46 $p < .005$.

Table A1.14. *Degree of Agreement Between Groups of Judges on Three Dimensions of Evaluation*

Judges	Art Teachers	Mathematics Students	Business Students
	Correlations of Ratings on Overall Value		
Artists	.75***	.30*	.14
Art teachers		.43**	.29
Mathematics students			.76***
	Correlations of Ratings on Originality		
Artists	.77***	.56**	.64**
Art teachers		.67***	.66***
Mathematics students			.83***
	Correlations of Ratings on Craftsmanship		
Artists	.73***	.33*	.30
Art teachers		.35*	.38*
Mathematics students			.85***

*p < .05
**p < .01.
***p < .001

Table A1.15. *Career Progress of Thirty-One Former Art Students Five to Six years After Graduation*

Success Score	N	Percent
0 (known to have left art)	7	
0 (unavailable)	8	
		48
1	7	
		23
2	2	
3	1	
4	2	
6	2	
7	1	
9 (maximum success)	1	
	31	
		29
		100

263

Table A1.16. Demographic Differences Between Former Fine Art Students Who Have and Have Not Abandoned Art Five to Six Years After Graduation

Demographic Variables	Unsuccessful Artists (N = 15)	Successful Artists (N = 16)	Significance of the Difference Between Two Groups by Fisher's Exacta
1. *Father's occupation*			
White collar and below	73%	50%	*p* = n.s.
Junior executive and above	27	50	
	100	100	
2. *Mother's occupation*			
Housewife	80	38	*p* = .01
Employed	20	62	
	100	100	
3. *Family income*			
Below $7500	53	25	*p* = .08
Above $7500	47	75	
	100	100	
4. *Father's education*			
No college	80	56	*p* = .06
Some college or more	20	44	
	100	100	
5. *Mother's education*			
No college	87	56	*p* = .08
Some college or more	13	44	
	100	100	
6. *Marital status of parents*			
Living together	60	87	*p* = .08
Separated, divorced, or deceased	40	13	
	100	100	
7. *Sibling position*			
Eldest son	33	81	*p* = .008
Other	67	19	
	100	100	
Middle son	53	0	*p* = .0008
Other	47	100	
	100	100	

Table A1.16   (Continued)

8. *Religion*
   Protestant
   Other or none

Protestant	60	19	.02
Other or none	40	81
	100	100

9. *Church attendance*

Once a month	33	31	n.s.
Less often than once a month	67	69
	100	100

ts and Method of Administration

ind Scoring Procedures

IVE TESTS

c Personnel Test, Form I. A 12-minute speed test, this is a
intelligence which can be converted into Otis Test of Higher
lities scores; it is described, among other places, in the *Wonder-*
l Test Manual (Wonderlic, 1961). Scoring objective.*

iality Factors, Form A, Factor B. This is a power test of "general
e," included in the 16 PF Personality battery. Described in
Stice (1962). Scoring objective.

Uses. Performance on this test is said to measure "divergent
us flexibility." It is described in Guilford et al. (1951), and was
ording to the 1963 scoring guide. Scoring reliability was com-
veen two raters ($N = 20$) by rank-order correlattion; $rho = .951$.

ses. Believed to measure "divergent semantic fluency" and
." Described in Guilford et al. (1951). In our study only 5
ere given for the completion of this test instead of the usual 10.
cording to the 1962 guide. Reliability between two raters, $N =$
order: fluency, $rho = 1.00$; flexibility, $rho = .877$.

ed tests that are scored objectively, scoring reliability was not computed.

(e) *Thing Categories (Ideational Fluency)*. A measure of "divergent semantic fluency." Included in several test batteries by other authors, it was used by Guilford and Merrifield (1960) to measure ideational fluency. No scoring guide was available for this test. The instructions are: *List the names of things that are round or that could be called round.* In this study, responses giving such objects as "cigar" or "pencil"—that is, primarily cylindrical objects—were not counted. Also, objects which could be round, but are not usually so, were disregarded, such as "letter," "painting," and "hams." Accepted responses included circular or spherical objects—"wheels," "bosoms," "fish eggs," "some heads," "buttons," and so on. Reliability between two scorers, $N = 20$, $rho = .962$.

(f) *Object-Question Test*. This instrument, described in a manual by R. C. Burkhart and G. Bernheim (1963), has been found to measure divergent evaluative questioning power. The test instructs subjects to ask as many questions as possible about six objects. The responses are scored according to how divergent and personal the resulting questions are. For this study, the scoring of the manual was slightly modified. Each question was given a score between 0 and 4. The highest score (4) was given to questions judged to be both divergent and personal (e.g., "Do paper clips have any feelings knowing they're just paper clips?"). Three points were given to divergent factual questions (e.g., "Could people live on grass for breakfast?"). Two points were given for complex personal questions (e.g., "What is it about ice trucks that fascinates children?"). Finally, one point was given to simple personal questions (e.g., "Is the color of grass why cows enjoy it?"). Complex factual and simple factual questions were not given any points. Examples of the two latter types of questions are, "How does the sea move the sea shell?" (complex factual) and "By what authority is the biological classification of the living shells correct?" (simple factual). Scoring reliability for the test was established between two judges, on four samples of 20 subjects each. Rank order correlations thus obtained ranged from .851 on the first 20 cases to .906 on the last 20. Percentage agreement between two raters on placement in a specific category ranged from 50 percent (divergent personal) to 78 percent (complex factual). Average agreement was 68 percent.

(g) *Word-Association Test*. A similar test was included in the "divergent" category by Guilford and Merrifield (1960). This instrument was identical with the homonymous test used by Getzels and Jackson (1962). It can be scored for fluency and flexibility of associations. Rank-order *rho*, two raters, 20 cases = .992.

2. PERCEPTUAL TESTS

(a) *Hidden Shapes*. Part of the *Objective-Analytic Test Battery* by Cattell
(1958). It supposedly measures "flexibility of closure," or "convergent
figural transformations" (Guilford and Merrifield, 1960). In the present
study, two minutes and 30 seconds were allowed for the completion of
the test, since it had seemed to have a low ceiling for this population.
Scoring objective.

(b) *Match Problems III*. A measure of "divergent figural transformations,"
used by Guilford and Merrifield (1960) to measure "figural adaptive
flexibility." Instead of allowing the required 12 minutes for this test, 8½
minutes were given for the completion of both its parts. This perhaps
accounts for the unsatisfactory results obtained through this instrument.
Scoring objective.

(c) *Spatial Visualization*. Part VI of the Guilford-Zimmermann Aptitude
Survey (Guilford and Zimmerman, 1956). A measure of "cognitive figural
transformations." Scoring objective.

(d) *Perceptual Memory*. This instrument was developed for the purposes of
this study by M. Csikszentmihalyi. It was expected to measure memory
for perceptual content, structure, and detail. The subjects are shown two
slides, each exposed for 40 seconds on a screen. Slide 1 is a design
composed of geometrical shapes. Slide 2 is a line drawing of a simple still
life (adapted from a painting by Morandi). Following the first slide, the
subjects are allowed three minutes to reproduce on a sheet of paper the
design shown on the screen. Following the second slide, the subjects are
allowed four minutes to reproduce the second design, and to mark the
correct alternative from nine pairs of illustrations, where in each pair one
illustration has a detail that was not present on the slide.

The scoring of the protocols is objective: Number of errors in the
content and the structure of the reproduced designs are counted. There
are five partial error scores, and a total error score. For the comparisons in
the present study, only the total error score was used. Reliability of
scoring between two judges, on four samples of 20 cases each, ranged
from .805 to .955, rank-order *rho*.

(e) *Welsh Figure Preference Test*. The Revised Art Scale of this instrument
measures subjects' visual preference against that of recognized artists.
Described in the *Manual* (Welsh, 1959). Scoring objective.

3. PERSONALITY TESTS

(a) *The Allport-Vernon-Lindzey Study of Values.* This measures the relative strength of six basic values which are thought to underlie a person's general orientation toward life. Described in the *Manual* (Allport, Vernon, and Lindzey, 1960). Scoring objective.

(b) *Sixteen Personality Factors Questionnaire.* Developed by Cattell, the 16 PF is an inventory that "covers planfully and precisely all the main dimensions along which people can differ" (Cattell and Stice, 1962). Among the 16 traits measured are ego-strength, sensitivity, and self-sufficiency. A combination of 10 of the factors has also been used to measure "creative personality" (*IPAT*, 1963). Scoring objective.

(c) *Sentence Completion.* This is a slightly modified version of a similar instrument used by Getzels and Jackson (1962). In the first battery, the test was worded in the third person ("When John [or, for females, Mary] was asked to be in charge, he [she] . . ."). In the third battery of tests, the same instrument was given again, this time worded in the first person ("When I am asked to be in charge, I . . ."). The number of negative responses was counted. Thirty of the 50 items implied either a positive or negative completion, and the score was based on these 30 items. Completions were counted as negative when they expressed despair, hostility, aggression—in general, an "acting out" of unsocialized impulses. Three scores were derived: (1) negative responses to third person; (2) negative responses to first person; and (3) differences between 1 and 2. Scoring reliability between two raters, $N = 17$, ranged between $rho = .773$ for the difference score to $rho = .952$ for the third person score. Percentage scoring agreement on single items ranged from 87 percent (first person) to 93 percent (third person).

(d) *Semantic Differential.* An instrument developed and used by Hess, Sims, and Henry (1963), it is based on Erikson's theory of ego identity, and is designed to measure identity diffusion. Scoring objective.

(e) *Thematic Apperception Test.* Group administration. Scored for novelty of productions. As with the usual TAT, the subjects are required to write stories to a picture shown to them. The administration and scoring procedures followed those used by Maddi et al. (1962). Four slides were shown on a screen for 20 seconds each, and four minutes were allotted following each picture for composing and writing the story. The stories were then scored for the unusual character of their plots, imagery, and so forth, and a total "novelty" score was obtained for each subject. Scoring reliability between two raters ranged from $rho = .878$ ($N = 18$) to $rho = .960$ ($N = 15$). The agreement in scoring the various categories ranged from 85 percent to 94 percent.

4. RATINGS

Ratings on originality and artistic potential were already available in the files of the art school, since it is the usual procedure for the teachers employed by the school to fill out a rating sheet for each of the students at the end of each semester. These ratings become part of the permanent record of the students.

(a) *Originality and Artistic Potential Rating I. (OAP-1).* Each student is rated by the teachers on 10 variables, including reliability, working habits, common sense, originality, and artistic potential. For each variable the student is given a rating from 1 (very low) to 4 (very high). For purposes of this study only the ratings on originality and artistic potential were used. Originality was defined by the teachers as "ability to originate ideas and to draw on personal resources in preparing assignments." Artistic potential was defined as "capacity for growth and development of innate talent in pursuit of positive professional success in chosen field."

Each student had in his files between three and five ratings on each dimension given by as many teachers. Agreement on artistic potential computed on a sample of 58 students each rated by four teachers was as follows. In 8 (14%) cases there was perfect agreement; in 18 (31%) cases there was perfect agreement among three teachers, the other teacher differing in 17 cases by one scale point, and in one case by two scale points; in 16 (28%) cases two of the teachers agreed on one rating and the other two on another rating only one scale point removed. That is, 42 cases (72%) were rated with a discrepancy that was no greater than of the type-3,3,2,2. No disagreement was greater than the type-3,3,2,1.

The originality ratings were averaged, and this average was added to the averaged artistic potential ratings. The new ratings therefore had a range from 2.0 to 8.0. The mean ratings on originality correlated with the mean ratings on artistic potential between .72 ($N = 44$ males) and .77 ($N = 33$ females). OAP-1 refers to the rating obtained as outlined above, based on teachers' ratings given at the end of the students' first year at the school.

(b) *Originality and Artistic Potential Rating II. (OAP-2).* This rating was obtained in the same way as OAP-1, but was based on teachers' rating given at the end of the students' second year.

5. GRADES

(a) *Art Grades.* This is an average based on all the grades a student received in art courses, obtained from the files of the school. Following the system used by the administration, a letter grade A was given 12 points, A− 11 points, B+ 10 points, and so on until F = 0 points.
(b) *Academic Grades.* This is a similarly obtained average in courses other than art (history, humanities, mathematics, etc.)

6. QUESTIONNAIRE

Personal and family background data were collected by means of a general questionnaire adapted from one used in a study by Hess, Sims, and Henry (1963).

Administration of Tests

The instruments were divided into three batteries, to be administered at different times. Within each battery, cognitive tests were alternated with personality inventories, speed tests with untimed tests, and so on, to achieve a maximum of diversity. Below is a list of the order in which the tests were given, and the time that each test took to be completed, instructions included.

Lists of Tests Included in the Three Batteries and Time with Instructions

A. *Battery 1*

   1. Questionnaire, 14 minutes (average)*
   2. Unusual Uses (10 minutes), 13 minutes**

*"Average" refers to the average time that the last student in a given testing session finished a nonspeed test.
**Amount of time in minutes provided for tests with time limits is given in parentheses.

3. Value Scale, 29 minutes (average)
4. Spatial Visualization (10 minutes), 14 minutes
5. Brick Uses (5 minutes), 7 minutes
6. Sentence Completion (Third person), 18 minutes (average)
7. Hidden Shapes (2.5 minutes), 3 minutes
   Total, 1 hour, 38 minutes

B. *Battery 2*

1. Semantic Differential, 12 minutes (average)
2. Thing Categories (3 minutes), 4 minutes
3. TAT (4 minutes for each of 4 slides), 21 minutes
4. Match Problems (8.5 minutes), 10 minutes
5. Color Association, 10 minutes (average)
6. 16 PF, 55 minutes (average)
   Total, 1 hour, 52 minutes

C. *Battery 3*

1. Wonderlic (12 minute), 13 minutes
2. Word Association (8 minutes), 10 minutes
3. Perceptual Memory, 13 minutes
4. Sentence Completion (First person), 17 minutes
5. Object-Question Test (9 minutes), 10 minutes
6. Welsh Figure-Preference, 31 minutes
   Total, 1 hour, 34 minutes

The testing was conducted in the lecture hall of the art school. Recruitment of subjects was handled by the school administration. Each second- and third-year student was invited by a letter (signed by the dean of the school) to participate in the testing session. To collect as many cases as possible, the first battery was administered three times, the second battery five times, and the third battery five times. Thus, 13 two-hour testing sessions were given.

APPENDIX 3

■

Bibliographical Note

The number of articles and books published in the last few years on creativity and on the psychology of art is so large as to defy a complete catalogue. An up-to-date bibliography would require a volume in its own right and is not attempted here. We limit ourselves to listing only those works which, to a greater or a lesser extent, have influenced our own research. Wherever appropriate, we mention the latest bibliographies on the topics with which this book deals, so that interested readers may find their own way into the bypaths of this vast literature.

Modern scientific approaches to creative thinking, or "genius," are traditionally held to begin with the genetic studies of Galton (1892) and the psychopathological investigations of Lombroso (1891). Most scholars who have been interested in understanding the dynamics of thought processes have made incidental observations about creativity, but without making a thorough study of the topic. Among those whose insights are still relevant are William James (1880), Souriau (1881), Baldwin (1900), Dewey (1910, 1929, 1938), Thurstone (1924), Terman (1926), Thorndike (1926), Tolman (1926), and Hull (1930); see also the reviews by Campbell (1960, 1974).

Cognitive psychologists had been by and large uninterested in creativity until Guilford's presidential address to the American Psychological Association (Guilford, 1950), which—possibly in conjunction with the challenge of the 1957 Russian space probe—helped to make creativity a popular subject of investigation. Since that time, the number of entries under the heading "creativity" in *Psychological Abstracts* has increased exponentially from an average of less that 10 per year to several hundred a year in the sixties and seventies. The interest shows no sign of abating.

274 Appendix 3

Recent reviews of the field which contain extensive bibliographies include Stein and Heinze (1964) on the personality and psychiatric aspects of creativity; Brunelle (1967) and Freeman, Butcher, and Christie (1968) on creative problem-solving processes; Child (1972) on aesthetics and creative thinking; Stievater (1973) on problem solving and the stimulation of creativity; and Getzels and Dillon (1973) on the educational implications of giftedness.

Even when creativity was more or less ignored by researchers in psychology, many important books on the subject were being published. At least four major types of writing may be discerned in this literature. The first includes restropective accounts of the creative process by artists or scientists. Among these some classics foreshadow the problem-finding approach: Kandinsky (1912) in relation to abstract art; Poincaré (1914) and Hadamard (1954) as applied to mathematics; Einstein in terms of physics (Einstein and Infeld, 1938); and Stravinski (1947) in regard to music. Another source of statements by creative individuals may be found in anthologies on the subject; five of the richest in material are Rossman (1931) for technological inventions; Montmasson (1932) for discoveries in general; Ghiselin (1952) for the arts; Schwartz and Bishop (1958) for scientific discoveries; and Garrett (1963) for chemistry.

A third set of writings on creativity outside the psychometric literature consists in the Gestalt approach, which has been developing a formal structural model to understand creative thinking. In this field one might mention Köhler (1940), Duncker (1945), Arnheim (1943, 1971, 1974), Wertheimer (1959), and Gruber, Terrell, and Wertheimer (1967).

The psychoanalytic literature is especially rich in references to creativity. After the early essays of Freud on poetry (1908) and art (1914, 1947), some of the major contributions have been those of Kris (1952), Neumann (1959), Weissman (1965), Ehrenzweig (1967), and Klein (see Segal, 1973). Jungian psychology has also provided important contributions to the field; see especially Jung (1922, 1930a, 1942), and Storr (1972).

The contemporary, experimentally-oriented approach to creativity is too voluminous to review in a short space. Any list of the major works should include Anderson (1959), Thompson (1959), Taylor (1964), Guilford (1967, 1968), Torrance and Myers (1970), Berlyne (1971), and in a more speculative vein Koestler (1964). A useful compendium of the psychology of the visual arts is the one by Hogg (1969).

Articles are still being written about the difference between intelligence and creativity, or between convergent and divergent thinking. Some of the participants in this controversy are Butcher (1972), Carlier and Roubertoux (1972-1973), Stievenart (1972), Schubert (1973), and Nash (1975). The earlier work by Wallach and Wing (1969) should also be noted. . Writers who have commented on the importance of understanding how problems are *found* rather than limiting the inquiry to how they are solved include Dewey (1929, 1938), Einstein and Infeld (1938), Duncker (1945), Beveridge (1951), Polànyi (1958), Wertheimer (1959), Thelen (1960), Boirel (1961), Mackworth (1965), Stephenson, Gantz, and Erickson (1971), and Henle (1975).

Among recent approaches to the study of the creative personality, especially that of artists, one may list the work of Roe (1946), Drevdahl (1956), MacKinnon (1964), Cross, Cattell, and Butcher (1967), Barron (1969, 1972), Roubertoux (1970), Albert and Elliott (1973), and Dellas (1974).

Since the *Journal of Creative Behavior* was started in 1966, many articles have been published concerning the possibility of increasing creativity through training, special encounter groups, and the like. For examples, see Parnes (1972), Parnes and Noller (1972), Whiting (1973), and Stein (1974). Other studies relating environmental effects to creativity are Blottenberg (1972) and Goyal (1973).

The analysis of art as a part of the social and cultural fabric has a long history, dating back at least to the Renaissance [e.g., Alberti (1435) and Vasari (1550)]. Among recent sociologists, Sorokin (1963) has written a trenchant review of the vicissitudes of aesthetic styles as related to social change and Hauser (1960) has provided the most thorough history of art from the sociological viewpoint. The function of the artist in society, and the tensions he experiences as a result of conflicts within his social environment, have been vividly analyzed by the Marxist critic György Lukács (e.g., Lukács, 1973, 1975). Other reading in this area might include Gombrich (1966), who as an art historian is eminently sensitive to the social context of art; Wilson (1964), Read (1969); and Gillespie and Perry (1973).

Art is so intimately bound up with the description of other cultures that the anthropological literature includes many references to it. Recent readers by Jopling (1971) and Forge (1974) contain some typical works, and different approaches are represented by Barry (1957), Fisher (1961), Lévi-Strauss (1964), and Adams (1973). A rare study of creativity in cultural evolution is the book by Mead (1965).

Finally, our own previous work, which has contributed to this volume, includes the two technical monographs reporting the results of the early study of art students (Getzels and Csikszentmihalyi, 1964, 1965); analyses of the criterion problem in creativity (Getzels and Csikszentmihalyi, 1966a, 1969); articles on problem finding (Csikszentmihalyi and Getzels, 1970, 1971); the personality of artists (Getzels and Csikszentmihalyi, 1968a, 1968b; Csikszentmihalyi and Getzels, 1973); and several theoretical articles (Getzels, 1964; Getzels and Csikszentmihalyi, 1966b, 1967, 1975).

Bibliography

■

Adams, M-J. Structural aspects of village art. *American Anthropologist*, 1973, **75**, 1, 265–279.

Albert, R. S., & Elliott, R. C. Creative ability and the handling of personal and social conflict among bright sixth graders. *Social Behavior and Personality*, 1973, **1**, 2, 169–181.

Alberti, L-B. *On Painting*. New Haven: Yale University Press, 1970 (original date: 1435).

Allport, G. W. *Personality–A Psychological Interpretation*. New York: Henry Holt and Co., 1937.

Allport, G. W., Vernon, P. E., & Lindzey, G. *Manual, Study of Values*. 3rd ed. Boston: Houghton Mifflin, 1960.

Anderson, H. H. (Ed.) *Creativity and Its Cultivation*. New York: Harper, 1959.

Andreasen, N. J., & Powers, P. S. Creativity and psychosis: An examination of conceptual style. *Archives of General Psychiatry*, 1975, **32**, 1, 70–73.

Arendt, H. *The Human Condition*. Chicago: University of Chicago Press, 1958.

Arlin, P. K. Problem finding: The relation between cognitive variables and problem finding performance. Unpublished Ph.D. thesis, University of Chicago, 1974.

Arnheim, R. Gestalt and art. *Journal of Aesthetics and Art Criticism*, 1943, **2**, 71–75.

Arnheim, R. *Entropy and Art*. Berkeley: University of California Press, 1971.

Arnheim, R. *Art and Visual Perception: A Psychology of the Creative Eye*. Berkeley: University of California Press, 1974.

Bachtold, L. M. & Werner, E. E. Personality characteristics of creative women. *Perceptual and Motor Skills*, 1973, **36**, 1, 311–319.

Baldwin, J. M. *Mental Development in the Child and the Race*. New York: Macmillan, 1900.

Barron, F. X. *Creative Person and Creative Process*. New York: Holt, Rinehart and Winston, 1969.

Barron, F. X. *Artists in the Making*. New York: Seminar Press, 1972.

Barry, H., III. Relationship between child training and the pictorial arts. *Journal of Abnormal and Social Psychology*, 1957, **54**, 38–83.

Berger, P. L., & Luckmann, T. *The Social Construction of Reality*. Garden City, N.Y.: Doubleday, 1967.

Berlyne, D. E. Novelty and curiosity as determinants of exploratory behavior. *British Journal of Psychology*, 1950–1951, **41**, 68–80.

277

Berlyne, D. E. *Aesthetics and Psychobiology*. New York: Meredith, 1971.

Beveridge, W. I. B. *The Art of Scientific Investigation*. New York: Norton, 1951.

Bexton, W. H., Heron, W., & Scott, J. H. Effects of decreased variation in sensory environment. *Canadian Journal of Psychology*, 1954, **8**, 70–76.

Blottenberg, E. H. Problems in the assessment of pictorial-artistic performance ability under special consideration of aesthetic judgment. *Psychologie und Praxis*, 1972, **16**, 1, 1–24.

Boirel, R. *Théorie générale de l'invention*. Paris: Presses Universitaires Françaises, 1961.

Bronowski, J. *Science and Human Values*. New York: Julian Messner, 1956.

Bruch, C. B., & Morse, J. A. Initial study of creative (productive) women under the Bruch-Morse model. *Gifted Child Quarterly*, 1972, **16**, 4, 282–289.

Brunelle, E. A. *Creativity and Problem Solving*. Buffalo, N.Y.: Creative Education Foundation, 1967.

Burkhart, R. C., & Bernheim, G. *Object Question Test Manual*. Pennsylvania State University Department of Education, May 1963.

Buros, O. K. *Personality Tests and Reviews*. Highland Park, N. J.: Griphon, 1970.

Butcher, H. J. Divergent thinking and creativity. In W. D. Wall & V. P. Varna (Eds.), *Advances in Educational Psychology*. New York: Barnes & Noble, 1972.

Campbell, D. T. Blind variation and selective retention in creative thought as in other knowledge processes. *Psychological Review*, 1960, **67**, 380–400.

Campbell, D. T. Evolutionary epistemology. In P. A. Schilpp (Ed.), *The Philosophy of Karl Popper*. Vol. 14, *The Library of Living Philosophers*. La Salle, Ill.: Open Court, 1974, 413–463.

Carlier, M., & Roubertoux, P. Creativity and plans of exploration. *Bulletin de Psychologie*, 1972–1973, **26**, 1–4, 22–25.

Cattell, R. B. *Objective-Analytic Test Battery*. Champaign, Ill.: Institute for Personality and Ability Testing, 1958.

Cattell, R. B. & Drevdahl, J. E. A comparison of the personality profile (16 PF) of eminent researchers with that of eminent teachers and administrators, and of the general population. *British Journal of Psychology*, 1955, **46**, 248–261.

Cattell, R. B., & Stice, G. F. *Handbook for the Sixteen Personality Factors Questionnaire*. Champaign, Ill.: Institute for Personality and Ability Testing, 1962.

Child, I. L. Esthetics. *Annual Review of Psychology*, 1972, **23**, 669–694.

Collingwood, R. *The Principles of Art*. New York: Galaxy Books, 1958.

Cross, P. G., Cattell, R. B., & Butcher, H. J. The personality pattern of creative artists. *British Journal of Educational Psychology*, 1967, **37**, 292–299.

Csikszentmihalyi, M. *Beyond Boredom and Anxiety: The Experience of Play in Work and Games*. San Francisco: Jossey-Bass, 1975.

Csikszentmihalyi, M., & Getzels, J. W. Concern for discovery: An attitudinal component of creative production. *Journal of Personality*, 1970, **38**, 1, 91–105.

Csikszentmihalyi, M., & Getzels, J. W. Discovery-oriented behavior and the originality of creative products: A study with artists. *Journal of Personality and Social Psychology*, 1971, **19**, 1, 47–52.

Csikszentmihalyi, M., & Getzels, J. W. The personality of young artists: An empirical and theoretical exploration. *British Journal of Psychology*, 1973, **64**, 1, 91–104.

Dellas, M. Effects of affective expression on divergent thinking production. *Journal of Psychology*, 1974, **88**, 2, 325–331.

Dewey, J. *How We Think.* Boston: Heath, 1910.

Dewey, J. *The Quest for Certainty.* New York: Putnam, 1929.

Dewey, J. *Logic: The Structure of Inquiry.* New York: Putnam, 1938.

Drevdahl, J. E. Factors of importance to creativity. *Journal of Clinical Psychology,* 1956, **12,** 21–26.

Dubos, R. *Louis Pasteur.* Boston: Little, Brown, 1950.

Duncker, K. *On Problem Solving.* Westport, Conn.: Greenwood, 1972 (original date: 1945).

Ecker, D. The artistic process as qualitative problem solving. *Journal of Aesthetics and Art Criticism,* 1963, **21,** 283–290.

Ehrenzweig, A. *The Hidden Order of Art: A Study in the Psychology of Artistic Imagination.* London: Weidenfeld & Nicolson, 1967.

Einstein, A., & Infeld, L. *The Evolution of Physics.* New York: Simon & Schuster, 1938.

Eliot, A. Encounters with artists. *Atlantic Monthly,* 1972, **230,** 4, 99–104.

Fisher, J. L. Art styles as cognitive maps. *American Anthropologist,* 1961, **63,** 79–93.

Forge, A. *Primitive Art and Society.* Oxford: Oxford University Press, 1974.

Freeman, J., Butcher, H. J., & Christie, T. *Creativity: A Selective Review of Research.* London: Society for Research in Higher Education, 1968.

Freud, S. The relation of the poet to day-dreaming. *Collected Papers.* New York: Basic Books, 1959, Vol. 4, 173–183 (original date: 1908).

Freud, S. The Moses of Michelangelo. *Collected Papers.* New York: Basic Books, 1959, Vol. 4, 257–287 (original date: 1914).

Freud, S. *Leonardo da Vinci: A Study in Psychosexuality.* New York: Random House, 1947

Galton, F. *Hereditary Genius: An Inquiry into Its Laws and Uniqueness.* London: Macmillan, 1892.

Garrett, A. B. *The Flash of Genius.* Princeton: Van Nostrand, 1963.

Getzels, J. W. Creative thinking, problem-solving, and instruction. In E. R. Hilgard (Ed.), *Theories of Learning and Instruction,* 63rd Yearbook of the National Society for the Study of Education, Part I. Chicago: University of Chicago Press, 1964, 240–267.

Getzels, J. W., & Csikszentmihalyi, M. *Creative Thinking in Art Students: An Exploratory Study.* Cooperative Research Report No. E-008, Chicago, 1964.

Getzels, J. W., & Csikszentmihalyi, M. *Creative Thinking in Art Students: The Process of Discovery.* Cooperative Research Report No. S-080, Chicago, 1965.

Getzels, J. W., & Csikszentmihalyi, M. The study of creativity in future artists: The criterion problem. In O. J. Harvey (Ed.), *Experience, Structure and Adaptability.* New York: Springer, 1966 (a).

Getzels, J. W., & Csikszentmihalyi, M. Portrait of the artist as an explorer. *Trans-action,* 1966, **3,** 6, 31–35 (b).

Getzels, J. W., & Csikszentmihalyi, M. Scientific creativity. *Science Journal,* 1967, **3,** 9, 80–84.

Getzels, J. W., & Csikszentmihalyi, M. The value-orientation of art students as determinants of artistic specialization and creative performance. *Studies in Art Education,* 1968, **10,** 5–16 (a).

Getzels, J. W., & Csikszentmihalyi, M. On the roles, values, and performance of future artists: A conceptual and empirical exploration. *Sociological Quarterly,* 1968, **9,** 516–530 (b).

Getzels, J. W., & Csikszentmihalyi, M. Aesthetic opinion: An empirical study. *Public Opinion Quarterly,* 1969, **33,** 34–45.

Getzels, J. W., & Csikszentmihalyi, M. From problem-solving to problem-finding. In I. A. Taylor & J. W. Getzels (Eds.), *Perspectives in Creativity*. Chicago: Aldine, 1975.

Getzels, J. W., & Dillon, J. T. The nature of giftedness and the education of the gifted. In R. M. W. Travers (Ed.), *Second Handbook of Research on Teaching*. Chicago: Rand McNally, 1973, 689–731.

Getzels, J. W., & Jackson, P. W. *Creativity and Intelligence: Explorations with Gifted Students*. New York: Wiley, 1962.

Ghiselin, B. (Ed.) *The Creative Process*. New York: Mentor, 1952.

Gillespie, D. F., & Perry, R. W. Research strategies for studying the acceptance of artistic creativity. *Sociology and Social Research*, 1973, **58**, 1, 48–55.

Gombrich, E. H. *The Story of Art*. New York: Phaidon, 1966.

Goyal, R. P. Creativity and school climate: An exploratory study. *Journal of Psychological Research*, 1973, **17**, 2, 77–80.

Gruber, H. E., Terrell, G., & Wertheimer, M. (Eds.) *Contemporary Approaches to Creative Thinking*. New York: Atherton, 1967.

Guilford, J. P. Creativity. *American Psychologist*, 1950, **5**, 9, 444–454.

Guilford, J. P. Brick Uses Scoring Guide. Reports of the Psychological Laboratory of the University of Southern California, May, 1962.

Guilford, J. P. Unusual Uses Scoring Key. *Reports of the Psychological Laboratory of the University of Southern California*, February, 1963.

Guilford, J. P. *The Nature of Human Intelligence*. New York: McGraw-Hill, 1967.

Guilford, J. P. *Intelligence, Creativity, and their Educational Implications*. San Diego: R. R. Knapp, 1968.

Guilford, J. P., et al. A factor-analytic study of creative thinking. I. Hypotheses and description of tests. *Reports of the Psychological Laboratory of the University of Southern California*, 1951, **4.**

Guilford, J. P., & Merrifield, P. R. The structure of intellect model: Its uses and implications. *Reports of the Psychological Laboratory of the University of Southern California*, 1960, **24.**

Guilford, J. P., & Zimmerman, W. S. *Guilford-Zimmerman Aptitude Survey. A Manual of Instructions and Interpretations*. 2nd ed. Beverly Hills: Sheridan Supply Co., 1956.

Hadamard, J. *An Essay on the Psychology of Invention in the Mathematical Field*. New York: Dover, 1954.

Hauser, A. *The Social History of Art*. New York: Vintage, 1951.

Hebb, D. O., & Thompson, R. The social significance of animal studies. In G. Lindzey (Ed.), *Handbook of Social Psychology*. Vol. 1. Reading, Mass.: Addison Wesley, 1954, 532–561.

Henle, M. Fishing for ideas. *American Psychologist*, 1975, **30**, 8, 795–799.

Hess, R. D., Sims, J., & Henry, W. E. Identity and identity diffusion: The professional actor. Paper delivered at the annual meeting of the American Sociological Association, Los Angeles, September, 1963.

Hogg, J. (Ed.) *Psychology and the Visual Arts*. Harmondsworth: Penguin, 1969.

Hull, C. L. Knowledge and purpose as habit mechanisms. *Psychological Review*, 1930, **37**, 511–525.

Hunt, J. McV. *Intelligence and Experience*. New York: Ronald, 1961.

IPAT Information Bulletin No. 10. Champaign, Ill.: Institute for Personality and Ability Testing, 1963.

IPAT, 16PF Test, Preliminary Norms. Champaign, Ill.: Institute for Personality and Ability Testing, 1962.

James, W. Great men, great thoughts, and the environment. *The Atlantic Monthly*, 1880, **46**, 276, 441–459.

Jopling, C. F. *Art and Esthetics in Primitive Societies.* New York: Dutton, 1971.

Jung, C. G. On the relation of analytical psychology to poetry. *Collected Works.* Vol. 15, Princeton: Princeton University Press, 1966, 65–83 (original date: 1922).

Jung, C. G. Psychology and literature. *Collected Works.* Vol. 15, Princeton: Princeton University Press, 1966, 84–105 (original date: 1930) (a).

Jung, C. G. Psychology and poetry. *Transition*, 1930, June, 19–20 (b).

Jung, C. G. The gifted child. *Collected Works.* Vol. 17, Princeton: Princeton University Press, 1954, 135–145 (original date: 1942).

Kandinsky, W. *Über das Geistige in der Kunst.* Munich: Piper Verlag, 1912.

Koestler, A. *The Act of Creation.* New York: Macmillan, 1964.

Köhler, W. *Dynamics in Psychology.* New York: Liveright, 1940.

Komarik, E. Creativity and orthogonal factors in personality. *Sbornik Praci Filosoficke Fakulty Brneske University*, 1972, **20**, 1, 115–124.

Kris, E. *Psychoanalytic Explorations in Art.* New York: International Universities Press, 1952.

Lawrence, D. H. Making pictures. In B. Ghiselin (Ed.), *The Creative Process.* New York: Mentor, 1952, 68–73.

Lévi-Strauss, C. *Tristes Tropiques.* New York: Atheneum, 1964.

Lombroso, C. *The Man of Genius.* London: W. Scott, 1891.

Lukács, G. *Marxism and Human Liberation.* New York: Dell, 1973.

Lukács, G. *Az Esztétikum Sajátossága* (The Specific Nature of the Aesthetic). Budapest: Akadémiai Kiadó, 1975.

MacKinnon, D. W. The nature and nurture of creative talent. *American Psychologist*, 1962, **17**, 484–495.

MacKinnon, D. W. The creativity of architects. In C. W. Taylor (Ed.), *Widening Horizons in Creativity.* New York: Wiley, 1964.

Mackworth, N. H. Originality. *American Psychologist*, 1965, **20**, 51–66.

Maddi, S. R., Charles, A. M., Maddi, D., & Smith, A. J. Effects of monotony and novelty on imaginative productions. *Journal of Personality*, 1962, **30**, 513–527.

Marchal, G. Contribution à l'etude du sentiment esthétique. *BINOP*, 1958, **14**, 82–93.

May, M. A. The Foundations of Personality. In P. S. Achilles (Ed.), *Psychology of Work.* New York: McGraw-Hill, 1932, 81–101.

Mead, M. *Sex and Temperament in Three Primitive Societies.* New York: Morrow, 1935.

Mead, M. *Continuities in Cultural Evolution.* New Haven: Yale University Press, 1965.

Montmasson, J-M. *Invention and the Unconscious.* New York: Harcourt, Brace, 1932.

Moore, H. Notes on Sculpture. In B. Ghiselin (Ed.), *The Creative Process.* New York: Mentor, 1955, 73–78.

Nash, W. R. The effects of warm-up activities on small group divergent problem-solving with young children. *Journal of Psychology*, 1975, **89**, 2, 237–241.

Neumann, E. *Art and the Creative Unconscious.* New York: Harper & Row, 1959.

Nietzsche, F. W. *The Will to Power.* New York: Frederick, 1960.

Overy, P. *Kandinsky.* New York: Praeger, 1969.

Parnes, S. J. *Creativity: Unlocking Human Potential.* Buffalo: D. O. K. Publishers, 1972.

Parnes, S. J., & Noller, R. B. Applied creativity: The creative studies project II. Results of the two-year program. *Journal of Creative Behavior,* 1972, **6,** 3, 164–186.

Parsons, T. *The Social System.* Glencoe, Ill.: Free Press, 1951.

Parsons, T. *Societies: Evolutionary and Comparative Perspectives.* Englewood Cliffs, N.J.: Prentice-Hall, 1966.

Piaget, J. *The Origins of Intelligence in Children.* New York: International Universities Press, 1952 (original date 1936).

Piaget, J. *Play, Dreams, and Imitation in Childhood.* New York: Norton, 1951 (original date 1945).

Poincaré, H. *Science and Method.* New York: Dover, 1914.

Polànyi, M. *Personal Knowledge.* Chicago: University of Chicago Press, 1958.

Rau, L. Interpersonal correlates of perceptual-cognitive functions. Paper read at the Society for Child Research and Development meeting, University of California, Berkeley April, 1963.

Read, H. *Art and Alienation.* New York: Viking, 1969.

Roe, A. The personality of artists. *Educational and Psychological Measurement,* 1946, **6,** 401–408.

Rosenberg, H. *The Anxious Object.* New York: Macmillan, 1973.

Rossman, J. *The Psychology of the Inventor: A Study of the Patentee.* Washington, D.C.: Inventors Publishing Co., 1931.

Roubertoux, P. Personality variables and interest in art. *Journal of Personality and Social Psychology,* 1970, **16,** 665–668.

Schachtel, E. G. *Metamorphosis: On the Development of Affect, Perception, Attention, and Memory.* New York: Basic Books, 1959.

Schubert, D. S. Intelligence as necessary but not sufficient for creativity. *Journal of Genetic Psychology,* 1973, **122,** 1, 45–47.

Schulze, F. Tripping with M. C. Escher and his fool-the-eye art. *Chicago Daily News,* September 23, 1972.

Schulze, F. *Fantastic Images.* New York: Follett, 1972.

Schwartz, G., & Bishop, P. W. (Eds.) *Moments of Discovery.* New York: Basic Books, 1958.

Segal, H. *Introduction to the Work of Melanie Klein.* New York: Basic Books, 1973.

Sorokin, P. *Modern Historical and Social Philosophies.* New York: Dover, 1963.

Souriau, P. *Théorie de l'invention.* Paris: Hachette, 1881.

Stein, M. I. *Stimulating Creativity.* New York: Academic Press, 1974.

Stein, M. I., & Heinze, S. I. *Creativity and the Individual: Summaries of Selected Literature in Psychology and Psychiatry.* Glencoe, Ill.: Free Press, 1964.

Stephenson R. W., Gantz, B. S., & Erickson, C. O. Use of analogies in order to facilitate invention. *Proceedings of the 79th Annual Convention of the American Psychological Association,* 1971, **6,** 2, 487–488.

Stievater, S. M. Bibliography of recent books on creativity and problem-solving: Supplement IV. *Journal of Creative Behavior,* 1973, **7,** 3, 208–213.

Stievenart, M. Influence of Guilford's model of the structure of the intellect on a study of creativity. *Revue Belge de Psychologie et de Pédagogie,* 1972, **34,** 139, 65–78.

Storr, A. *The Dynamics of Creation.* London: Secker & Warburg, 1972.

Stravinski, I. *Poetics of Music.* Cambridge: Harvard University Press, 1947.

Taylor, C. W. (Ed.) *Creativity: Progress and Potential.* New York: McGraw-Hill, 1964.

Terman, L. M. *Genetic Studies of Genius.* Stanford: Stanford University Press, 1926.

Thelen, H. A. *Education and the Human Quest.* Chicago: University of Chicago Press, 1960.

Thompson, R. *The Psychology of Thinking.* Baltimore: Penguin, 1959.

Thorndike, E. L. *Measurement of Intelligence.* New York: Bureau of Publications, Teachers College, Columbia University, 1926.

Thurstone, L. L. *The Nature of Intelligence.* New York: Harcourt, Brace, 1924.

Tolman, E. C. A behavioristic theory of ideas. *Psychological Review,* 1926, **33,** 352–369.

Torrance, E. P. Current research on the nature of creative talent. *Journal of Counseling Psychology, 1959,* **6,** 309–316.

Torrance, E. P. Problems of highly creative children. *Gifted Child Quarterly,* 1961, **5,** 31–34.

Torrance, E. P. Creative women in today's world. *Exceptional Children,* 1972, **38,** 8, 597–603.

Torrance, E. P., & Myers, R. E. *Creative Learning and Teaching.* New York: Dodd, Mead, 1970.

Vasari, G. *Lives of the Most Eminent Painters, Sculptors, and Architects.* New York: Random House, 1959 (original date: 1550).

Wallach, M. A. & Wing, C. W. *A Validation of the Creativity-Intelligence Distinction.* New York: Holt, Rinehart and Winston, 1969.

Watson, J. B. *Behaviorism.* New York: W. W. Norton, 1930.

Weissman, P. *Creativity in the Theater: A Psychoanalytic Study.* New York: Basic Books, 1965.

Welsh, G. S. *Welsh Figure Preference Test, Preliminary Manual.* Palo Alto: Consulting Psychologists Press, 1959.

Wertheimer, M. *Productive Thinking.* New York: Harper & Row, 1945.

White, R. W. Motivation reconsidered: The concept of competence. *Psychological Review,* 1959, **66,** 297–331.

Whiting, B. G. How to predict creativity from biographical data. *Journal of Creative Behavior,* 1973, **7,** 201–207.

Willingham, W. W. Predicting success in graduate education. *Science,* 1974, **183,** 4122 273–278.

Wilson, R. N. *The Arts in Society.* Englewood Cliffs, N.J.: Prentice-Hall, 1964.

Wonderlic, E. F. *Wonderlic Personnel Test Manual.* Northfield, Ill.: E. F. Wonderlic & Associates, 1961.

Zavalloni, R., & Giordani, N. Ricerche sulla sensibilità estetica nell'età evolutiva. *Problemi Pedagogici,* 1958, **6,** 904–919.

Zervos, C. Conversation with Picasso. In B. Ghiselin (Ed.), *The Creative Process.* New York: Mentor, 1952, 55–60.

Author Index

Subject Index